BAZI

The
DESTINY CODE
REVEALED

八字解碼

八
字
解
碼

BaZi - The Destiny Code Revealed

The author can be reached at:

Mastery Academy of Chinese Metaphysics Sdn. Bhd. (611143-A)
19-3, The Boulevard, Mid Valley City,
59200 Kuala Lumpur, Malaysia.
Tel   : +603-2284 8080
Fax   : +603-2284 1218
Email   : info@masteryacademy.com
Website: www.masteryacademy.com

DISCLAIMER:

Published by JY Books Sdn. Bhd. (659134-T)

INDEX

八字
解碼

PREFACE

20 months ago, *The Destiny Code* was published. I'm pleased to say that the book has had a good reception amongst Chinese Astrology practitioners and enthusiasts on the subject. I had planned for this book to come out much earlier. However, this book has been rewritten several times since its inception late last year. Writing this book has been a real exercise in persistence and determination. Originally it was meant to go out in April 2006 but in light of feedback from students, practitioners, members of the public and colleagues in the field, I went back and added more content, notably more examples. I felt it was important not to replicate the content of Chinese books on this subject as in my research of Chinese language BaZi books, I discovered that the important elemental relationships in BaZi were often only briefly and vaguely explained – Punishments, Clashes, Destructions, Harms and Combinations were accorded one or two lines, a page at most. Hence, I felt it was important that *The Destiny Code Revealed* was thorough on these subjects, but without being unduly complex and dense. Hence, the many numerous rewrites that this text went through.

As a result, *The Destiny Code Revealed* is a slightly thicker book than its predecessor.

If you have not read *The Destiny Code*, this book may be a little hard to follow because it makes certain assumptions with regard to certain types of information, such as how to plot a chart, and the Five Elements and Five Element relationships, as well as basic chart interpretation. Hence, it is probably best if you read *The Destiny Code* first, before moving on to this book, unless you have some background in BaZi.

Many people ask if they can learn BaZi through my books, without attending a class. I think a class has its own unique benefits. You get to meet like minded people and have interaction with an instructor. But at the same time, some people handle personal study better. To be a practitioner, you probably need both – formal training with an instructor, and some texts to help clarify certain concepts or give you insight and ideas. But if you just want to utilise the knowledge of BaZi for yourself, or family members, then probably reading books is good enough.

Think of it as being like brain surgery. If you want to be a brain surgeon, you probably have to read the textbooks and cut a few brains under the guidance of a brain surgeon. But if you're going for brain surgery, reading the textbooks is probably helpful so you understand what you're getting yourself into, but you don't really need to cut a few brains.

For someone who wishes to make use of the services of a BaZi consultant, I am certain that my books in the BaZi series will be helpful in enabling you to maximise any BaZi consultation because you will have a better understanding of where the BaZi consultant is coming from and whether you are getting your money's worth in the consult. If a BaZi consultant only delivers the technical analysis but no interpretation or clear line of advice on what to do, then you might as well have done it yourself, with the help of this book.

八字
解
碼

Lao Tzu once said: "He who knows others is wise, he who knows himself is enlightened". If every person felt more confident about themselves, and understood themselves better, there would be fewer disgruntled, unhappy and displeased people. Most people out there don't know what they want in life – they are going through life on cruise control. It is because they do not understand their purpose in life or perhaps, even why they are here on this planet. I truly believe that BaZi has the ability to illuminate for people this very important question of their purpose in this universe. Unconsciously, most people know the answer to this question. They probably just don't dig hard enough, even though they really want to know the answer. A motivational seminar, a self-help session or going for NLP is an external method of finding your answer. BaZi lets you tackle this problem from the inside out – to seek the answer from within.

Many people also constantly seek guidance or answers to the difficult questions in life: career questions, financial questions, relationship issues. People want certainty in their life. BaZi is an excellent tool for finding the answers and certainty that you need in life. And with the information in this book, certainly some of the basic questions on career, wealth, relationship and even health, can be determined by you, for yourself.

This book is also designed to help the public understand the difference between classical BaZi and what I term 'New Age BaZi'. Classical BaZi is about making improvements to yourself through your own actions. New Age BaZi is kind of like retail therapy – change your hair, change your clothes, wear some jewellery, decorate your house, and your life will change overnight. I have no opposition to New Age BaZi and New Age practices – however, I do feel that they should not be confused with Classical BaZi and a more serious and studied approach towards BaZi. So I hope this book will help you differentiate between New Age BaZi practices and the more Classical BaZi practice.

I hope you will find this book a useful companion on your journey towards a deeper understanding of BaZi and the first, or many steps, towards understanding yourself better and achieving your goals, dreams and aspirations in life.

Joey Yap
October 20, 2006

Author's personal website :
www.joeyyap.com

Academy websites :
www.masteryacademy.com I www.maelearning.com I www.baziprofiling.com

Joey Yap on Facebook :
www.facebook.com/joeyyapFB

MASTERY ACADEMY
OF CHINESE METAPHYSICS™

At **www.masteryacademy.com**, you will find some useful tools to ascertain key information about the Feng Shui of a property or for the study of Astrology.

The Joey Yap Flying Stars Calculator can be utilised to plot your home or office Flying Stars chart. To find out your personal best directions, use the 8 Mansions Calculator. To learn more about your personal Destiny, you can use the Joey Yap BaZi Ming Pan Calculator to plot your Four Pillars of Destiny – you just need to have your date of birth (day, month, year) and time of birth.

For more information about BaZi, Xuan Kong or Flying Star Feng Shui, or if you wish to learn more about these subjects with Joey Yap, logon to the Mastery Academy of Chinese Metaphysics website at **www.masteryacademy.com.**

八字解碼

MASTERY ACADEMY
E-LEARNING CENTER
www.maelearning.com

www.maelearning.com

Bookmark this address on your computer, and visit this newly-launched website today. With the E-Learning Center, knowledge of Chinese Metaphysics is a mere 'click' away!

Our E-Learning Center consists of 3 distinct components.

1. Online Courses

These shall comprise of 3 Programs: our Online Feng Shui Program, Online BaZi Program, and Online Mian Xiang Program. Each lesson contains a video lecture, slide presentation and downloadable course notes.

2. MA Live!

With MA Live!, Joey Yap's workshops, tutorials, courses and seminars on various Chinese Metaphysics subjects broadcasted right to your computer screen. Better still, participants will not only get to see and hear Joey talk 'live', but also get to engage themselves directly in the event and more importantly, TALK to Joey via the MA Live! interface. All the benefits of a live class, minus the hassle of actually having to attend one!

3. Video-On-Demand (VOD)

Get immediate streaming-downloads of the Mastery Academy's wide range of educational DVDs, right on your computer screen. No more shipping costs and waiting time to be incurred!

Study at your own pace, and interact with your Instructor and fellow students worldwide... at your own convenience and privacy. With our E-Learning Center, knowledge of Chinese Metaphysics is brought DIRECTLY to you in all its clarity, with illustrated presentations and comprehensive notes expediting your learning curve!

Welcome to the Mastery Academy's E-LEARNING CENTER...YOUR virtual gateway to Chinese Metaphysics mastery!

Chapter One:
A BaZi Moment

In many Asian countries such as Hong Kong, Singapore, Taiwan and Malaysia, it is not uncommon for BaZi consultants to be engaged by top business tycoons, prominent corporate leaders, and other well-known personalities, as in-house advisors to help them make important decisions, based on their own personal Destiny Chart or BaZi and Luck Pillars.

BaZi advisors also play an important role in the selection of key corporate personnel. A business leader, for example, cannot do everything himself and at some point, he has to rely on his manager. And a business is really only as good as its managers and other key personnel. This is where the services of a BaZi consultant is useful in helping to select key corporate personnel.

Working hand in hand with their Feng Shui counterparts, BaZi advisors are also consulted for appropriate dates for the opening of major businesses, hotels and offices. The BaZi charts of all key members of an organisation are taken into consideration in order to find the 'perfect' day of the year for the launching of the enterprise. Why the need to select a good day? Every day the Earth is affected by different forms of Qi. The exact timing of Qi (year, month, day and hour) is selected to facilitate the Qi patterns (or BaZi) of the key individuals involved in the business to ensure smooth sailing and a good start to business. So Feng Shui and BaZi, or Zi Wei (Purple Star) Astrology, if you are into other types of Chinese Astrology, go hand-in-hand and, if you are planning to use the services of a Feng Shui practitioner, it is always advisable to look for someone who is also a highly skilled BaZi or Destiny consultant.

As I have stated many times in my articles and earlier books, no Feng Shui practitioner can offer a complete service without some knowledge of Destiny analysis. Feng Shui is the prescription, and Destiny analysis is the means to make a diagnosis. If your Feng Shui consultant has no idea what your problem is in the first place, how can he be expected to fix your problem? Would you go to a doctor who cuts you open first in order to find out what is wrong with you?

BaZi for Public

Okay, but you are not a business tycoon you say. Not even anywhere near a superstar unless one counts singing in the bathroom. Perhaps you are just a modest millionaire. Or a hard-working blue-collar worker. How is BaZi useful to you?

BaZi and knowledge of BaZi is infinitely more useful in many respects to the average person than a big business tycoon or a superstar. Tycoons, superstars and millionaires have the advantage of being able to throw money at a problem if they encounter any obstacles. Most people do not have this kind of luxury. Tycoons, superstars and millionaires can afford an entourage of advisors to help them make every decision with all the information and knowledge that money can buy. The average person has, at best, whatever free advice the Internet offers. The tycoons, superstars and millionaires, to some degree, can afford to make a mistake, or lose some money. Of course they may feel the pinch, but not in the same way as the average individual who cannot afford to lose a couple of thousand of their life savings on a failed business venture.

BaZi is a powerful tool that levels the knowledge playing field. Sure, you may not be able to call upon an in-house BaZi advisor like the truly rich and wealthy can, but access to BaZi, be it for knowledge or consultations, is no longer only the purview of the fabulously wealthy.

Let's be a little bit honest as well - if the super rich are using it, and it works so well for them, why not empower yourself with the same skills and techniques?

八字解碼

BaZi for Life

Let's talk practical and not hypothetical. Different situations, scenarios, events, outcomes, actions and behaviors can all be defined as types of Destiny Codes. Even colours, sounds, places and attitudes can be converted to Destiny Codes. It is simply a matter of determining what type of Qi represents the variable in question, adding the Five Elements layer and then deriving the Destiny Code. By converting various situations, decisions, opportunities and issues into BaZi Code, and then analysing the Code into the context of an individual's Destiny Code, a BaZi consultant can determine if the outcome, decision, action or inaction will be favourable or unfavourable.

Should I move or should I stay?

A good practical example is the issue of migration. Migration is something that almost every one contemplates or considers at one point or another in their lives. It's a major decision. And it's a decision that is most effectively decided with the help of your personal BaZi.

Your BaZi can reveal to you whether your decision to move is wise or unwise generally, and more specifically, whether the period of time you are choosing to move is favourable or unfavourable. BaZi can also help you determine whether or not the country or destination you wish to move to is suitable. Why?

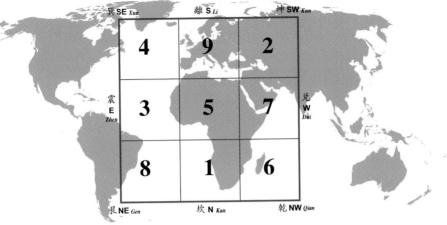

Geographical directions have an elemental value as well, derived from the Luo Shu. So every town, country, and continent, has an elemental value to it. By reviewing these elements, and co-relating them to a person's BaZi, a BaZi consultant can determine if the movement is favourable or unfavourable for the person from many angles. A move may yield greater financial rewards, but the person could feel deeply unhappy living in a foreign city or country. Alternatively, the move could bring about greater personal satisfaction, but there could be some compromises when it comes to financial rewards or perhaps, career opportunities. Sometimes, a move makes good career sense but may produce problems for the person in other areas.

Moving to another country and uprooting yourself should be an informed decision but being informed does not mean visiting the country and deciding you can live there. Remember, a place you like may not necessarily be 'good' for you from a BaZi perspective. Sometimes, a place you are not comfortable working in could be favourable to your personal development. BaZi takes the stress out of a move, takes the stress out of a decision, and allows you to truly understand the pros and cons of 'making the Big Move'.

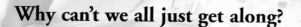

Why can't we all just get along?

Today, we're a society that's all about understanding people. Since 'Men are from Mars, Women are from Venus', why not use Chinese Astrology to further your understanding of your Other Half? Life would be a lot easier if relationships were less complicated. And relationships can be easier to manage if we simply understood the other person better - their motivations, their beliefs, their personal ideals, their innate character. A person's Destiny Chart affords us this understanding and depth of knowledge of the person, making it easier for us to communicate with them in the appropriate manner or fashion.

Health is Wealth

Health-care is estimated to be one of the rising costs facing the world today. Medical advances mean we are better able to treat many health conditions but that also means higher medical bills. Understanding your potential health issues through BaZi means you can focus on spending your money on managing your health better or making sure you detect any health problems early.

A person's BaZi reveals their potential health conditions during various points in time. The harmony and inter-relationship of the Five Elements explain which parts of the body are likely to break down or experience ailments, at certain points in time. Some people smoke all their life and die of natural causes at 98. Yet there are non-smokers out there who get lung cancer just by breathing in second-hand smoke! Understanding your health through BaZi is like having an annual medical or blood screening, except with BaZi, you have a better idea of which body parts should be monitored closely.

Queen Bee or Worker Ant?

BaZi doesn't get any more practical than when it's used to answer questions about money and one's ability to make money or venture into entrepreneurial endeavours. Is it a good time to start on a new business venture? Is this business partner trustworthy? Should I change jobs? Is the new job opportunity better? Does my new business partner have a hidden agenda? These are issues that could be converted into BaZi elements and analysed through a person's BaZi.

If you are not suited inherently for partnership, then you should not participate in one. But if you chose to participate in a partnership, then be prepared for certain problems. If you are suited for partnership, what kind of partner should you look for? What are the skillsets that this person will bring to the table that will complement your own abilities? Can you be sure this person will be able to work with you? Can you see how BaZi can be illuminating in so many ways?

BaZi is applicable to almost every major decision you will make in your life. When all the knowledge is at your fingertips, all you have to do is make the right decision. Press the right button. Hit the right gears.

Who says BaZi isn't for everyone?

Helping you, help yourself

Self-Help is a big business these days and there are many people who feel that the answer to their problems is first, to understand their problems. I completely agree. That is exactly what BaZi is all about. Understanding your problems, and then fixing them. Sounds easy, right?

Perhaps you have heard about this very famous international best-seller called 'Who Moved My Cheese' by Dr Spencer Johnson. It's a great story that applies to BaZi as well. In 'Who Moved My Cheese', Dr Johnson talks about two mice who discover one day that someone has 'moved their cheese'. He then talks about the mouse who goes looking for cheese after it disappears from the maze, and the other mouse who keeps going back to the same place in the maze, hoping the cheese will appear again.

When it comes to BaZi, people fall broadly into two categories. Those who, having decoded their Destiny, act positively upon what they have learnt and see themselves as empowered by the knowledge, irrespective of whether or not what they learn is what they want to hear; and those who do nothing but continue to hope that their wildest dreams and ambitions will magically appear.

Every single BaZi has a dynamic and static component to it. It has an unchanging value, as well as a changing value. Today, we no longer have the fatalistic approach to Destiny that prevailed in the old days. Destiny is not only what is already made, but what you make of it also.

In other words, there are always options.

So why then do some people come out of a BaZi consultation feeling dissatisfied? Or how it is that some people, upon decoding their Destiny, become demoralised rather than empowered? The difference, in my experience as a consultant, lies in how the person approaches the situation.

As a BaZi consultant, I tell a person what is in the chart. That means the good, and the bad. My role as a consultant is not to tell a person - give up on your dream, unless that dream is truly unattainable. My role is to encourage a person in the areas that they need and deserve encouragement, and also offer them advice on avoiding the wayward path. There is a big difference between hope, and false hope. BaZi is not about false hope.

Sometimes, we have to tell people things they don't want to hear. One of the most obvious examples of telling people what they don't want to hear includes making it known that they will not become rich beyond their wildest dreams and they are not about to strike the lottery. It is often devastatingly hard for people to accept that they are going to have to make their money the old-fashioned way: through hard-work!

Do I tell people to accept mediocrity? Mediocrity is a state of mind. It is a matter of perception. If you are a modest school-teacher, but your children are great successes - are you mediocre? If you are not rich, but you are blissfully married and contented with your life, are you mediocre?

Do I tell people to accept that they will never be millionaires? No. I tell them to realise that they will have to work hard and smart to become a millionaire. That for some, opportunities for them are fewer so they must make the most of what comes their way. That thinking about short-cuts will not get them anywhere.

Sure, everyone wants to be a millionaire at 30. But does it matter if you didn't achieve it by 30, if you got there eventually?

In BaZi, there are always solutions. But people who feel that BaZi offers no solution are people who don't like what they have heard or refuse to move the goalposts. They insist on holding on to something which they haven't even grabbed hold of in the first place. They are impatient, focused on the now and cannot see how 'bad news' can be good. If it was the case that bad news is never good, then CNN would be out of business. If it was the case that bad news is never good, we wouldn't have weather forecasts.

Empowerment is not just about working with the positive. It is also about the negative. Sometimes, people only make progress after a jolt or a scare.

Other times, they need hope and the knowledge that there is a light at the end of the tunnel. BaZi is not a 'need to know basis' type of knowledge. It is a 'the more you know, the better' field of knowledge.

People who win with BaZi and who gain the most out of BaZi are those with the ability to first, accept a situation, and then, figure out how to make the most of the situation.

Okay, it's hard to accept sometimes. You know what? Go home, have a cry, stay in bed for 10 days, eat gallons of ice cream, call your best-friend and tell them about it, whine, grumble, complain, shake your fist at the heavens, beat a boxing bag, throw darts at Bill Gates' picture - whatever. (By the way, BaZi will also tell you which works best for you when it comes to situations like this!)

Then, take decisive action. Make the change you have to make. Re-align your goals to what is best for you at this point in time. Adjust your expectations if you have to. Bide your time. Strategise. Craft your response, for the right time.

Your Destiny is shaped by the actions you take and the decisions you make based on your chart!

Many a time, people forget that the 33 percent of BaZi comes hand in hand with the 33 percent of Man Luck. And let's face it, not enough of us make use of Man Luck. There are many things that are within the power of a person to change. 99.9 percent of the time, it is a question of whether they want to, or do not want to do what is needed. Can they bite the bullet? Man Luck refers to what you do (or don't do), your thoughts, your goals, your principles and basically your virtues. Anything within your control is Man Luck – the 33% component in the Heaven, Earth and Man Cosmic Trinity.

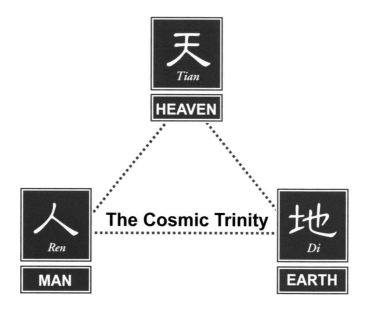

I didn't say it would be easy. But nothing is worth doing if it is easy now, is it? And the greatest rewards come to those who are prepared to do what it takes, to achieve their goals, whatever that may be.

It is not about being 'governed' by destiny, it is about 'shaping' our destiny. If our destiny is good, follow it. If the destiny is unfavourable, then don't walk down that path. Why do you think that in military academies, they still teach military officers about retreat? Because in war, pride is not a factor. Winning is what counts. And if you have to retreat to avoid defeat, then you retreat.

BaZi offers the answer to the question of what is the problem. Man Luck - your own efforts, your actions, your deeds, your choices, is the solution.

Every person in their life, has a moment. That point in their life, when all is as it should be. You can stand by, and let that moment slip past you, or you can grab it and run with it.

What if it has already passed you by? Then you grab what is on the plate now, and make the most of that. Complaining or feeling sorry for yourself gets you nowhere. Doing something, at the very least, means you have made an effort.

The power is in your hands. You can be what my English students call 'a moaning minnie' and complain about your lot in life, or you can get on with the business of achieving your goals, modified of course, to the circumstances and situation of your Destiny Code, and strive to be the best YOU can be, knowing what that is. The choice is yours.

The world has no room for losers today. But being a winner is not about crossing the finish line first, or being one of the richest persons on the planet. Being a winner is living your life on your terms, and being firmly in the driver's seat, rather than being dictated by backseat drivers. It is taking control of your life and facing up to yourself, and making the best of your situations, warts and all. It is understanding who you are, being comfortable with that person, and achieving happiness.

Delving Deeper into your Destiny Code

In my previous book, *The Destiny Code*, we talked about BaZi as a tool for personal empowerment, and most importantly, the basics of deriving your personal Destiny Code. I showed you how to plot your personal BaZi chart, plot the Luck Pillars, as well as the Age Luck Limits, which tells you when your Luck Pillars change. Another important component of the basics of BaZi is the Five Elements and the Five Element cycles.

You can also obtain your personal Destiny Code by visiting my website **www.joeyyap.com** and using the BaZi Ming Pan calculator there. Of course, plotting by hand is preferred at this stage to familiarise yourself with all the characters, but if you want to be fast or perhaps you just don't want to carry *The Ten Thousand Year Calendar* around with you, then using the calculator is convenient.

So by this stage, you would know your personal Day Master 日元, be familiar with your personal BaZi chart, be aware of your current Luck Pillar and know which of the Five Elements represent the Five Factors for your Day Master. Incidentally, you should note that the Age Limits for the Luck Pillars is your Chinese Age. So to get your Western Age, minus one year off the Age Limit. All the examples that are used in this book refer to the Chinese Age, so minus one year for the Western Age.

In case you've forgotten, briefly, the Five Factors are Wealth 財星, Companion 比劫, Influence 官殺, Output 食傷 and Resource 印星. Here's a quick recap of the Five Factors for each of the 10 Day Masters.

Day Master	財星 Wealth Element	食傷 Output Element	官殺 Influence Element	印星 Resource Element	比劫 Companion Element
木 Wood 甲,乙 Jia Yi	Earth	Fire	Metal	Water	Wood
金 Metal 庚,辛 Geng Xin	Wood	Water	Fire	Earth	Metal
水 Water 壬,癸 Ren Gui	Fire	Wood	Earth	Metal	Water
土 Earth 戊,己 Wu Ji	Water	Metal	Wood	Fire	Earth
火 Fire 丙,丁 Bing Ding	Metal	Earth	Water	Wood	Fire

The next step in decoding your Destiny is to understand the relationships that are present within your personal Destiny Chart. What do I mean by relationships?

Every element in your chart has an elemental relationship or interaction with the other elements in your chart. The next stage in decoding a BaZi is understanding and appreciating how the Heavenly Stems in your BaZi interact with each other and also how the Earthly Branches in your BaZi interact with each other. To do this, you will need to understand the different types of relationships that Heavenly Stems and Earthly Branches can have. Hence, *The Destiny Code Revealed* is very much about understanding the relationships of the codes in your chart.

八字解碼

合 Clash 沖

合 Combination

害 Harm

刑 Punishment

破 Destruction

As with broaching any new subject, we must always begin at the basics. So in this book, I will be exploring the key basic relationships between the elements in a Destiny chart that you will need to know. These relationships go by the names of Combination 合, Clash 沖, Harm 害, Punishment 刑 and Destruction 破. As we delve deeper into the study of BaZi and your appreciation of BaZi becomes more sophisticated, these basic relationships will take on a new dimension and the information you derive from these relationships will also become more precise.

These key basic relationships are a new level of codes that unlock new information and bring dimension and depth to a Destiny Code. By understanding how the various elements of the BaZi chart interact with each other, and understanding who or what these relationships relate to or involve in (i.e.: objects, individuals, events), we can then decode the kinds of challenges, or the possibilities that are open to a person, during a specific period of time in their life, as well as during their life journey. Combination, Clash, Harm, Punishment and Destruction relationships give us indications on all aspects of a person's life - marriage, business partnerships, health, moving house, gaining new assets and even, if you're going to be forgetful or lose your keys.

Now, like I have said before, do not be alarmed by the names of these BaZi terms. Treat them as technical terms used to describe an elemental relationship between two components of your BaZi chart. No doubt, as you read through the chapters and study your personal Destiny chart, you will find that some of the elemental relationships are present in your chart. Don't be alarmed or concerned or get negative about the situation - remember, the point of BaZi is to get information and empower yourself.

That means that if you have decoded something negative or perhaps less-desirable in your BaZi, you need to DO SOMETHING ABOUT IT.

In BaZi, Action Matters

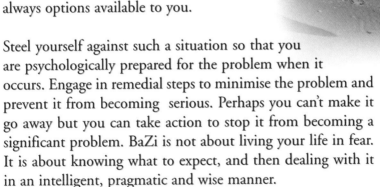

If you look back at my introduction to BaZi in *The Destiny Code*, you will notice that I constantly talk about 'taking action'. That is what BaZi is all about. Knowing the problem, and then taking active steps to prevent the problem from occurring. When faced with a situation, there are always options available to you.

Steel yourself against such a situation so that you are psychologically prepared for the problem when it occurs. Engage in remedial steps to minimise the problem and prevent it from becoming serious. Perhaps you can't make it go away but you can take action to stop it from becoming a significant problem. BaZi is not about living your life in fear. It is about knowing what to expect, and then dealing with it in an intelligent, pragmatic and wise manner.

In many cases, you might find that there are some positive codes in your chart! Then, more than anything, you need to TAKE ACTION because only then can you benefit from the opportunities when they arrive! Perhaps you discover that you have some latent talents that have yet to be awakened – then it's time to take action and unleash those hidden abilities! Your destiny is in your hands. Understand your life path, make better decisions to shape your destiny and live a better life. That should be your goal in studying your own personal Destiny Code.

Let the BaZi decoding process begin!

Chapter Two:
Composing the Code

A person's Destiny Code or BaZi (sometimes called 'Eight Characters' or 'Four Pillars of Destiny') is derived from a person's birth data: the year, month, day and hour of birth. A BaZi comprises of Heavenly Stems, which form the top four characters of a BaZi, and Earthly Branches, which form the bottom four characters of a BaZi.

	時 Hour	日 Day	月 Month	年 Year	
Heavenly Stems	辛 *Xin* **Yin Metal**	壬 *Ren* **Yang Water**	丙 *Bing* **Yang Fire**	乙 *Yi* **Yin Wood**	天干 Heavenly Stems
Earthly Branches	亥 *Hai* **Pig** Yin Water	戌 *Xu* **Dog** Yang Earth	戌 *Xu* **Dog** Yang Earth	未 *Wei* **Goat** Yin Earth	地支 Earthly Branches
	壬 *Ren*　甲 *Jia*	丁 *Ding*　戊 *Wu*　辛 *Xin*	丁 *Ding*　戊 *Wu*　辛 *Xin*	乙 *Yi*　己 *Ji*　丁 *Ding*	藏干 Hidden Stems

You might be wondering: how did the Chinese create this system of BaZi? It all started with the Chinese calendar. The Chinese calendar traditionally was produced and distributed by the Imperial Palace, under the auspices of the reigning emperor. A specialised department within the Imperial Palace was tasked with coming up with the calendar every year, with information on eclipses, astrological observations and of course, information about the harvest for agricultural needs. The Chinese have always had both a lunar and solar calendar but around 2BC, a consistent date for the Winter Solstice was introduced, resulting in the use of a dual-system calendar.

The solar calendar uses a sexagenary cycle to count the years, months and days but in the early days of the calendar, it was only the days that were counted.

The result of this calendaring system was that in any one month, there are only a maximum of three repetitions of any one day. Finding that this system was still not quite ideal, the 12 Earthly Branches were paired with each Heavenly Stem, creating sixty pairs, each pair known as a pair of Jia Zi 甲子. Hence, the Chinese Solar calendar consists of 60 paired pillars or Jia Zi 甲子, for each Year, Month, Day and Hour.

The 60 Jia Zi 甲子 Table

八字
解碼

甲 寅 *Jia Yin* Wood Tiger	甲 辰 *Jia Chen* Wood Dragon	甲 午 *Jia Wu* Wood Horse	甲 申 *Jia Shen* Wood Monkey	甲 戌 *Jia Xu* Wood Dog	甲 子 *Jia Zi* Wood Rat
乙 卯 *Yi Mao* Wood Rabbit	乙 巳 *Yi Si* Wood Snake	乙 未 *Yi Wei* Wood Goat	乙 酉 *Yi You* Wood Rooster	乙 亥 *Yi Hai* Wood Pig	乙 丑 *Yi Chou* Wood Ox
丙 辰 *Bing Chen* Fire Dragon	丙 午 *Bing Wu* Fire Horse	丙 申 *Bing Shen* Fire Monkey	丙 戌 *Bing Xu* Fire Dog	丙 子 *Bing Zi* Fire Rat	丙 寅 *Bing Yin* Fire Tiger
丁 巳 *Ding Si* Fire Snake	丁 未 *Ding Wei* Fire Goat	丁 酉 *Ding You* Fire Rooster	丁 亥 *Ding Hai* Fire Pig	丁 丑 *Ding Chou* Fire Ox	丁 卯 *Ding Mao* Fire Rabbit
戊 午 *Wu Wu* Earth Horse	戊 申 *Wu Shen* Earth Monkey	戊 戌 *Wu Xu* Earth Dog	戊 子 *Wu Zi* Earth Rat	戊 寅 *Wu Yin* Earth Tiger	戊 辰 *Wu Chen* Earth Dragon
己 未 *Ji Wei* Earth Goat	己 酉 *Ji You* Earth Rooster	己 亥 *Ji Hai* Earth Pig	己 丑 *Ji Chou* Earth Ox	己 卯 *Ji Mao* Earth Rabbit	己 巳 *Ji Si* Earth Snake
庚 申 *Geng Shen* Metal Monkey	庚 戌 *Geng Xu* Metal Dog	庚 子 *Geng Zi* Metal Rat	庚 寅 *Geng Yin* Metal Tiger	庚 辰 *Geng Chen* Metal Dragon	庚 午 *Geng Wu* Metal Horse
辛 酉 *Xin You* Metal Rooster	辛 亥 *Xin Hai* Metal Pig	辛 丑 *Xin Chou* Metal Ox	辛 卯 *Xin Mao* Metal Rabbit	辛 巳 *Xin Si* Metal Snake	辛 未 *Xin Wei* Metal Goat
壬 戌 *Ren Xu* Water Dog	壬 子 *Ren Zi* Water Rat	壬 寅 *Ren Yin* Water Tiger	壬 辰 *Ren Chen* Water Dragon	壬 午 *Ren Wu* Water Horse	壬 申 *Ren Shen* Water Monkey
癸 亥 *Gui Hai* Water Pig	癸 丑 *Gui Chou* Water Ox	癸 卯 *Gui Mao* Water Rabbit	癸 巳 *Gui Si* Water Snake	癸 未 *Gui Wei* Water Goat	癸 酉 *Gui You* Water Rooster

That is why a person's Destiny Code comprises of Eight Characters or Four Pillars. It is one Jia Zi 甲子 for the year, month, day and hour of birth.

八字
解
碼

The Ten Heavenly Stems (十天干) and 12 Earthly Branches (十二地支) are the central focal point of BaZi as a field of study. There are a total of 22 characters to commit to memory and it is important to know them at your fingertips in order to speed up the process of learning BaZi.

Now, here is the magic of the system of BaZi. Each character carries a different meaning, depending on the context. A single character can represent a diverse range of objects, subject matter, relationships, people and events. And each character's value is changed, enhanced, or weakened, depending on how the character presents in a chart.

By judging the quality of these characters in a person's Destiny Code, we can find out a range of details about their lives, their aspirations, their hopes, their ambitions, their talents, their abilities, their relationships and their deepest dreams. That is the power of BaZi.

The Building Blocks of BaZi

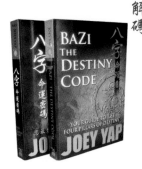

In my first book, *The Destiny Code*, I exposed readers to the ten Heavenly Stems and twelve Earthly Branches. As the Stems and Branches are an essential component of a BaZi, they bear repeating.

Let's first review the Ten Heavenly Stems first, with the diagram below:

甲	乙	丙	丁	戊	己	庚	辛	壬	癸
Jia	*Yi*	*Bing*	*Ding*	*Wu*	*Ji*	*Geng*	*Xin*	*Ren*	*Gui*
Yang Wood	Yin Wood	Yang Fire	Yin Fire	Yang Earth	Yin Earth	Yang Metal	Yin Metal	Yang Water	Yin Water

As you will remember in *The Destiny Code*, I mentioned the importance of trying to approach BaZi from a pictorial standpoint, early on. Many of the attributes of the Stems and Branches are derived from the sages' observations of nature, planetary movements and the universe. So it is important to think in pictures as often as you can, when you are looking at a BaZi.

Jia 甲 Wood is the first of the Ten Heavenly Stems. Jia 甲 Wood is Yang Wood. When picturing Jia 甲 Wood, think of tall trees, big trees, timber and big logs. This wood is tough, hard and rough.

Yi 乙 Wood is the second of the Ten Heavenly Stems. Yi 乙 Wood is Yin Wood. To picture Yi 乙 Wood, think of flowers, twigs, leaves or grass. Yi 乙 Wood is flexible and supple.

Bing 丙 is a Fire Element Heavenly Stem. It is Yang Fire. Picture Bing 丙 Fire as the great ball of fire we call the Sun. This fire gives warmth, and nurtures life and all living beings on earth. Its warmth is felt across the planet.

Ding 丁 is Yin Fire. Picture Ding 丁 as a candle, or the glowing embers from the fireplace. It can brighten up a small room, and illuminate the darkness.

Wu 戊 Earth should be pictured as boulders or large rocks. Wu 戊 is tough, hard and stable. It is strong and unyielding. Wu 戊 Earth can barricade water and stop fire from spreading. Wu 戊 Earth is Yang Earth.

Ji 己 Earth is the earth from the fields or from the soil. Picture wet, fertile, volcanic soil, which grows crops. Ji 己 Earth is easily dispersed by water. Ji 己 Earth is Yin Earth.

Picture Geng 庚 Metal as a chunk of raw metal ore. It can also be seen as a large sword or an axe. Unyielding, tough, strong, and cutting are some of the attributes of Geng 庚 Metal. It is the Yang manifestation of the Metal element.

Gold, silver and platinum jewelry, a finely crafted pen, or a beautiful ring - these are some of the visual images of Xin 辛 Metal It is delicate, beautiful and attractive. Xin 辛 Metal is the Yin manifestation of the Metal element.

Ren 壬 Water is the great sea, the roaring river. It is always moving and gushing. It is Yang Water.

Gui 癸 Water represents mist, cloud, dew and gentle rains. It is subtle, gentle, refined in nature. Gui 癸 Water is Yin Water.

八字
解
碼

It is important to know which is the Yin and Yang variation of each of the Five Elements that form the ten Heavenly Stems. However, as you advance through your journey of understanding BaZi, you must also speak the language of BaZi. Begin by calling the ten Heavenly Stems by their names, rather than their element and polarity. What do I mean by their names? Say Jia 甲 Wood instead of Yang Wood. Say Ren 壬 Water when you mean Yang Water.

You should also try to appreciate the pictorial quality of the Stems. Every time you think of Jia 甲 Wood, imagine a soaring California redwood. Each time you think of Ding 丁 Fire, imagine a slim, flickering candle in the night. By understanding BaZi by elements, polarity and 'image', you are starting the process of learning BaZi in the right dimension.

There's another very good reason for referring to the ten Heavenly Stems by their names and also, keeping the pictorial image of the Stems in mind. It relates to a core concept of BaZi analysis, which requires all analysis be related to and defined by the Heavenly Stem of your Day of Birth.

Day Master ◄————————┐

時 Hour	日 Day	月 Month	年 Year	
辛	壬	丙	乙	天干 Heavenly Stems
Xin Yin Metal	Ren Yang Water	Bing Yang Fire	Yi Yin Wood	
亥	戌	戌	未	地支 Earthly Branches
Hai Pig Yin Water	Xu Dog Yang Earth	Xu Dog Yang Earth	Wei Goat Yin Earth	
壬 甲 Ren Jia	丁 戊 辛 Ding Wu Xin	丁 戊 辛 Ding Wu Xin	乙 己 丁 Yi Ji Ding	藏干 Hidden Stems

The Heavenly Stem of your Day of Birth is known as the 'Day Master'. Your Day Master 日元 is not JUST the Heavenly Stem of your day of birth. It is not just a calendar symbol. Your Day Master is YOU. It represents you - your basic nature, your characteristics, your behaviour, even your appearance! The Day Master is your personal element.

So, from this page on, begin to think of yourself in the context of BaZi. If you are born on a Bing 丙 Day, call yourself a Bing 丙 Fire Day Master. If your Day Master is Yin Water, refer to yourself as a Gui 癸 Water Day Master.

This is the first and very essential step towards using your personal Destiny Code to understand yourself better, and in turn, better yourself.

Know YOUR Day Master, Know Yourself!

By this stage, you would have plotted your own BaZi and identified your Day Master. If you are unfamiliar with plotting a BaZi chart, visit my website, **www.joeyyap.com** and you'll find a BaZi Ming Pan calculator that you can use. There's also a CD and PDA version for those who want to be able to do charts on the move. Personally, I advocate anyone interested in BaZi to learn how to plot the chart manually and you can find out how it is done by looking at the chapter on Plotting a BaZi chart in my first book, *The Destiny Code*. But for speed, the software makes life a lot easier.

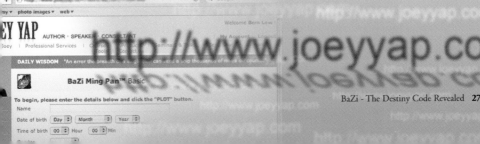

八字解碼

You probably have already begun to notice you have some personal characteristics, attributes or parts of your personality or innate nature that correspond to your Day Master. It's time to delve deeper into the Ten Heavenly Stems and understand more about the characteristics of each of the ten Heavenly Stems.

You might be wondering - why are we still on the subject of the Day Master? What about the other 7 characters in the Destiny Chart?

Day Master ←

時 Hour	日 Day	月 Month	年 Year	
辛 *Xin* **Yin Metal**	壬 *Ren* **Yang Water**	丙 *Bing* **Yang Fire**	乙 *Yi* **Yin Wood**	天干 Heavenly Stems
亥 *Hai* **Pig** Yin Water	戌 *Xu* **Dog** Yang Earth	戌 *Xu* **Dog** Yang Earth	未 *Wei* **Goat** Yin Earth	地支 Earthly Branches
壬 甲 *Ren* *Jia*	丁 戊 辛 *Ding* *Wu* *Xin*	丁 戊 辛 *Ding* *Wu* *Xin*	乙 己 丁 *Yi* *Ji* *Ding*	藏干 Hidden Stems

The Day Master is the central focus of a BaZi chart - it provides context, background and definition for a chart. Also, remember, we must not under-estimate the importance of basics. As you delve deeper into BaZi, or if you are keen to do some reading of your own, you will discover that many BaZi classics, such as Di Tian Sui 滴天髓, are all dedicated to the finer attributes of each Day Master! So, while the Day Master is but one of the characters in a BaZi, it is definitely a Very Important Character!

So, let's find out more about each of the 10 Day Masters.

Knock on Wood

In the study of BaZi, Jia 甲 and Yi 乙 Wood are seen as pieces of Wood. Most of us have seen a piece of Wood. As the name implies, these people are usually straight, and unchanging. After all, when was the last time you saw a piece of wood that was curved unless it has become warped. In which case, it's not a good piece of wood, is it?

Wood people tend to be quite set in their ways, but are sentimental at heart. Trees (even the little weeds), never stray far from where they have been planted. Hence, Wood people often need to stay in the same spot and remain rooted. Naturally, uprooting carries a more severe effect on Wood people than other types of Day Masters.

However, it is this rooting that makes Wood people able to persist at their chosen field and eventually, their efforts will bear fruit. Thus, Wood people rarely are people without some kind of progress in life and they usually have a great deal of determination and drive. It may not be obvious but remember, we rarely see trees grow, but that does not mean they are not growing!

Within these broad characteristics, the Yin and Yang manifestation of the Wood element adds layers and complexity to the basic make-up and character of Wood people. Now, it is important to remember that each Jia 甲 Wood Day Master will be further qualified by their month of birth - you get different types of wood from different parts of the world as climate and conditions affect the Wood. But it is possible to derive some fairly general characteristics.

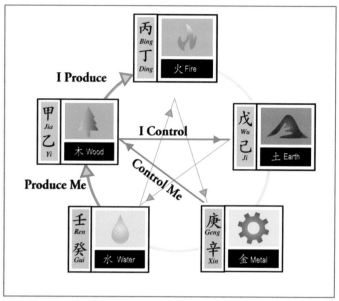

Wood's Elemental Relationship

甲 *Jia* **Yang Wood**

Jia 甲 Wood Day Masters are commonly steady, forthright, direct (sometimes, tactless) and stern, generally not very animated types. Stiff, is probably a good way to describe Jia Wood Day Masters. They can also be thick, not in terms of lacking in intelligence, but with regard to their perception of what is going on around them. They sometimes appear unfeeling but it is not because they are not sentimental, but rather, they simply are not tuned in to what is going on around them.

Jia Wood types are usually determined and keen to improve their lives. However, they also tend to be quite conservative and reluctant to make changes, until these changes are forced on them. This sometimes stymies their personal development and growth but often, Jia Wood will spring back eventually and recover from the change, just as a tree eventually recovers from being struck by an axe. It just takes a very long time!

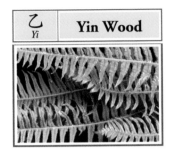

| 乙
_{Yi} | **Yin Wood** |

The potted plants, beautiful flowers and twines that are Yi 乙 Wood are quite the opposite of their 'stiff' Jia Wood brethren. One of Yi Wood's defining characteristics is its flexible and adaptable nature. Like twines that eventually reach the sunlight at the top of the forest canopy, Yi Wood types always 'find' their way in life. They have a survivalist nature. Yi Wood people are generally not ruthless and their ability to adapt to changes quickly is always a strong point in their favour. These are people who avoid trouble by ducking out of the way or slinking away until the trouble dies down! However, Yi Wood types also tend to be like grass in the wind - they are fickle and rarely commit one way or another. They change their minds quickly and can be difficult to keep up with because they refuse to stick to one course of action.

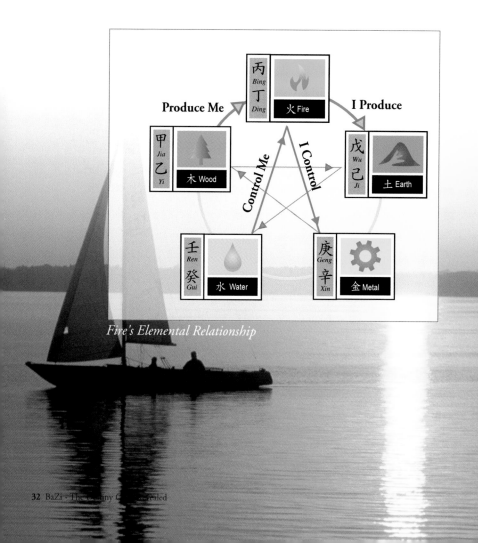

Burning Flames

It is rare to meet a Fire Day Master who is not passionate, expressive, compassionate, warm and friendly. Bing 丙 and Ding 丁 Fire people usually have an illuminating quality about them - they can create warmth and bring out the best in people.

Of course, just telling someone they are passionate is a bit on the thin side, so let's see how the two Fire elements stack up against each other.

Fire's Elemental Relationship

丙 *Bing*	**Yang Fire**

Bing 丙 Fire, like the fire of the sun, 'radiates' warmth. It's rare to meet a Bing Fire who hasn't touched someone's life. Bing Fire types are usually generous and open. Of course, depending on the brightness and radiance of their Day Master, Bing 丙 Fire types can be vibrant, vivacious, and yes, sunny in disposition, or gloomy and not very good at expressing their feelings.

However, generally, most Bing Fire people are sincere, just and upright, noble types. They rarely have a hidden agenda and are frequently not the type to carry a 20-Year grudge. They are sentimental, charitable and if you dig deep enough, you'll find they are passionate about a cause, a belief or a principle. Of course, when you are the center of the universe, that comes with a certain amount of pride and ego. Sometimes, Bing Fire types think the world revolves around them (it does, but that's just from the astrological perspective!). And like the sun, they are often very routine-orientated and easily reach a plateau, becoming bored with their jobs or work.

丁 *Ding*	**Yin Fire**

Illuminating is what best describes Ding 丁 Fire Day Masters. These are people who are born leaders, or often, people who take pride in showing people the way. Sometimes, they are fickle (just as the light of a candle flickers) but they also have a tremendous ability to rise to great occasions, just like a small fire can suddenly become a great bonfire. Meticulous, detail-orientated and sentimental, Ding Fire people are great motivators. The downside is, sometimes, they are easily de-motivated, because they forget to light their own fire!

I am a Rock

Trust is one of the most important values in life. Without trust, relationships would not work, society could not function and the world would not be a pleasant place to live in. Some people automatically inspire trust; others, no matter how hard they work, can't shake that shifty image.

In the study of Five Elements, Earth represents trust as it is the only element that is unmoving and eternal. Mountains have been here since the dawn of time, and they will still be there, at the end of time. Unmoving, strong, and protective. We come from Mother Earth, and in death, we return to Mother Earth. In the Chinese classics, it is said that Earth is the sum of ten thousand things.

Earth's nature is sincere but tough. Earth is often silent, but that does not mean that it is not thinking. Earth knows much, but does not offer up its secrets.

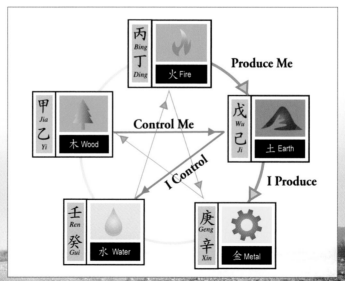

Earth's Elemental Relationship

 戊 Wu	**Yang Earth**

Wu 戊 is the Earth of stones and rocks. Wu Earth Day Masters are almost always solid, steady, dependable types, who are trustworthy and loyal. Wu Earth is very protective so if your best friend is a Wu Earth Day Master, they will definitely be someone you can count on to watch your back. Wu Earth types, however, tend to be unwavering and stubborn. They are at best inflexible, at worst, immovable, be it when it comes to taking action or their personal nature. Sometimes, it is this pigheadedness that proves costly.

 己 Ji	**Yin Earth**

Like the soft pliant soil from which crops spring forth, Ji 己 Earth is nurturing, productive and resourceful. Ji Earth Day Masters are usually good-hearted and are people to count on. Just like the earth tolerates the pollution that human beings create, Ji Earth usually puts up with quite a bit of abuse and will not withdraw its support just because of a little bit of unpleasantness. Ji Earth types are always 'understanding' of other people's weaknesses and fallacies. They rarely see the worst in people. The common weakness of Ji Earth Day Masters is a lack of adaptability, and frequently, an inability to make quick decisions or spontaneous decisions.

The Justice League

Joseph Campbell probably had Metal people in mind when he wrote about the Hero Myth. Just, righteous, standing up for the weak, enduring against the challenges to prevail, overcoming hardship and adversity - these are the common attributes associated with Metal Day Masters. Fair and square is very important to Metal Day Masters.

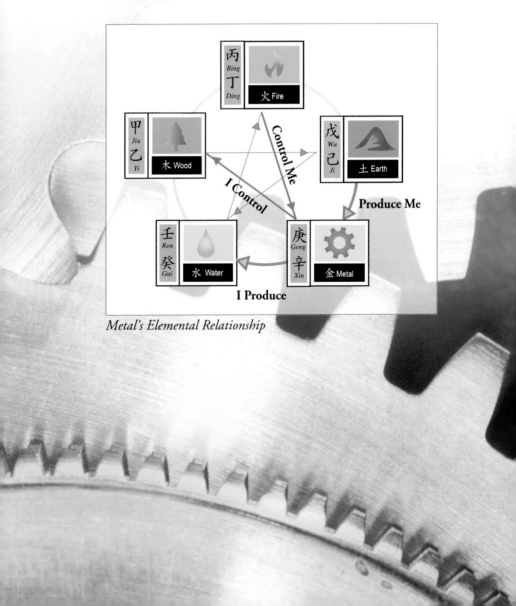

Metal's Elemental Relationship

 庚 *Geng*	**Yang Metal**

Geng 庚 Metal, like the sword and the axe, represents endurance and stamina. Geng Metal types are usually tough people who can tolerate hardship and endure suffering. They often achieve their goals through blood, sweat and tears and through their own hardwork and efforts. Geng Metal people are usually hands-on types who will not hesitate to do something themselves, if they think that is the better way to get something done. Geng Metal people are altruistic types, who value friendship and brotherhood. They are also usually leaders or strong characters. Their weakness however is a lack of flexible thinking and sometimes, they are hasty in their actions.

 辛 *Xin*	**Yin Metal**

Xin 辛 Metal, being fine jewelry, beautifully engraved items and beautiful metal, loves attention. Xin Metal Day Masters usually are attention-getters - sometimes it is their looks, sometimes it is their intellect. But whatever it is, they are people who love being in the spotlight and the focal point of everyone and if they are not, well, you can count on them to make a scene and one heck of a scene too!

Xin 辛 Metal types often seem tough and unyielding but bending their ear is not difficult if you know how to go about persuading them. Here's a hint: subtlety works, the sledgehammer approach doesn't! Xin Metal people often value relationships and are sentimental but their tendency to steal the show, or hog the limelight, can be annoying. Face value is also very important to Xin Metal, and this can sometimes be their downfall.

Am I Intelligent?

Most people wants to know whether they are smart and intelligent. Some people believe they are, genuinely, while others don't think they are 'smart enough'. What element governs intelligence? Water. Water represents wisdom in the study of the Five Elements.

Water's shape changes a thousand forms. Water is formless and shapes according to whatever condition it is presented with. Water is deep and the bottom is unseen. Just like a person's thoughts cannot be seen – water is deep and infinite.

Water is always on the move. Even in a still state, its particles move.

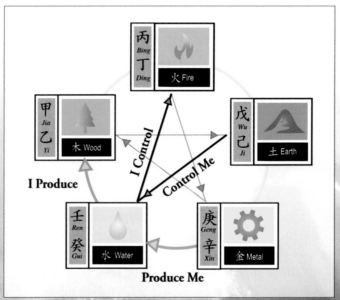

Water's Elemental Relationship

| 壬 Ren | Yang Water |

Ren 壬 Water people, like the water of the river and sea, are always on the move. Adaptive, intelligent and usually unable to stand or sit still, Ren Water people are also usually extroverts. They always have something on the boil (Water is always moving) but run the risk of becoming easily distracted and lacking focus. Ren Water types are adventurous people who enjoy robust activities. When they put their mind to it, Ren Water people are unstoppable! They are however often rebellious and dislike being made to conform.

| 癸 Gui | Yin Water |

Gui 癸 Water people, like the clouds and mist that drift and move, are usually also not the type to sit still. They make good teachers, since Gui Water's role is to water the plants, feed and grow a new generation. They are however usually introverts. Frequently imaginative and creative, they value principles and often think of the greater good. Gui Water people have one disadvantage and that is the lack of staying power with any endeavour.

The 12 Earthly Branches

Now that you are familiar with the ten Heavenly Stems and the Day Masters, it is time to move on to the second component of a BaZi, the Earthly Branches.

The table below shows you the 12 Earthly Branches. You will notice that they correspond with what is often loosely termed 'the animal signs'. Initially of course, you will find you prefer to refer to the Earthly Branches by their animal call signs as it were. However, try to familiarise yourself with the proper names and use these proper names. To learn BaZi, one must speak the language of BaZi. So, try to think of Rat as Zi 子, and Pig as Hai 亥, rather than just Rat and Pig.

子	丑	寅	卯	辰	巳	午	未	申	酉	戌	亥
Zi	Chou	Yin	Mao	Chen	Si	Wu	Wei	shen	You	Xu	Hai
Rat	Ox	Tiger	Rabbit	Dragon	Snake	Horse	Goat	Monkey	Rooster	Dog	Pig

The 12 Earthly Branches are used to represent 'time' and 'seasonal Qi' in the study of BaZi. Earthly Branches contain stronger 'Qi' than the Heavenly Stems. This is because the Branches represent the sector of the earth's orbit around the sun, whereas the Heavenly stem is only 'Prevailing Qi'.

Branches are grouped into the 'seasons'. Now, you may remember this term from *The Destiny Code*. Just to refresh your memory, the seasons do not actually refer to the actual Four Seasons, although it is derived from the sages' observation of the seasons. For now, think of it as a descriptive language to describe the strength and cyclical nature of Qi.

The table below explains how the Earthly Branches are grouped by season.

The Hidden Stems: Keys to the Code

Earth contains ten thousand things. This is the saying in Chinese. In the study of BaZi, the Earthly Branches each 'contain' or store certain 'Heavenly Stems'. These are called the Hidden Stems and they play a major role in a complete BaZi analysis. In BaZi terminology, this is called Zi Cang Ren Yuan 支藏人元. To gain the full benefit of BaZi, it is essential to know the Hidden Stems contained in EACH of the 12 Earthly Branch.

The true nature of a Branch is determined by the main element or Main Qi hidden inside the Earthly Branch. The old books of BaZi write of 'Heavenly Qi' being pure and clear, and Earthly Qi being sophisticated and dense. Earthly Qi is sophisticated because it contains hidden Heavenly Stems inside. When we add all three together, we get the Cosmic Trinity: Heaven-Earth-Man in each pillar.

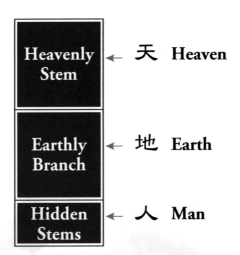

The table below explains what Hidden Stems are contained within each of the 12 Earthly Branches.

So, within the Earthly Branch of Yin 寅 (Tiger), there is Jia 甲 Wood, Bing 丙 Fire and Wu 戊 Earth. Inside the Zi 子 (Rat), there is Gui 癸 Water. Within the Xu 戌 (Dog), you will find hidden Wu 戊 Earth, Xin 辛 Metal and Ding 丁 Fire.

Some Earthly Branches contain just one Hidden Stem, while others contain up to three. The main thing to remember at this point, when it comes to Hidden Stems, is we are interested in the Main Qi of the branch. The Main Qi is the core Qi of that particular Earthly Branch.

春 Spring		
寅	卯	辰
Yin	Mao	Chen
Tiger	**Rabbit**	**Dragon**
Yang Wood	Yin Wood	Yang Earth
戊甲丙 Wu Jia Bing	乙 Yi	癸戊乙 Gui Wu Yi

夏 Summer		
巳	午	未
Si	Wu	Wei
Snake	**Horse**	**Goat**
Yin Fire	Yang Fire	Yin Earth
庚丙戊 Geng Bing Wu	丁己 Ding Ji	乙己丁 Yi Ji Ding

秋 Autumn		
申	酉	戌
Shen	You	Xu
Monkey	**Rooster**	**Dog**
Yang Metal	Yin Metal	Yang Earth
戊庚壬 Wu Geng Ren	辛 Xin	丁戊辛 Ding Wu Xin

冬 Winter		
亥	子	丑
Hai	Zi	Chou
Pig	**Rat**	**Ox**
Yin Water	Yang Water	Yin Earth
壬甲 Ren Jia	癸 Gui	辛己癸 Xin Ji Gui

People often get confused between the polarity of the Earthly Branch and the polarity of the Hidden Stems inside. Polarity here refers to whether it is Yin or Yang. For example, Wu 午 (Horse) has a Yang polarity, but inside, it contains Ding 丁 Fire or Yin Fire Stem! The polarity of the Earthly Branch can be different from the polarity of the Main Qi of the Hidden Stems. The polarity of the Earthly Branches and Hidden Stems do not always have to be the same.

The Hidden Stems (Cang Gan 藏干) in BaZi represent the 'auxiliary' stars in a BaZi. Like the name implies, these are hidden details. They represent the facets of a person, their relationships, their fears, their secrets and their aspirations that they don't tell anyone about! In some cases, they represent aspects of a person's personality or nature that even they do not know they have within them. The Hidden Stems tell the true story of the Destiny Code.

Not knowing the Hidden Stems is like not knowing how to plot a BaZi chart. Any kind of BaZi analysis must include an analysis of the Hidden Stems. Without the Hidden Stems, you are effectively only seeing 25% of the Code. It's like knowing a strand of DNA belongs to a mammal, but not knowing if it is a dog, whale or human being!

Of course students always like to ask, what is the easiest way to remember these Hidden Stems? Here is a quick summary to help you learn them better but remember, there's no substitute for good old fashioned memory work sometimes. So if you want to be good in BaZi, you MUST commit the Hidden Stems to memory.

One way is to group all 12 Earthly Branches into the following THREE groups:

Zi 子 (Rat), Wu 午 (Horse), Mao 卯 (Rabbit) and You 酉 (Rooster) as one group. Call this group the Four Cardinals (四正) group.

The 4 Cardinals 四正			
子 *Zi*	午 *Wu*	卯 *Mao*	酉 *You*
Rat	Horse	Rabbit	Rooster

Yin 寅 (Tiger), Shen 申 (Monkey), Si 巳 (Snake) and Hai 亥 (Pig) are another group. We call this the Four Growths (四生) group.

The 4 Growths 四生			
寅 *Yin*	申 *Shen*	巳 *Si*	亥 *Hai*
Tiger	Monkey	Snake	Pig

And lastly, the Chen 辰 (Dragon), Xu 戌 (Dog), Chou 丑 (Ox) and Wei 未 (Goat) are the group called the Four Graveyards (四墓).

The 4 Graveyards 四墓			
辰 *Chen*	戌 *Xu*	丑 *Chou*	未 *Wei*
Dragon	Dog	Ox	Goat

The Four Cardinals (四正)

The Four Cardinals are the 'direct' or pure Qi Earthly Branches. All of these 4, with the exception of Wu 午 (Horse), contain ONLY one Hidden Stem. Only Wu 午 (Horse) contains two Hidden Stems. And you will notice that they ALL contain Yin Hidden Stems.

四正 The 4 Cardinals	藏干 Hidden Stems	
子 Zi Rat	癸 Gui - Yin Water	
午 Wu Horse	丁 Ding - Yin Fire	己 Ji - Yin Earth
卯 Mao Rabbit	乙 Yi - Yin Wood	
酉 You Rooster	辛 Xin - Yin Metal	

The Four Growths (四生)

The Four Growths derive their name from the fact that in the study of advanced BaZi, these four branches are positioned in the 'Chang Sheng 長生' or growth stage of Qi. With the exception of Hai 亥 (Pig) branch, ALL the branches in this group have 3 Hidden Stems. Only Hai 亥 (Pig) contains 2 Hidden Stems. You will also notice that ALL of the Hidden Stems are Yang.

四生 The 4 Growth	藏干 Hidden Stems		
寅 Tiger Yin	甲 Jia - Yang Wood	丙 Bing - Yang Fire	戊 Wu - Yang Earth
申 Monkey Shen	庚 Geng - Yang Metal	壬 Ren - Yang Water	戊 Wu - Yang Earth
巳 Snake Si	丙 Bing - Yang Fire	戊 Wu - Yang Earth	庚 Geng - Yang Metal
亥 Pig Hai	壬 Ren - Yang Water	甲 Jia - Yang Wood	

The Four Graveyards (四墓)

The Four Graveyards are aptly termed to represent the four Earth element Earthly Branches. These four branches are sometimes also referred to as 'storage' because they store excess Qi. With the exception of the main Qi of Chen 辰 (Dragon) and Xu 戌 (Dog), ALL the Hidden Stems in the Four Graveyards are YIN Heavenly Stems and each of them contain 3 Heavenly Stems. Chen 辰 (Dragon) and Xu 戌 (Dog) are the ONLY two Earthly Branches in the system of twelve that contain both Yin and Yang Stems inside them.

四墓 The 4 Graveyards	藏干 Hidden Stems		
辰 Chen **Dragon**	戊 Wu - Yang Earth	乙 Yi - Yin Wood	癸 Gui - Yin Water
戌 Xu **Dog**	戊 Wu - Yang Earth	辛 Xin - Yin Metal	丁 Ding - Yin Fire
丑 Chou **Ox**	己 Ji - Yin Earth	癸 Gui - Yin Water	辛 Xin - Yin Metal
未 Wei **Goat**	己 Ji - Yin Earth	丁 Ding - Yin Fire	乙 Yi - Yin Wood

The Earthly Branches and Hidden Stems Summary Chart

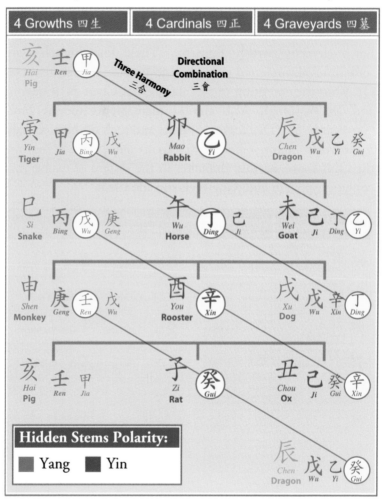

Some students of BaZi need to have an understanding before they can learn the Earthly Branches and Hidden Stems. Of course, the rote approach is best because it is FAST. Otherwise, you can use the grouping method I've described above. The key to proceeding through this book is familiarity with the Hidden Stems and the Earthly Branches. So take some time at this juncture to process and store the information I've given you here before continuing to Chapter 3.

Chapter Three:
Common BaZi Mistakes

You might be wondering why I have included a chapter on common BaZi mistakes. One of the major obstacles to successfully learning and making use of BaZi is starting off on the wrong foot. The basics are incorrect - so naturally, decoding the chart becomes wrong. How can you decode a Destiny Chart if the code is wrong to begin with?

So in this chapter, I want to highlight some common misconceptions and mistakes in order that you may proceed on your BaZi journey with the right perspective and understanding of the subject. The basics and fundamentals of any field of study are important - they are the roots in which you build your knowledge upon, so it is essential that the foundation is well set before proceeding to more advanced and sophisticated topics like Clashes, Combinations, Harms and Punishment Relationships.

八字
解碼

The BaZi Chart: Getting the Code Right

Do you recognise any of these symbols?

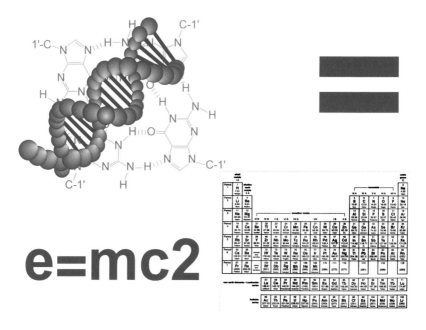

These are all mathematical and chemical tables, physics formulas and medical codes. From the time Crick and Watson posited the concept of the double helix, till today, it has remained more or less similar in its presentation form, only more sophisticated. The Equals sign has been used in mathematics for centuries. The Periodic Table hasn't changed since it was first invented. Hence, we must show the same respect for BaZi.

We cannot change the way the BaZi is presented simply to cater to whims and fancies or just to make it 'a little easier' for everyone to understand. Some fundamentals do not change.

This is an incorrect way to write a BaZi chart.

This is the correct way to present the Chart.

The Hidden Stems are another area where mistakes are common. Hidden Stems are sometimes regarded as an 'advanced subject', which is why many people who independently study BaZi are sometimes unaware of Hidden Stems. The most common mistake when it comes to Hidden Stems is getting the wrong polarity for the Main Qi of the Hidden Stems.

This mistake is common with the Wu 午 (Horse) and Hai 亥 (Pig) Hidden Stem. Now, the reason for this mistake is simple enough. As I mentioned in Chapter 2, the polarity of the Earthly Branch, and the polarity of the Hidden Stem inside the Earthly Branch, are not one and the same.

The above are examples of incorrectly written Hidden Stems for Wu 午 (Horse) and Hai 亥 (Pig) Branches

Take a look at this table, which illustrates for you the polarity of the Earthly Branches.

The Wu 午 (Horse) is a Yang Branch and the Hai 亥 (Pig) a Yin Branch. The ill-informed would presume that the Wu 午

(Horse) must contain Bing 丙 Fire since Wu 午 (Horse) is a Yang Branch and therefore, it must contain Yang Fire, which is Bing 丙 Fire. The same (incorrect!) assumption is extended to the Hai 亥 (Pig), which is a Yin Branch and so is assumed to contain Yin Water or Gui 癸 Water.

BaZi classics make it clear that the polarity of the Earthly Branch, especially when it comes to Fire and Water Branches, must not be confused with the polarity of the Hidden Stems. This is because Earthly Branches are, in Chinese Astrological terms, Palaces, with each palace containing certain Stars. The Stars, what we know as the Hidden Stems, each contain their own polarity. This is particularly the case with the Fire and Water Earthly Branches, which have a reverse polarity with the Hidden Stems they contain.

Here's the technical explanation for those who are interested in understanding this difference. Fire and Water are the transition between Yin and Yang. Hence, these Branches are Yin on the outside, but Yang on the inside, or vice versa.

Separate the polarity of the Earthly Branch from the polarity of the Hidden Stem in your mind, and you won't be making this mistake. Assume you are cleverer than the system (seriously, would all the classics be making the same mistake?), and that's when you get into trouble!

Some Branches, such as Chen 辰 (Dragon) and Xu 戌 (Dog) contain both Yin and Yang Hidden Stems. There is also a reason behind that but it is very complex so we shall leave that to another time. For now, the main thing to remember is that the polarity of the Earthly Branch and the Hidden Stems inside that Branch are not always the same.

Getting the Luck Pillars Right

Another area, where mistakes are frequent, relate to the Luck Pillars. Chapter Four of my previous book *The Destiny Code* explains how to correctly plot the Luck Pillars, so I shall not go into detail on that. Presentation of the Luck pillars should follow the technique of writing the BaZi from right to left, a form that all Chinese writing follows.

So, it is incorrect to present the Luck Pillars as follows:

16	26	36	46	56	66	
丙 *Bing* Yang Fire	乙 *Yi* Yin Wood	甲 *Jia* Yang Wood	癸 *Gui* Yin Water	壬 *Ren* Yang Water	辛 *Xin* Yin Metal	大運 Luck Pillars
辰 *Chen* Dragon Yang Earth	卯 *Mao* Rabbit Yin Wood	寅 *Yin* Tiger Yang Wood	丑 *Chou* Ox Yin Earth	子 *Zi* Rat Yang Water	亥 *Hai* Pig Yin Water	

This is the correct way to present the Luck Pillars:

86	76	66	56	46	36	26	16	6	
己 *Ji* Yin Earth	庚 *Geng* Yang Metal	辛 *Xin* Yin Metal	壬 *Ren* Yang Water	癸 *Gui* Yin Water	甲 *Jia* Yang Wood	乙 *Yi* Yin Wood	丙 *Bing* Yang Fire	丁 *Ding* Yin Fire	大運 Luck Pillars
酉 *You* Rooster Yin Metal	戌 *Xu* Dog Yang Earth	亥 *Hai* Pig Yin Water	子 *Zi* Rat Yang Water	丑 *Chou* Ox Yin Earth	寅 *Yin* Tiger Yang Wood	卯 *Mao* Rabbit Yin Wood	辰 *Chen* Dragon Yang Earth	巳 *Si* Snake Yin Fire	
辛	丁戊辛	壬甲	癸	辛己癸	戊甲丙	乙	癸戊乙	庚丙戊	

Common sense will tell you that it's easier to read the BaZi when both the BaZi and Luck pillars are written using the same form, which is from right to left. Imagine how hard it would be if you had to read the BaZi characters from right to left, and then the Luck Pillars from left to right - how confusing would that be?

As people say, if it isn't broken, don't fix it. BaZi has been written in this form since the days of its founder Master Xu Zi Ping 徐子平 and even before his time! So why change it when there is nothing wrong with it?

It may seem like I am harping on a minor point but just like learning BaZi requires appreciating its language, so we must respect the forms. You don't see modern mathematicians changing the equals sign, or rewriting e=mc2 to make it look more 'marketable' or 'easier to understand' - why do that with BaZi?

Quality, not Quantity

This mantra bears repeating, ad nauseam. I rarely use so strong a word as 'never' but in the case of counting the elements in a chart, it is not only the wrong way to approach BaZi, but it is something you should NEVER do.

The objective in any BaZi analysis is to unlock the coded information within the chart, and then determine how to bring balance to the chart through the elements.

By balance, we are referring to the balance of the elemental energies in the chart and the flow of Qi. This is because when the chart is balanced, then the Qi is flowing smoothly between the elements and so the person is comfortable, happy and able to perform at their best and maximise the opportunities that come their way.

Just because you have an equal number of the Five Elements, does not mean your BaZi is balanced. In classical BaZi, there are techniques for evaluating whether or not a BaZi is balanced, but these are not based on mathematical considerations as simple as counting the elements. For that matter, just because a particular element shows a zero value, does not mean that the element is entirely absent from the chart. In some instances, the element is still regarded as present, even though through 'counting', there is a zero value. (You need to check the Hidden Stems!)

Counting your wealth, before it hatches

Ultimately, when it comes to evaluating a BaZi chart, quantity is never the deciding factor. Otherwise, everyone with a high 'Wealth Element' count would effectively be millionaires. But yet, you can encounter charts where there is a preponderance of Wealth Elements in the chart, but the person is not anywhere near a millionaire. To illustrate the danger of counting the elements in the chart, take a look at this example below. It was brought to me by a student. I will first tell you the analysis derived by this student and then explain the correct approach to decoding the chart.

時 Hour	日 Day	月 Month	年 Year	
辛	丙	丁	丙	天干 Heavenly Stems
Xin	Bing	Ding	Bing	
Yin Metal	Yang Fire	Yin Fire	Yang Fire	
卯	戌	酉	辰	地支 Earthly Branches
Mao	Xu	You	Chen	
Rabbit	Dog	Rooster	Dragon	
Yin Wood	Yang Earth	Yin Metal	Yang Earth	
乙	丁 戊 辛	辛	癸 戊 乙	藏干 Hidden Stems
Yi	Ding Wu Xin	Xin	Gui Wu Yi	

82	72	62	52	42	32	22	12	2	
丙	乙	甲	癸	壬	辛	庚	己	戊	大運 Luck Pillars
Bing	Yi	Jia	Gui	Ren	Xin	Geng	Ji	Wu	
Yang Fire	Yin Wood	Yang Wood	Yin Water	Yang Water	Yin Metal	Yang Metal	Yin Earth	Yang Earth	
午	巳	辰	卯	寅	丑	子	亥	戌	
Wu	Si	Chen	Mao	Yin	Chou	Zi	Hai	Xu	
Horse	Snake	Dragon	Rabbit	Tiger	Ox	Rat	Pig	Dog	
Yang Fire	Yin Fire	Yang Earth	Yin Wood	Yang Wood	Yin Earth	Yang Water	Yin Water	Yang Earth	
丁己	庚丙戊	癸戊乙	乙	戊甲丙	辛己癸	癸	壬甲	丁戊辛	

1 October 1976 at Rabbit Hour (5.45 am), MALE

八字
解碼

Based on the 'counting method', the student declared the chart to be weak but yet due to the other two Fire elements and the two Wood elements, was not that weak since Wood and Fire support the Bing 丙 Fire Day Master. Wealth was strong in this chart according to this student because of the number of Wealth elements (3 in total) and the fact that there is additional wealth from the extra element of metal that comes into the picture through the You 酉 (Rooster) and Chen 辰 (Dragon) combination. When will the person become rich? I asked this student casually - it is a learning exercise after all! The answer was during the Geng Zi 庚子 Luck Pillar, as Water was favourable to the chart since there is only one Water element, based on the counting method.

Of course, if you're counting the elements, I'm sure that's the correct interpretation. And even then, this interpretation is just technical mumbo-jumbo. It tells us nothing about the person, which is part of the study of BaZi. But since counting is the wrong way to analyse a BaZi, the analysis is not quite correct.

Here is the correct interpretation. This is a weak Bing 丙 Fire Day Master but not because of the number of elements, but because of the SEASON of birth. Remember in *The Destiny Code*, we talked about the seasons and which element is strongest in what season? Well in Autumn, Fire is weak to begin with.

死 Dead	囚 Trap	休 Weak	相 Strong	旺 Prosperous	Strength / Season
土 Earth	金 Metal	水 Water	火 Fire	木 Wood	春 Spring
金 Metal	水 Water	木 Wood	土 Earth	火 Fire	夏 Summer
木 Wood	火 Fire	土 Earth	水 Water	金 Metal	秋 Autumn
火 Fire	土 Earth	金 Metal	木 Wood	水 Water	冬 Winter

Bing 丙 Fire cannot be read like the other Day Master's when it comes to the strength of the Day Master. Bing 丙 is the fire of the sun. Since when does burning Wood make the sun brighter? When you reach a more sophisticated level of BaZi, your appreciation of the elements will change and you will realise, not all Fire is strengthened by Wood. Wood in fact, only helps the Ding 丁 Fire in the chart. Finally, this Bing 丙 Fire Day Master is born at the Rabbit Hour (5am-7am). The sun is dim at this hour of the morning.

What does it tell us about the person? This BaZi belongs to a person who is outshined by the people around him and lives in the shadow of other people's achievements. The person is timid.

As this Bing 丙 Fire Day Master is weak, it cannot control the Wealth Element in this chart. Granted, Wealth is strong in this chart but it is not because of the NUMBER of elements, but because this person is born in the season of Metal and thus, Metal is strong in the chart. Now, Metal, specifically Xin 辛 Metal, represents the wealth AND wife star of this person. Since Metal is vastly stronger than the Fire in this chart, we can conclude that this person's wife bosses him around and is more capable than he is.

時 Hour	日 Day	月 Month	年 Year	天干 Heavenly Stems
辛 Xin Yin Metal	丙 Bing Yang Fire	丁 Ding Yin Fire	丙 Bing Yang Fire	
卯 Mao **Rabbit** Yin Wood	戌 Xu **Dog** Yang Earth	酉 You **Rooster** Yin Metal	辰 Chen **Dragon** Yang Earth	地支 Earthly Branches
乙 Yi	丁 戊 辛 Ding Wu Xin	辛 Xin	癸 戊 乙 Gui Wu Yi	藏干 Hidden Stems

82	72	62	52	42	32	22	12	2	大運 Luck Pillars
丙 Bing Yang Fire	乙 Yi Yin Wood	甲 Jia Yang Wood	癸 Gui Yin Water	壬 Ren Yang Water	辛 Xin Yin Metal	庚 Geng Yang Metal	己 Ji Yin Earth	戊 Wu Yang Earth	
午 Wu Horse Yang Fire	巳 Si Snake Yin Fire	辰 Chen Dragon Yang Earth	卯 Mao Rabbit Yin Wood	寅 Yin Tiger Yang Wood	丑 Chou Ox Yin Earth	子 Zi Rat Yang Water	亥 Hai Pig Yin Water	戌 Xu Dog Yang Earth	
丁 己	庚 丙 戊	癸 戊 乙	乙	戊 甲 丙	辛 己 癸	癸	壬 甲	丁 戊 辛	

Will this person become rich in the Geng Zi 庚子 pillar? Unlikely. Firstly, the Metal is on the surface, appearing only at the Heavenly Stem level and is not rooted in the Earthly Branch. So the Metal or Wealth is superficial in nature. The Zi 子 (Rat) combines with the Chen 辰 (Dragon), destroys the You 酉 (Rooster) and punishes the Mao 卯 (Rabbit). Don't worry if it doesn't make sense now - it will as you get through this book.

All these interactions between the Zi 子 (Rat) Earthly Branch and the BaZi tell us that things look good during this period, but in fact, are far from it. Zi 子 (Rat) also contains Gui 癸 Water - Gui 癸 Water is the clouds, the mist. Guess what makes the sunlight look dim? The clouds and the mist. So this Bing 丙 Fire Day Master can expect career and emotional setbacks during this period.

See what is the danger of counting the elements? Not only do you get an inaccurate picture of the situation, but the analysis lacks precision, accuracy and detail. This student wisely decided to re-evaluate the chart before giving any further advice to his friend.

八字
解碼

Remember, when it comes to judging the elements, determining dominance and weakness is based on the season and the roots of the element, not merely by the number of elements present. There is no magic formula on how many elements a person should have in their BaZi. Every Destiny Code is unique and so should be interpreted dynamically and not mechanically through set formulas on the number of elements.

Also, as you advance in your study of BaZi, you will realise that when you over-lay the principles of Five Elements theory over the BaZi, interpreting the strength of the chart becomes an even more sophisticated process.

BaZi is like peeling an onion - the deeper you go into it, the more you 'see' and the more sophisticated your thinking and approach to it becomes. Of course, this is only the beginning of your journey in decoding a BaZi chart but as you go through this book, you will realise that you are seeing the charts in a new light as you gain more insight into how the Five Elements work and see the many levels in the analysis.

Reading the Pillars in Totality

Another common 'interpretative' error that novice students make early on is to assume that the Hidden Stem affects the first five years of the 10-year Luck Pillar, and the Earthly Branch affects the last five years. This is incorrect.

時 Hour	日 Day	月 Month	年 Year	
己 Ji Yin Earth	己 Ji Yin Earth	丁 Ding Yin Fire	乙 Yi Yin Wood	天干 Heavenly Stems
巳 Si **Snake** Yin Fire	亥 Hai **Pig** Yin Water	亥 Hai **Pig** Yin Water	亥 Hai **Pig** Yin Water	地支 Earthly Branches
庚 丙 戊 Geng Bing Wu	壬 甲 Ren Jia	壬 甲 Ren Jia	壬 甲 Ren Jia	藏干 Hidden Stems

84	74	64	54	44	34	24	14	4		
戊 Wu Yang Earth	己 Ji Yin Earth	庚 Geng Yang Metal	辛 Xin Yin Metal	壬 Ren Yang Water	癸 Gui Yin Water	甲 Jia Yang Wood	乙 Yi Yin Wood	丙 Bing Yang Fire	大運	*5 years on the Heavenly Stem*
89	**79**	**69**	**59**	**49**	**39**	**29**	**19**	**9**	Luck Pillars	*5 years on the Earthly Branch*
寅 Yin Tiger Yang Wood	卯 Mao Rabbit Yin Wood	辰 Chen Dragon Yang Earth	巳 Si Snake Yin Fire	午 Wu Horse Yang Fire	未 Wei Goat Yin Earth	申 Shen Monkey Yang Metal	酉 You Rooster Yin Metal	戌 Xu Dog Yang Earth		
戊甲丙	乙	癸戊乙	庚丙戊	丁己	乙己丁	戊庚壬	辛	丁戊辛		

The influence of the Heavenly Stem in each Luck Pillar is the Qi that the Day Master will be initially influenced by during the start of each Luck Pillar. But that does not mean or is the same as saying the Heavenly Stem governs the luck of the first 5-Years. On the contrary, the impact and indeed, the outcome of the 10-year Luck Pillar, is largely influenced and determined by the quality of the Earthly Branch.

We read the pillars holistically as ONE. We don't call it a Pillar for no reason. At the highest level of BaZi, pillars are perceived pictorially, as a single unit. So this 5-Years Stem and 5-Years Branch approach is plainly incorrect. If that was the case, if the Heavenly Stem was a favourable element and the Earthly Branch unfavourable, that means 5-Years of good luck and 5-Years of bad luck and that's just illogical.

84	74	64	54	44	34	24	14	4	
戊	己	庚	辛	壬	癸	甲	乙	丙	大運 Luck Pillars
Wu Yang Earth	Ji Yin Earth	Geng Yang Metal	Xin Yin Metal	Ren Yang Water	Gui Yin Water	Jia Yang Wood	Yi Yin Wood	Bing Yang Fire	
寅	卯	辰	巳	午	未	申	酉	戌	
Yin Tiger Yang Wood	Mao Rabbit Yin Wood	Chen Dragon Yang Earth	Si Snake Yin Fire	Wu Horse Yang Fire	Wei Goat Yin Earth	Shen Monkey Yang Metal	You Rooster Yin Metal	Xu Dog Yang Earth	
戊甲丙	乙	癸戊乙	庚丙戊	丁己	乙己丁	戊庚壬	辛	丁戊辛	

									流年 Year pillars
2018 戊戌	2008 戊子	1998 戊寅	1988 戊辰	1978 戊午	1968 戊申	1958 戊戌	1948 戊子	1938 戊寅	
2019 己亥	2009 己丑	1999 己卯	1989 己巳	1979 己未	1969 己酉	1959 己亥	1949 己丑	1939 己卯	
2020 庚子	2010 庚寅	2000 庚辰	1990 庚午	1980 庚申	1970 庚戌	1960 庚子	1950 庚寅	1940 庚辰	
2021 辛丑	2011 辛卯	2001 辛巳	1991 辛未	1981 辛酉	1971 辛亥	1961 辛丑	1951 辛卯	1941 辛巳	
2022 壬寅	2012 壬辰	2002 壬午	1992 壬申	1982 壬戌	1972 壬子	1962 壬寅	1952 壬辰	1942 壬午	
2023 癸卯	2013 癸巳	2003 癸未	1993 癸酉	1983 癸亥	1973 癸丑	1963 癸卯	1953 癸巳	1943 癸未	
2024 甲辰	2014 甲午	2004 甲申	1994 甲戌	1984 甲子	1974 甲寅	1964 甲辰	1954 甲午	1944 甲申	
2025 乙巳	2015 乙未	2005 乙酉	1995 乙亥	1985 乙丑	1975 乙卯	1965 乙巳	1955 乙未	1945 乙酉	
2026 丙午	2016 丙申	2006 丙戌	1996 丙子	1986 丙寅	1976 丙辰	1966 丙午	1956 丙申	1946 丙戌	
2027 丁未	2017 丁酉	2007 丁亥	1997 丁丑	1987 丁卯	1977 丁巳	1967 丁未	1957 丁酉	1947 丁亥	

Each Annual Pillar interacts with the Luck Pillar

Each year interacts differently with the entire Luck Pillar

The correct way to look at the impact of the Luck Pillar is to see how it relates or interacts with the individual years in the Luck Pillar. The Earthly Branch relationships that you will learn about in the chapters to come will show you how the Luck Pillar interacts with the individual years and with the BaZi. That tells you how a person's Luck will be within those 10-Years. Hence, the pillars must be read in totality and not separated.

Colour Therapy, Food Therapy, Element Therapy, Name Therapy, Retail Therapy?

八字
解碼

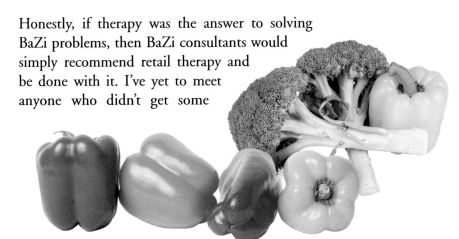

I have written extensively in my books on Feng Shui about what I like to term 'the placebo effect'. Many laypeople tend to place faith in what I call the 'Put Therapy' to resolve Feng Shui issues. 'Put Therapy' refers to the mentality that every problem can be resolved with a placement or "Putting" of a figurine or by placing something in a corner somewhere. As long as you know what that something (object, item, symbol) is, everything will be just fine. Unfortunately, it does not work this way.

The idea of using colours, food, or surrounding yourself with certain types of furniture or elements has sprung forth from the 'Put Therapy', I believe. Now, even in BaZi consultations, clients ask about what they should put in their rooms, what symbols to put in their offices, colours they should wear or even, elements they should make more use of in order to solve problems diagnosed from their BaZi charts.

Honestly, if therapy was the answer to solving BaZi problems, then BaZi consultants would simply recommend retail therapy and be done with it. I've yet to meet anyone who didn't get some

happiness from spending money! For that matter, if the solution to an elemental imbalance is a matter of changing the furniture or elements of the objects around us, then the whole swathes of people are potentially living in houses that are elemental time bombs (since they don't know what elements they should have around them or the elements are mixed) and we would have to re-draw the entire population map of the world because certain people should, or shouldn't live, in certain places or houses!

Oh, and not to mention the thousands of people living without Chinese names who will now have to find inventive ways to 'incorporate' their helpful elements into their names. Perhaps the Queen (a Geng 庚 Metal lady) should reconsider using the name 'Windsor'.

Let's face it - this is just unreal. And that is why the 'Put Therapy' and its resultant therapies are simply not in tune with the correct approach to BaZi.

This is not to say that colours are not helpful, or that geographical location is not relevant. But colours at best carry a negligible advantage only and I always say, don't just wear a colour because it's a favourable colour according to your BaZi elemental requirements. If you hate the colour, you're not going to be comfortable wearing it and any nominal benefit is instantly cancelled out. Your luck is not going to change just because you are wearing something. Your luck may change if you do something about the situation that relates to the problem.

Let me pose this question: If Water is your unfavourable element, should you stop drinking water? Obviously not. So if you're not about to stop consuming an element because it's bad for you, so clearly adding or wearing more of an element physically is not going to improve things.

For that matter, if you are told a certain symbol (say a 如意 Ru Yi) is helpful to you, and hey, the bigger it is, the better right? - Are you going to lug around a giant 如意 Ru Yi with you everywhere you go?

An object or a symbol cannot change or influence an elemental problem. But your actions in tackling that problem correctly can.

Otherwise, we might as well ask all the people who need water to move into biospheres at the bottom of the sea or work out of their bathtubs at home!

BaZi - It Ain't no Miracle

Solutions in BaZi are not always easy. But there is always a solution. Often, it is not a case that there is no solution, as much as the solution is unpalatable or unpleasant to consider. Changing your character to overcome weaknesses is never easy. Changing the way you think about yourself is accomplished not without effort. But that is why you have that 33.3 percent Man Luck factor.

Destiny is in your hands - the question is, do you have what it takes to take control, or are you content to just go along with the ride and be a backseat driver?

But where clients (in the case of those who seek a professional consultation) and individuals are prepared to do what it takes, and are willing to face up to the obstacles and challenges, mental or otherwise, then Destiny has a chance to be fulfilled, and your dreams have a chance to come true.

BaZi, as you all know, is about taking action. Doing the right thing, at the right time, with the right person or in the right place. However, the 'Put Therapy' is hardly what we consider taking action in BaZi. Placing certain objects around you is

not the solution to a missing element, or a weak element or an element needed to balance your BaZi. Instead, in BaZi, the solution is derived from determining what the missing or weak element is, and then translating that element into action, thoughts, attitude or behaviour.

The 'add physical element solution' is not the way BaZi is done and I will show you an example of how 'put therapy' can be misguided. The following chart was shown to me by an American student. It belonged to a friend of his and his friend had recently gone for a BaZi consult. The consultant's advice was to build a swimming pool as the Jia 甲 Wood Day Master's chart was too dry and needed Water. The person was also advised to wear blue colour and paint her office blue.

時 Hour	日 Day	月 Month	年 Year	
己	甲	甲	己	天干 Heavenly Stems
Ji Yin Earth	Jia Yang Wood	Jia Yang Wood	Ji Yin Earth	
巳	戌	戌	未	地支 Earthly Branches
Si Snake Yin Fire	Xu Dog Yang Earth	Xu Dog Yang Earth	Wei Goat Yin Earth	
庚 丙 戊 Geng Bing Wu	丁 戊 辛 Ding Wu Xin	丁 戊 辛 Ding Wu Xin	乙 己 丁 Yi Ji Ding	藏干 Hidden Stems

82	72	62	52	42	32	22	12	2	
癸 Gui Yin Water	壬 Ren Yang Water	辛 Xin Yin Metal	庚 Geng Yang Metal	己 Ji Yin Earth	戊 Wu Yang Earth	丁 Ding Yin Fire	丙 Bing Yang Fire	乙 Yi Yin Wood	大運 Luck Pillars
未 Wei Goat Yin Earth	午 Wu Horse Yang Fire	巳 Si Snake Yin Fire	辰 Chen Dragon Yang Earth	卯 Mao Rabbit Yin Wood	寅 Yin Tiger Yang Wood	丑 Chou Ox Yin Earth	子 Zi Rat Yang Water	亥 Hai Pig Yin Water	
乙己丁	丁己	庚丙戊	癸戊乙	乙	戊甲丙	辛己癸	癸	壬甲	

3 November 1979, Horse Hour (9am), Female

Let's do the analysis together. This is a Jia 甲 Wood Day Master, born in the Autumn season. Clearly, it is weak Wood. Yes, there are small tiny roots in the Wei 未 (Goat) branch but these roots are quite weak. It is also obvious that this chart has a missing element, namely Water.

Now, sometimes, people jump to the conclusion that an element is missing without checking the Hidden Stems. It is very important to make sure an element is really missing. One good way, if you are not sure, is to plot the chart using the BaZi Ming Pan calculator on **www.joeyyap.com** and check the elemental values table on the charts plotted. If there is a zero anywhere in the table, that means the element is really missing.

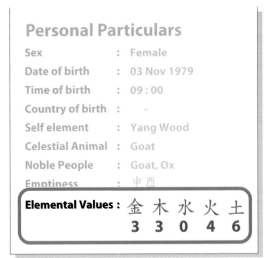

Personal Particulars

Sex	:	Female
Date of birth	:	03 Nov 1979
Time of birth	:	09 : 00
Country of birth	:	-
Self element	:	Yang Wood
Celestial Animal	:	Goat
Noble People	:	Goat, Ox
Emptiness	:	申 酉

Elemental Values :

金	木	水	火	土
3	3	0	4	6

Just because Water is missing from this chart, that does not mean that the solution to this person's BaZi is to 'add water'. We're not talking about cooking a stew here where the pot runs a bit dry and so you add water. An element being missing, does not mean that element is favourable to the chart. The correct question to ask is whether this charts NEEDS water, and also, whether it can USE Water effectively in the first place.

As Water is non-existent in this chart, this Jia 甲 Wood Day Master does not have any affinity with Water. That means that eventhough the Water element appears in the Luck Pillars or Annual Pillars, the Jia 甲 Wood Day Master is not receptive to it. So trying to 'add water' to this chart in the form of building a swimming pool doesn't help this Jia 甲 Wood Day Master for two reasons: firstly, building a swimming pool is not how we introduce an element into the chart in classical BaZi and secondly, this Jia 甲 Wood Day Master is not receptive to Water.

Accordingly, the advice this person received to build a swimming pool is highly debatable with regards to its efficacy, especially if the swimming pool is not located using Feng Shui principles. In fact, the lack of affinity with the Water element suggests that the swimming pool may end up giving her problems after it is constructed! Even if, for the sake of argument, building a swimming pool could be construed as a means of introducing Water into this person's BaZi chart, a swimming pool is Ren 壬 Water. Ren 壬 Water does not feed this dead Jia 甲 Wood - it is Gui 癸 Water that the Jia 甲 Wood needs. Perhaps, the consultant should have suggested she hire a medicine man to bring rain!

Feng Shui and BaZi: Heaven and Earth working together.

I have always emphasised the importance of looking at BaZi when it comes to Feng Shui audits or consultations. This is because BaZi is the means in which to diagnose a person's problem, and then Feng Shui is the prescription for resolving the problem. Many people are aware that Feng Shui and BaZi must be used in a complementary manner.

As this is a book about BaZi, I want to explore the issue from the reverse perspective and talk a little bit about how is Feng Shui used, to assist with problems identified through a BaZi consult. Firstly, this will help put to rest some of the misconceptions about using elements from a person's BaZi in their personal Feng Shui and secondly, it will help foster further appreciation of how these two complementary disciplines work together.

I think the best way to understand how BaZi and Feng Shui are complementary is by using an example. In this example I will show you how Feng Shui recommendations are offered to a client, when the problem is identified through BaZi,

時 Hour	日 Day	月 Month	年 Year	
庚 Geng Yang Metal	丙 Bing Yang Fire	庚 Geng Yang Metal	己 Ji Yin Earth	天干 Heavenly Stems
寅 Yin **Tiger** Yang Wood	子 Zi **Rat** Yang Water	午 Wu **Horse** Yang Fire	丑 Chou **Ox** Yin Earth	地支 Earthly Branches
戊 甲 丙 Wu Jia Bing	癸 Gui	丁 己 Ding Ji	辛 己 癸 Xin Ji Gui	藏干 Hidden Stems

83	73	63	53	43	33	23	13	3	
辛 Xin Yin Metal	壬 Ren Yang Water	癸 Gui Yin Water	甲 Jia Yang Wood	乙 Yi Yin Wood	丙 Bing Yang Fire	丁 Ding Yin Fire	戊 Wu Yang Earth	己 Ji Yin Earth	大運 Luck Pillars
酉 You **Rooster** Yin Metal	戌 Xu **Dog** Yang Earth	亥 Hai **Pig** Yin Water	子 Zi **Rat** Yang Water	丑 Chou **Ox** Yin Earth	寅 Yin **Tiger** Yang Wood	卯 Mao **Rabbit** Yin Wood	辰 Chen **Dragon** Yang Earth	巳 Si **Snake** Yin Fire	
辛	丁 戊 辛	壬 甲	癸	辛 己 癸	戊 甲 丙	乙	癸 戊 乙	庚 丙 戊	

When I met this gentleman, his chart revealed a Zi 子 (Rat) and Wu 午 (Horse) clash, which is indicative of, amongst other things, a heart problem. Ding 丁 Fire represents the heart and the clash is already present in his chart between the Ding 丁 Fire in the Wu 午 (Horse) and the Gui 癸 Water inside the Zi 子 (Rat). At the 53 Luck Pillar of Jia Zi 甲子, the Zi 子 (Rat) appears again and clashes with the Wu 午 (Horse) in the BaZi chart. This makes it very clear that a heart problem is on the boil.

Off we went to his house to have a look. Sure enough, in the South Sector of this house, there was an electric pole. The South sector is governed by the Li 離 Gua and Li Gua amongst other things, represents the heart.

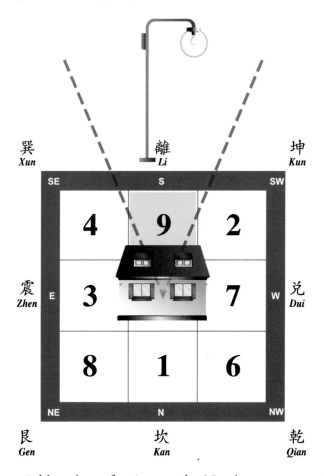

The neighbour's roof points at the Northwest sector of the property and the Northwest sector of his property is very small. The gentleman himself is Gua #6, Qian 乾 Gua. The Early Heaven Ba Gua of Qian 乾 Gua is Li 離 Gua. An Early Heaven relationship between the Gua's indicates health problems or matters.

What does all this analysis tell us? That the problems in a person's BaZi chart will always show up in their Feng Shui. Hence, the two are inter-related and should always be used together. Because this gentleman had a pre-disposition in his chart to a heart problem, he would invariably choose a home that 'confirmed' the likelihood of the problem.

What was the Feng Shui prescription, now that the BaZi diagnosis had been made?

First, the Northwest sector was expanded and tall trees were planted in the Northwest to block out the sharp roof from the neighbour's house pointing at the Northwest sector. Qian 乾 Gua, which represents him, is strengthened. He is also the head of the household, which Qian 乾 Gua represents. He was also advised to try and remove the pole in the South.

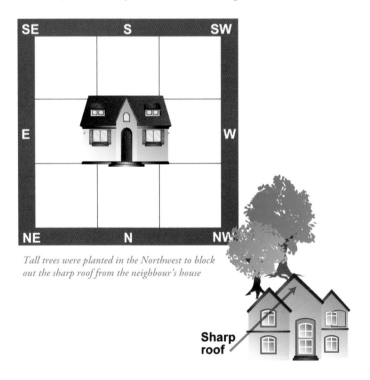

Tall trees were planted in the Northwest to block out the sharp roof from the neighbour's house

八字
解碼

Secondly, regular health check-ups, specifically with a cardiologist, had to be rigorously adhered to, especially in 2002 壬午 (Ren Wu) and 2008 戊子 (Wu Zi), which is when the clash with the Wu 午 (Horse) materialises.

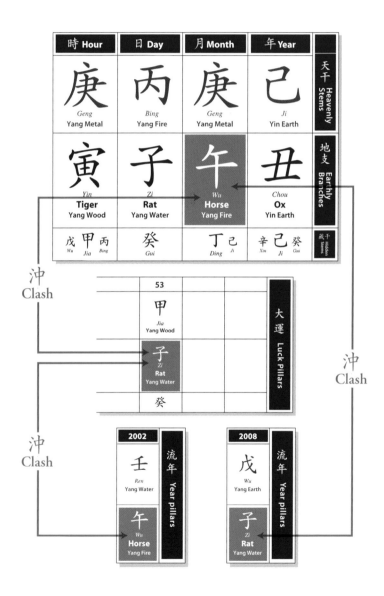

Take a deep breath...

八字解碼

Some of the analysis in this chart probably goes over your head - I have mentioned certain Earthly Branch relationships which you are unfamiliar with, talked a bit about Feng Shui. It's all a lot to absorb. But BaZi is one of those wonderful subjects where getting thrown into the deep end is one of the best ways to learn. Also, by illustrating the common errors made with examples, I hope it makes it easier for you to see why certain analysis techniques are simply not appropriate.

Of course, you should not reverse engineer too much when it comes to BaZi, but what is contained in this chapter's examples is just a flavour and taster of what is to come. When you get to the end of the book, revisit the chapter again and you'll see all the examples in a new light.

Chapter Four:
Combination Codes

Let's kick off the types of Earthly Branch relationship codes with something that I'm sure most of you have heard about before. Ever heard some people saying those born in the year of the Dog should avoid marrying (or for that matter working together with, embarking on a JV or even hiring!) people born in the year of the Dragon but they could do any of the above activities with someone born in the year of the Rabbit? Guess where this advice originates from? You guessed it - Combination Codes in BaZi.

Unfortunately, Combinations are also one of the most 'abused' BaZi principles, often employed to sell animal pendants or to give a BaZi basis for the theory of 'secret friends' or to justify why those born in the year of the Snake should marry Monkey-born spouses but not Pigs. All these are what I call 'New Age' BaZi ideas - they do not have any basis in classical BaZi studies and represent an incorrect use, interpretation and explanations of Combinations.

Remember in BaZi, the aim is to make informed decisions and take the right action. Buying a pendant, wearing a pendant, or being superstitious, is not considered 'taking the right action' or 'making an informed decision' by any stretch of imagination. Why not just marry someone born in the same year as you - that way, there would be absolutely no clashes because you'd both be of the same character and nature!

The real meaning behind Combination Codes

Combinations are in effect relationships between two Earthly Branches. It is one of the most important relationships that must be considered when analysing a Destiny Code because Combinations indicate a compatibility between two Heavenly Stems or two Earthly Branches. At its most basic level, the presence of Combinations in a BaZi tells us that two elements in a BaZi have a connection that we must consider or pay attention to.

What do I mean when I say 'compatibility' between two Heavenly Stems or Earthly Branches? This does not refer to compatibility within the context of a personal relationship between two people. Rather, it means the two Earthly Branches have a connection or an elemental association.

Combinations in BaZi are typically an indication of union or a connection between two aspects of a person's life. By determining what those two aspects are, using a technique in BaZi known as the Ten Gods 十神, it is possible to determine which two aspects of a person's life (be it relationships, objects or persons) have a connection or a union.

Essentially, there are TWO levels of combinations: Heavenly Stems combinations and Earthly Branches combinations. A Heavenly Stems combination refers to the presence of a connection between two Heavenly Stems in a BaZi chart.

An Earthly Branches combination, as the name suggests, involves a union or affiliation between two or three of the Earthly Branches. An Earthly Branches combination has stronger effect, while a Heavenly Stems combination is usually weaker and more superficial or surface level only. Because of this, I will first discuss the Earthly Branches Combinations here in this chapter.

The Earthly Branches Combination

Earthly Branches combinations are derived from astrological phenomenon - an Earthly Branch is a segment of the planet's location. Certain Qi and stars are compatible with the Qi and stars of that Branch and it is from here that the Combinations are derived.

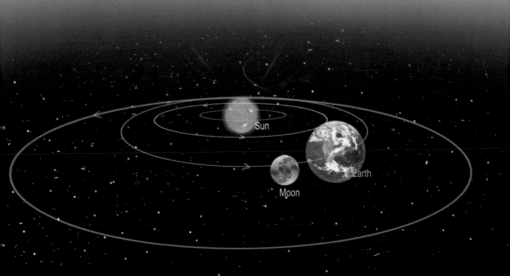

Earthly Branches Combinations indicate a strong union, link, bond or connection or nexus between the objects or relationships represented by the elements involved in the Combinations. These bonds or connections are less easily broken or challenged.

Connections, affiliations, relationships and associations are sometimes simple matters, sometimes complex matters, and can involve a diverse number of possibilities and subjects. So these are reflected in the types of Earthly Branches combinations. Sometimes a combination involves two Branches, sometimes three. It is a wise idea to try to commit to memory all these combinations but don't be too worried if you can't do it right away. Instead, look to appreciate how combinations work and the subtleties of combinations for now.

There are three types of Earthly Branches combinations:
• The Three Harmony Combination (三合)
• The Directional Combination (三會)
• The Six Harmony Combination (六合)

When working with combinations, remember that we must always consider if the Combination is favourable or unfavourable before arriving at a conclusion. Sometimes, there is a strong bond to something, but it is to something that could be harmful, such as an abusive or tormenting relationship. The Combination creates a situation where the person cannot let go, or is unable to close off the relationship or end the connection.

The Three Harmony Combination 三合

I like to call the Three Harmony Combination the 'three musketeers'. It helps my students differentiate this Combination from other Combinations.

Before we learn more about the Three Harmony Combination, I must touch upon the subject of 'Secret Friends'. You may have heard of this concept - it is quite popular in New Age Feng Shui and is often referenced in populist Chinese Astrology. The 'Secret Friends' concept states that individuals are more likely to be 'compatible' with individuals born in certain years and those compatible years are derived from animals within certain groups which are deemed to have a special affinity with each other.

For example, a person born it the year of the Rooster is supposedly more compatible with those born in the year of the Snake and Ox, according to the 'Secret Friends' concept. So what happens if you scrutinise your little black book and discover you have no friends born in those 'compatible' years? No big deal - buy a pendant of the animal that forms your 'Secret Friend' and your Secret Friend will soon turn up!

If only it was that easy!

There is absolutely no basis for the concept of wearing a pendant of the animal of 'Secret Friends' in classical BaZi , nor is there anything in BaZi called 'Secret Helpers Luck'. The so-called 'Secret Friends' is actually derived from the Three Harmony Combination or any combinations between the Earthly Branches. But all that has been distilled is the animals in the group. The actual meaning and application of the Three Harmony Combination has been conveniently excluded!

So, what is this Three Harmony Combination? Have a look at the chart below which shows the Three Harmony Combination:

申 *Shen* Monkey	子 *Zi* Rat	辰 *Chen* Dragon	水局 Water Structure
亥 *Hai* Pig	卯 *Mao* Rabbit	未 *Wei* Goat	木局 Wood Structure
寅 *Yin* Tiger	午 *Wu* Horse	戌 *Xu* Dog	火局 Fire Structure
巳 *Si* Snake	酉 *You* Rooster	丑 *Chou* Ox	金局 Metal Structure

If you are familiar with or have been an understanding of Feng Shui, you will realise that the Three Harmony Combination is derived from the Water, Fire, Metal and Wood Frames.

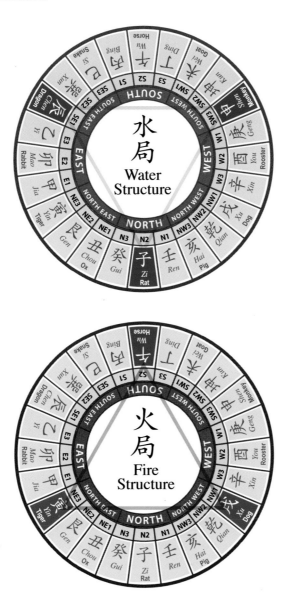

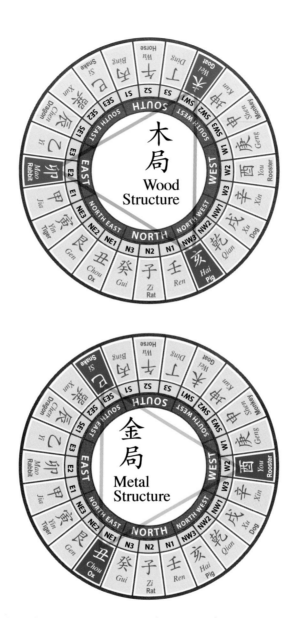

木局
Wood Structure

金局
Metal Structure

What the Three Harmony Combination does is empower one of the Five Elements in the chart, and enable it to become the dominant Element in the chart. The Three Harmony Combination in the BaZi chart typically indicates a powerful network or special relationships. When such a combination exists within a BaZi, in the correct sequence, and it is favourable to the Day Master, the person is usually someone who has a special connection or link to certain groupings in society or rub shoulders with many high-ranking or high-status individuals.

If the element that the Three Harmony combination produced is NOT favorable to the BaZi chart itself, it can denote troublesome relationships or complicated associations that run like the typical plot of a daytime soap opera. In other words, very complex, complicated and not fun.

Let's take a look at the example below:

時 Hour	日 Day	月 Month	年 Year	天干 Heavenly Stems
癸 Gui Yin Water	丙 Bing Yang Fire	壬 Ren Yang Water	壬 Ren Yang Water	
巳 Si Snake Yin Fire	申 Shen Monkey Yang Metal	子 Zi Rat Yang Water	辰 Chen Dragon Yang Earth	地支 Earthly Branches
庚 丙 戊 Geng Bing Wu	戊 庚 壬 Wu Geng Ren	癸 Gui	癸 戊 乙 Gui Wu Yi	藏干 Hidden Stems

Look at the Year Branch, Month Branch and Day Branch of this Bing Fire Day Master's chart. Do you see the Chen 辰 (Dragon), Zi 子 (Rat) and Shen 申 (Monkey)? Now, check the Three Harmony Combination table on page 84.

This BaZi chart has a Water Frame Three Harmony Combination.

Now, is this combination favourable or unfavourable?

This Bing 丙 Fire Day Master is weak. The presence of the Water Frame Three Harmony Combination diminishes further the quality of the sunlight in this chart and overwhelms the Bing 丙 Fire Day Master. The Water Frame therefore is clearly not favourable since Water is a negative element for the Day Master. From this, we can deduce that this individual's relationships with his superiors and legal issues are complicated, dramatic and frequently long, protracted and dragged out.

Now, let's look at an example of where a Three Harmony Combination is positive and favourable.

時 Hour	日 Day	月 Month	年 Year	
壬 *Ren* **Yang Water**	丁 *Ding* **Yin Fire**	癸 *Gui* **Yin Water**	己 *Ji* **Yin Earth**	天干 Heavenly Stems
寅 *Yin* **Tiger** Yang Wood	巳 *Si* **Snake** Yin Fire	酉 *You* **Rooster** Yin Metal	丑 *Chou* **Ox** Yin Earth	地支 Earthly Branches
戊 甲 丙 _{Wu} _{Jia} _{Bing}	庚 丙 戊 _{Geng} _{Bing} _{Wu}	辛 _{Xin}	辛 己 癸 _{Xin} _{Ji} _{Gui}	藏干 Hidden Stems

Again, look at the Year Branch, Month Branch and Day Branch. See the Chou 丑 (Ox), You 酉 (Rooster) and Si 巳 (Snake)? This is a Three Harmony Combination that forms the Metal Frame. Now, this Ding 丁 Fire Day Master is strong enough to handle the Metal element, even though it is not born in season, as it receives support from the Wood element in the Yin 寅 (Tiger) and the Fire element in the Si 巳 (Snake).

Accordingly, the combination is favourable. So how is it favourable to this Ding 丁 Fire Day Master? Metal, is the Wealth element of a Ding 丁 Fire Day Master. This person's business connections and networking are the key to his ability to amass great wealth.

A Three Harmony Combination can also be activated when the missing Earthly Branch required to complete the combination arrives through an annual pillar or 10-year Luck Pillar. Take a look at the example below:

In the above instance, the Three Harmony Combination is completed during the 10-year Luck Pillar beginning at the Chinese age of 33. This example shows the Three Harmony Combination of Hai 亥 (Pig)-Mao 卯 (Rabbit)-Wei 未 (Goat).

The Three Harmony Combination can also be activated during the one year when the missing Earthly Branch that completes the Combination arrives. Have a look at the example below:

Here, the Fire Frame combination of Yin 寅 (Tiger), Wu 午 (Horse) and Xu 戌 (Dog) is activated in the year 1966, during the Geng Yin 10-Year Luck Pillar, when the Fire Frame combination's component Earthly Branches are all present.

The Directional Combination 三會

Directional combinations are another type of combination that involves three Earthly Branches. A Directional Combination is present when, within a BaZi chart, all the Earthly Branches from a season are present in the chart. Just in case you have forgotten about the Branches of each season here is the list:

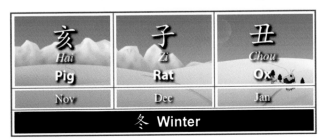

For example, a BaZi chart containing Yin 寅 (Tiger), Mao 卯 (Rabbit) and Chen 辰 (Dragon) can be said to contain the entire season of Spring. This Directional Combination is known as Eastern Wood.

時 Hour	日 Day	月 Month	年 Year	
癸 *Gui* **Yin Water**	丙 *Bing* **Yang Fire**	丁 *Ding* **Yin Fire**	甲 *Jia* **Yang Wood**	天干 Heavenly Stems
巳 *Si* **Snake** Yin Fire	辰 *Chen* **Dragon** Yang Earth	卯 *Mao* **Rabbit** Yin Wood	寅 *Yin* **Tiger** Yang Wood	地支 Earthly Branches
庚 丙 戊 *Geng Bing Wu*	癸 戊 乙 *Gui Wu Yi*	乙 *Yi*	戊 甲 丙 *Wu Jia Bing*	藏干 Hidden Stems

The Directional Combination produces one overwhelmingly strong and dominant element in the chart. This is because the entire season is present in the chart and so that particular Element is strongly supported. A Directional Combination may be favourable or unfavourable, depending on whether the strong, dominant element is a favourable element or an unfavourable element.

Spring   Summer   Autumn

春   夏   秋

春 Spring

寅 *Yin* **Tiger** Yang Wood	卯 *Mao* **Rabbit** Yin Wood	辰 *Chen* **Dragon** Yang Earth
戊 *Wu* 甲 *Jia* 丙 *Bing*	乙 *Yi*	癸 *Gui* 戊 *Wu* 乙 *Yi*

夏 Summer

巳 *Si* **Snake** Yin Fire	午 *Wu* **Horse** Yang Fire	未 *Wei* **Goat** Yin Earth
庚 *Geng* 丙 *Bing* 戊 *Wu*	丁 *Ding* 己 *Ji*	乙 *Yi* 己 *Ji* 丁 *Ding*

秋 Autumn

申 *Shen* **Monkey** Yang Metal	酉 *You* **Rooster** Yin Metal	戌 *Xu* **Dog** Yang Earth
戊 *Wu* 庚 *Geng* 壬 *Ren*	辛 *Xin*	丁 *Ding* 戊 *Wu* 辛 *Xin*

冬 Winter

亥 *Hai* **Pig** Yin Water	子 *Zi* **Rat** Yang Water	丑 *Chou* **Ox** Yin Earth
壬 *Ren* 甲 *Jia*	癸 *Gui*	辛 *Xin* 己 *Ji* 癸 *Gui*

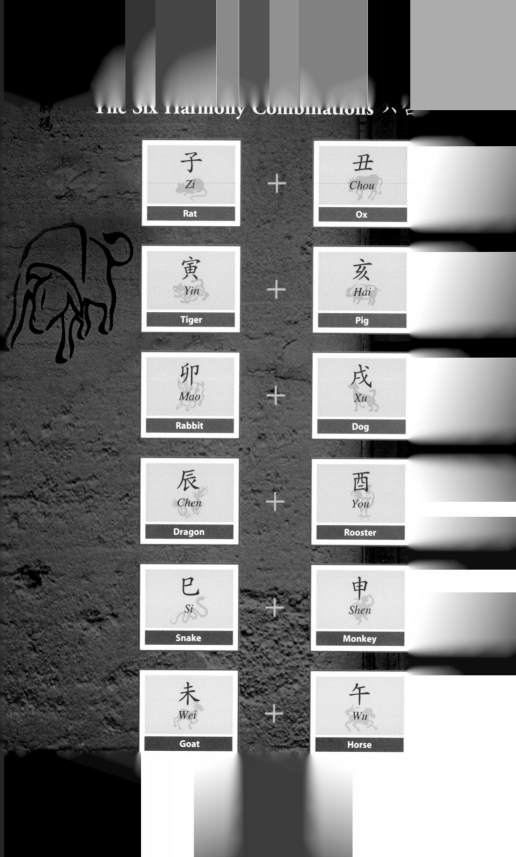

子 *Zi* **Rat**	+	丑 *Chou* **Ox**
寅 *Yin* **Tiger**	+	亥 *Hai* **Pig**
卯 *Mao* **Rabbit**	+	戌 *Xu* **Dog**
辰 *Chen* **Dragon**	+	酉 *You* **Rooster**
巳 *Si* **Snake**	+	申 *Shen* **Monkey**
未 *Wei* **Goat**	+	午 *Wu* **Horse**

The Six Harmony Combinations, like the Three Harmony Combination and The Directional Combination, can appear within a BaZi chart itself, known as an Internal Combination, or can materialise during certain Luck Pillars (a 10-year cycle) or during a particular year (Annual Pillars), known as an External Combination.

You will notice that sometimes, Combinations transform or produce an element. Now, the technical term for this is 'He Hua 合化' - transform or produce is not strictly speaking an accurate translation so do not take the term too literally.

A combination is like a union of two of the Earthly Branches. They unite and, under certain conditions, they may transform into another element.

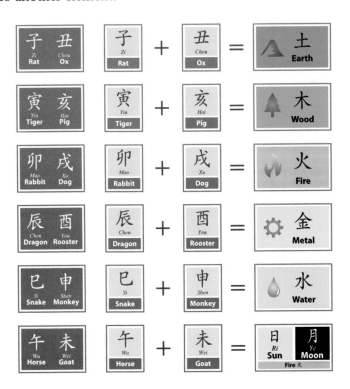

The Heavenly Stems Combinations

Heavenly Stems can also have Combination relationships. These usually represent obvious relationships, meetings and joint ventures, or obvious connections. But because Heavenly Stems represent only prevailing Qi, these relationships may not last, or may be superficial only in nature. There is the appearance of combination but it may not be a strong one, unless the combination is rooted.

The table below lists the Heavenly Stem Combinations.

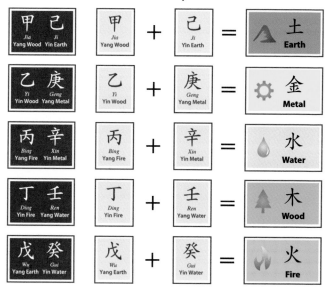

Heavenly Stem combinations all have specific meanings attached to them. Jia 甲 and Ji 己 is called the combination of benevolence. People with this combination are typically merciful and nice.

The Yi 乙 and Geng 庚 combination is a combination that indicates loyalty and altruism. People with a Yi 乙-Geng 庚 combination in their chart usually treat their friends like blood brothers or are extremely close to their friends. Yi and Geng combinations in a chart, especially where Geng Metal is the Day Master and is a male, usually means the moment the man is married, his wife becomes the most important person to him.

Bing 丙 and Xin 辛 is usually described as a betrayal combination. It can also mean that the person is lusty and sensual. Ding 丁 and Ren 壬 is a combination that marks out the person as a fiercely loyal person. Finally, Wu 戊 and Gui 癸 is known as a non-merciful combination (Wu Qing He 無情合) because the combination does not last.

Each combination also has the possibility of producing or transforming into a new element. For instance, Wu 戊 and Gui 癸 can combine and transform into the Fire Element. However, any transformation needs the correct conditions to facilitate the process. For instance, Wu 戊 and Gui 癸 will only transform when the person goes through Fire Luck Pillars, since conditions then become conducive in the chart for the successful transformation into Fire.

Combination Caveats

When looking at combinations, we are interested in looking at several issues. First, obviously, is determining if the combination is a favourable combination, or an unfavourable combination. Just like not all marriages turn out well, not all combinations bode well for a BaZi. Secondly, it is also relevant to consider if the combination transforms or produces an element. Just like not all marriages produce children, not every combination will successfully transform or produce the element in question. Thirdly, we must consider if the combination is an internal combination or external combination, because the impact of the combination varies in each instance.

八字
解
碼

The common assumption which is frequently made is that combinations indicate good relationships or marriages and that combinations are a good thing. In BaZi, we never assume, just like we never pre-judge, something to be instantly good or bad. Combinations basically just indicate a relationship between two Earthly Branches and a nexus or connection between two subjects, issues or persons in your life. It's always important to assess what aspects are in combination before determining whether it is something you want!

Consider the result, before making a judgment. If the Combination is favourable for the chart, then the relationship outcome between the elements is positive. If the combination is not favourable to the chart, then there is a union or a nexus between the elements that brings about an unfavourable outcome.

To Transform, or not to Transform?

Two of the most frequently asked questions by students of BaZi when it comes to Combinations are: When does a combination produce an outcome? And what does it mean? Does it add an extra element to the chart?

Whether or not a Combination will produce an additional element depends on the Combination itself. A combination does not always transform or produce an element, if the conditions within the BaZi chart are not conducive to a transformation. What does this mean?

Essentially, the Month Branch and Season must support the transformed or produced element. If the BaZi chart's month branch and season are not supportive of the transformed or produced element, then the transformation does not materialize.

Take a look at the example below:

時 Hour	日 Day	月 Month	年 Year	天干 Heavenly Stems
申 *Shen* **Monkey**	巳 *Si* **Snake**	Winter Month		地支 Earthly Branches

Shen 申 and Si 巳 combine; supposed to transform to water.

This BaZi has a Combination between the Si 巳 (Snake) in the Day Branch and Shen 申 (Monkey) in the Hour Branch. Based on the Six Harmony Combinations, this Combination produces Water. Now, if the person is born in the Winter months of Hai 亥 (Pig) and Zi 子 (Rat) then Water is strong and so the additional Water element will be produced.

時 Hour	日 Day	月 Month	年 Year	天干 Heavenly Stems
申 *Shen* **Monkey**	巳 *Si* **Snake**	Winter Month		地支 Earthly Branches

Will transform to water

However, if we change the positioning of the Combination slightly, as per the diagram below, then the situation is very different.

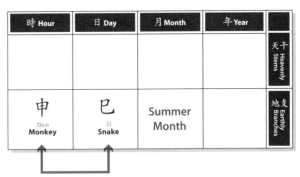

Does not transform to water

The Shen 申 - Si 巳 combination is still present, but this time, the season is Summer. During Summer, Fire is strong and it is dry. So, the combination between Si 巳 (Snake) and Shen 申 (Monkey) will not produce Water. However, when this person enters their Water 10-Year Luck Pillars, then this Combination will transform to become Water.

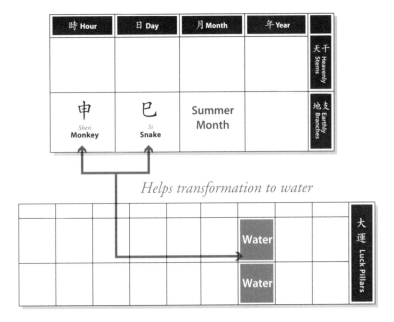

Helps transformation to water

There are some schools of BaZi which state that once the Si 巳 (Snake) and Shen 申 (Monkey) combine, the Branches lose their individual elements of Metal and Fire, and become Water. This is an incorrect explanation of how the Water element is derived. Again, let me use the analogy of a marriage to explain why this explanation is incorrect. When a woman marries a man, and they produce a child, the woman and man do not die upon the birth of the child.

Think of Combinations as a marriage of the BaZi chart's Earthly Branches. Sometimes an additional element is produced, sometimes an additional element is not. It depends on the fertility of the chart, so to speak.

When an additional element is present in the chart, that element represents one of the five factors in your life. Remember, Wealth, Influence, Companion, Resource Output? The question then is whether or not this element is favourable or not. This will answer the question of whether or not the Combination and its outcome are favourable or unfavourable.

You may have also heard of a concept known as 'Combined Away' but as this is slightly complicated, I will leave it for the next book in this series. Right now, as we are still on the basics level, let's keep things simple!

Combining with Who and What? Decoding Combinations

Generally, Combinations indicate a bonding, a joint venture, a union, a nexus between the elements, and what those elements represent. Getting an exact picture of what the combination involves however requires decoding the combination. How do we do this? By looking at the palaces involved, and determining whether or not the Combination is successful or unsuccessful, favourable or unfavourable and of course, the Ten Gods involved in the combination.

Let's look at how we can use the Palaces to decode a Combination.

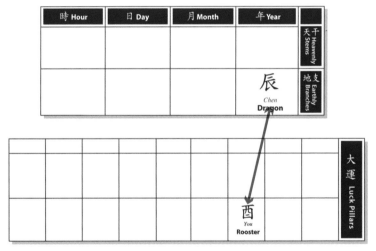

A combination between the Year Branch of the BaZi chart and the Luck Pillar.

When a combination involves the Year Pillar, this indicates that extended family is involved in the picture. If the combination involves the Month Pillar, then it hints at a relationship involving an immediate member of the family, or a superior. If it is the Day Branch that is involved in a Combination, the Combination relates to your spouse, your home or you personally. If the Hour Pillar is affected by the Combination, then it relates to your career or your children.

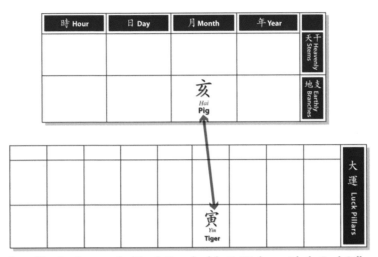

A combination between the Month Branch of the BaZi chart with the Luck Pillar.

The element produced, or affected by the combination, also indicates what the scenario or subject matter that the combination affects will be. For example, if the Influence Element is produced, or affected, then the combinations outcome or occurrence will affect the person's reputation, authority, superiors or relationships or objects under the person's control or dominion.

If the Resource element is impacted by the combination, health is the issue at hand. If the Companion Element is produced, this indicates meeting new friends. If the Wealth element is involved, and the combination is a favourable one, then it indicates making money. However, if the element produced is an unfavourable one, then you may lose money!

八字解碼

Will You Marry Me?
When a Combination Means Marriage

In certain circumstances, a combination does really denote a marriage or meeting a spouse, or a Significant Other. What is this circumstance? When the combination that takes place produces the element that is also the Spouse Star of the Day Master.

In case you've forgotten how to derive the Spouse Star, I've reproduced the table below, from *The Destiny Code*, for quick reference.

Male Day Master	Spouse Element			
火 Fire	丙, 丁 *Bing* *Ding*	庚 *Geng* Yang Metal	辛 *Xin* Yin Metal	申 *Shen* Yang Metal	酉 *You* Yin Metal
土 Earth	戊, 己 *Wu* *Ji*	壬 *Ren* Yang Water	癸 *Gui* Yin Water	子 *Zi* Yang Water	亥 *Hai* Yin Water
金 Metal	庚, 辛 *Geng* *Xin*	甲 *Jia* Yang Wood	乙 *Yi* Yin Wood	寅 *Yin* Yang Wood	卯 *Mao* Yin Wood
水 Water	壬, 癸 *Ren* *Gui*	丙 *Bing* Yang Fire	丁 *Ding* Yin Fire	巳 *Si* Yin Fire	午 *Wu* Yang Fire
木 Wood	甲, 乙 *Jia* *Yi*	戊 *Wu* Yang Earth 己 *Ji* Yin Earth	辰 *Chen* Yang Earth	戌 *Xu* Yang Earth	丑 *Chou* Yin Earth 未 *Wei* Yin Earth

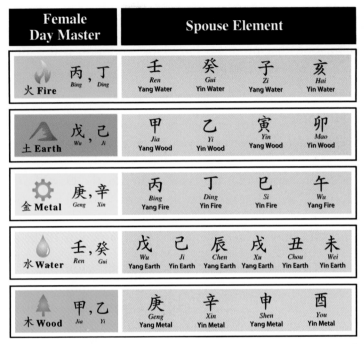

Female Day Master	Spouse Element			
火 Fire 丙,丁 Bing Ding	壬 Ren Yang Water	癸 Gui Yin Water	子 Zi Yang Water	亥 Hai Yin Water
土 Earth 戊,己 Wu Ji	甲 Jia Yang Wood	乙 Yi Yin Wood	寅 Yin Yang Wood	卯 Mao Yin Wood
金 Metal 庚,辛 Geng Xin	丙 Bing Yang Fire	丁 Ding Yin Fire	巳 Si Yin Fire	午 Wu Yang Fire
水 Water 壬,癸 Ren Gui	戊 Wu Yang Earth	己 Ji Yin Earth	辰 Chen Yang Earth	戌 Xu Yang Earth · 丑 Chou Yin Earth · 未 Wei Yin Earth
木 Wood 甲,乙 Jia Yi	庚 Geng Yang Metal	辛 Xin Yin Metal	申 Shen Yang Metal	酉 You Yin Metal

Let's take a look at this example. This is the BaZi chart of a male born on Dec 21, 1956 at You 酉 (Rooster) Hour, which is 5pm-7pm.

By modern standards, this man got married at a very early age, namely, the age of 23. Let's see what the BaZi chart tells us. This man is a Ren 壬 Water Day Master. Accordingly, his Wealth Element, which is also his Spouse Star, is Fire.

八字
解碼

In the Ren Yin 壬寅 Luck Pillar, in the year of Wu Wu 戊午 (1978) there is a Yin 寅-Wu 午-Xu 戌 Three Harmony Combination that produces Fire. Fire, we know, is this Ren Water Day Master's Spouse Star.

The Day Master here is strong, as it is born in season. So this Ren 壬 Water is strong enough to control the Fire element. You will notice this chart is also a bit cold, being born at the height of the Winter season. So, Fire is clearly a favourable element as it helps warm the chart and make the Day Master comfortable. So, the combination is clearly favourable, usable and needed by the Day Master. Since the combination produces the Spouse Star, the person got married in 1978.

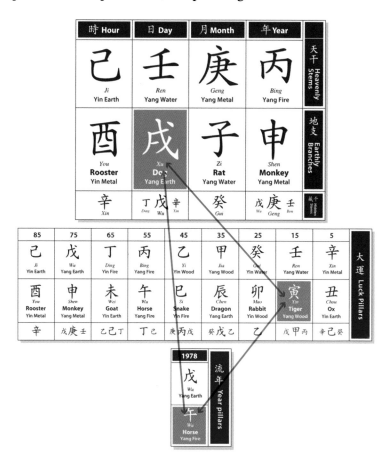

Let's All Get Rich Together -
When a Combination means Cooperation and Joint Venture

時 Hour	日 Day	月 Month	年 Year	
乙	壬	癸	丙	天干 Heavenly Stems
Yi Yin Wood	*Ren* Yang Water	*Gui* Yin Water	*Bing* Yang Fire	
巳	辰	巳	戌	地支 Earthly Branches
Si Snake Yin Fire	*Chen* Dragon Yang Earth	*Si* Snake Yin Fire	*Xu* Dog Yang Earth	
庚 丙 戊 *Geng Bing Wu*	癸 戊 乙 *Gui Wu Yi*	庚 丙 戊 *Geng Bing Wu*	丁 戊 辛 *Ding Wu Xin*	藏干 Hidden Stems

八字解碼

This BaZi chart belongs to an individual who, in his mid-twenties, commenced a business partnership manufacturing plastic household wares. His partnership was phenomenally successful, making both individuals in the partnership very wealthy in the process.

This Ren 壬 Water Day Master is born in the Summer season. Wealth and business ideas are strong in this individual as there is strong fire in the Year Pillar of Bing Xu 丙戌 and Fire is the Wealth Star for this Ren 壬 Water Day Master. And because this Ren 壬 Water Day Master is weak, having been born out of season, he has lots of ideas but is unable to execute them solo. This weak Water needs help from other 'Water' - a partner in the form of Gui 癸 Water.

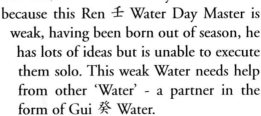

Gui 癸 Water will help this Ren 壬 Day Master control the Fire. What does this mean? It means the partner helps him achieve and materialise his goals. In the Bing Shen 丙申 (Fire Monkey) Luck Pillar, commencing at the age of 26, a combination is activated between the Shen 申 (Monkey) and the Si 巳 (Snake). This combination has a strong tendency to produce the water element. So, a combination is already waiting to happen and it involves a partner.

Now, telling a person that a business partner is about to come along any time during the 10 years is not very helpful to a person. He wants to know when is the big moment! So how do we know when the partnership kicked off?

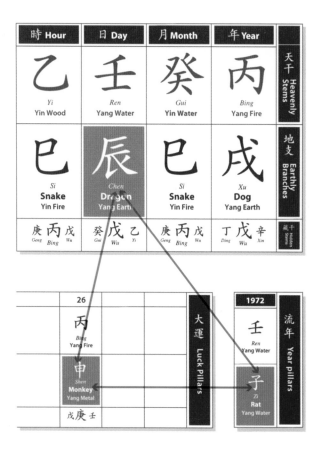

Take a look at 1972. That is the year of the Rat. Now, do you see that the Shen 申 - Zi 子 - Chen 辰 Three Harmony combination that produces the Water Frame is complete?

Water is the Companion Element of this Ren 壬 Water Day Master and is exactly what the weak Ren 壬 Water Day Master needs. The Ren Zi 壬子 year allows the Shen 申 - Si 巳 combination to transform into Water. A partnership was formed that year and the business ideas were able to materialise for this gentleman.

八字
解碼

These are of course just two illustrations of how combinations work and are very simple applications of combinations. As you progress through your understanding and learning of BaZi, particularly with the Ten Gods component added to the BaZi chart, greater depth of understanding of combinations will emerge. For now, focus on remembering what Stems and Branches have combination relationships with each other and practice identifying combination relationships in BaZi charts. As your acuity of combinations improves, and you start to think about the combinations in relation to the Day Master and the Five Relationships, so the combinations will make sense!

Chapter Five:
Clash Codes

This is one type of relationship between the Earthly Branches that is actually already familiar and known to most people. Perhaps you may have heard someone saying that a couple should never have a six-year difference in their ages because otherwise, the year of their birth 'clashes'. Or sometimes, people think that the reason they do not get along with certain people is because their animal signs clash. For example, Rats should not marry Horses, or Dogs should not have bosses who are Dragons, or Roosters will not get along with people who are born in the Year of the Rabbit.

Unfortunately, this is a wrong understanding and erroneous application of the Clash Relationship amongst the Earthly Branches. This incorrect understanding of the Clash Relationship is what has given rise to lots of fodder for annual horoscope books, the Sunday newspaper horoscopes and superstitious practices.

A Clash 沖, in BaZi theory, involves an opposing or a repelling relationship between the Branches, based on the elements or contrasting attributes of the elements. Each Branch represents a specific position of the Earth in relation to the sun. The Branches that have a clash relationship with each other are those which have opposing planetary positions.

In reality, a Clash brings about challenges, obstacles, deterrent, interruptions and difficulties. It represents opposition, change, and sometimes, loss or removal of something or someone.

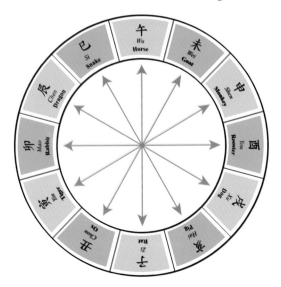

A Clash can manifest in many ways: it can mean an incompatibility with a situation or path you have chosen, it can make a person lose something, such as wealth or a spouse or a company, it can mean physical harm or danger such as an accident, it can mean a problem or incompatibility with certain people such as a spouse, a family member, a friend or a business partner.

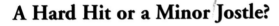

A Hard Hit or a Minor Jostle?

天 戰 猶 自 可 , 地 戰 急 如 火

The Heavenly Battle is bearable , but the Earthly Battle is swifter than the spread of fire - Di Tian Sui 滴天髓

The severity of a Clash in a BaZi chart is determined by several factors. The methodology for evaluating a Clash is usually first, to decode the Clash itself. We want to look at the type of Clash, and determine if, for example, it is an emotional Clash, or a physical Clash. We also want to see what is the element involved in or impacted by the Clash. If a favourable element is clashed, clearly, the Clash will not be a pleasant one. If it is the Useful God or Yong Shen 用神, which is the most important element in the BaZi, is clashed, then definitely it is not a pretty outcome.

Secondly, the Palace that is involved in the clash will also indicate the degree of severity. A Clash that impacts the Year Branch, manifests differently from a Clash that impacts the Month, Day and Hour Branches.

An Internal clash between the year branch and the month branch.

An Internal clash between the day branch and the hour branch.

A third consideration is whether the Clash is already present in the BaZi, known as an Internal Clash, or only occurs upon the arrival of certain Annual or Luck Pillars and thus, only occurs and affects the BaZi chart during certain points in time in the person's life, known as an External Clash. External Clashes are usually drastic or shocking change, that affects the person's health, their relationships or their business or work endeavours. However, they are also usually problems that you can see coming, and are challenges which if you are aware are on the horizon, you can take pro-active steps to handle or psychologically be prepared for. Internal Clashes by contrast usually involve a certain internalised questioning or debate by the person on a matter. They often involve change or events forced by circumstances that are already prevailing.

Finally, there is the practical question that must always be considered, which is, what exactly is being affected by the

Clash? Which of the Five Factors does the Clash relate to?
Is it an Output element? Resource? Influence? By looking at
the Clash, within the context of the 10 Gods, we can further
decode what the clash will affect, how it will affect the person
and the severity of the Clash. By knowing what is being
affected, only then, can we place the Clash within the context
of the person's life and determine if the Clash is a hard hit, or
just a little jolt.

As you make your way through this chapter, I want you to
bear something very important in mind. Do not assume that
a Clash is always bad or is automatically bad. The presence of
a Clash in itself is not cause to be upset or worried. Until the
Clash is properly decoded and understood within the context
of the person's life, keep an open mind and just treat it as an
elemental relationship between the Branches.

The Six Clashes 六沖

The table below shows which Earthly Branches have a Clash relationship with each other.

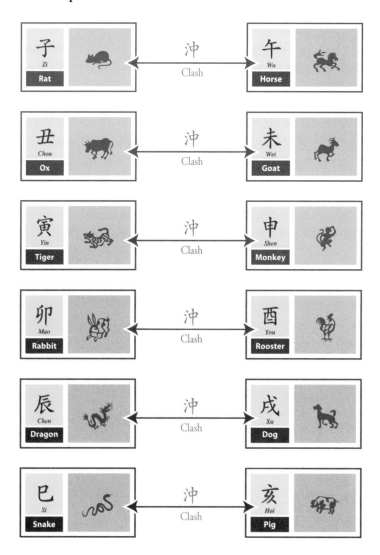

Clash, No Clash or Potential Clash?

The Earthly Branches that have a Clash relationship with each other MUST BE next to each other in the BaZi in order to be considered a Clash in the BaZi. If the two Branches skip a pillar, this is not considered a Clash in the strict sense although the Clash may be activated in certain special circumstances or may impact on the person in a mild or moderate form.

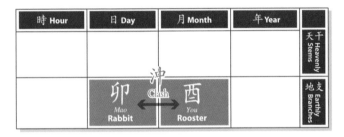

The Clash in this BaZi is between the You 酉 (Rooster) in the Month Branch and the Mao 卯 (Rabbit) in the Day Branch. It is side-by-side and therefore the impact of the Clash is more serious.

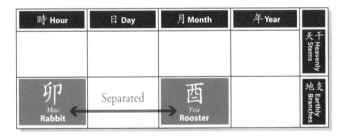

Now, take a look at this BaZi chart. Strictly speaking, the Clash is considered present because the two Clash elements, the You 酉 (Rooster) and the Mao 卯 (Rabbit) are present. However, as the Clash is separated, the elements are not close enough to cause substantial impact and so the Clash is not severe and it is usually tolerable.

This Clash is between the Month Branch and the Hour Branch. In my first book, *The Destiny Code*, I indicated that the Month Pillar is also known as the Parents' Palace whilst the Hour Pillar is also known as the Children's Palace. Hence we can say that the relationship between these two palaces is not favourable and there may be some incompatibility. In simple terms, the person's children will not get along or have an affinity with their grandparents.

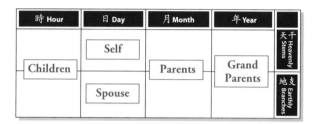

A person may also 'meet' with a Clash if the Earthly Branches in their BaZi have a Clash relationship with the Annual or Luck Pillar, as illustrated by the example below. This is referred to as an External Clash.

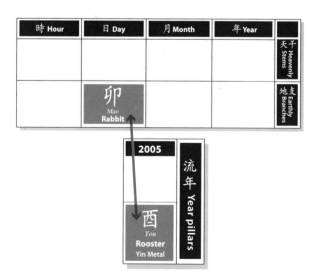

When the year 2005 arrives, there is a Clash between the Day Branch of the BaZi chart, which is Mao 卯 (Rabbit) and the Branch of the annual Luck Pillar, which is You 酉 (Rooster). Now, simple mathematics tell us that since there are only 12 animals signs, this means that every twelve years, a Clash will occur. So does that mean that this person has to be nervous and worried every time the Rooster year rolls around?

An annual clash is usually interpreted differently because the 10-Year Luck Pillar will function as a filter on the impact of the Annual Pillar on the BaZi. Depending on the 10-Year Luck Pillar, the impact of the Clash may be neutralised, or softened, or amplified.

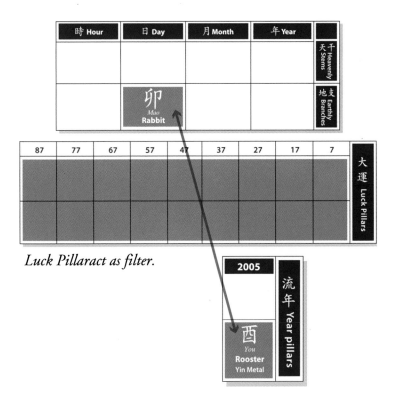

Luck Pillaract as filter.

Internal Clash

An Internal Clash refers to a Clash that is already present in a BaZi, and the Branches with a clash relationship are side-by-side. Take a look at the examples below.

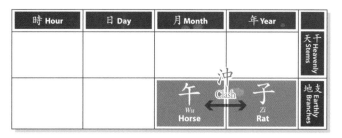

Internal Clash between the Year Branch and the Month Branch

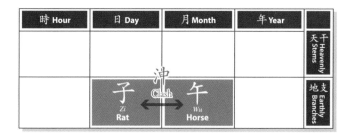

Internal Clash between the Month Branch and the Day Branch

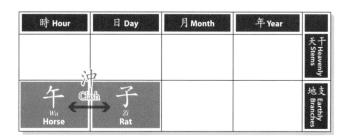

Internal Clash between the Day Branch and the Hour Branch

An Internal Clash represents a certain incompatibility that is present at the time of the person's birth, or an obstacle or change in the person's life that is just waiting to happen. So how do we go about decoding the Clash to understand what it means and what implications it carries?

One very powerful feature of BaZi is its ability to give us insight into the timing of events, and not just say that a certain event is likely to happen. Once the BaZi is decoded, it is possible to drill down to the precise year or month in which the event is likely to occur. When it comes to Clashes, knowing when it is going to happen is as important as knowing what is going to happen.

The Age Pillars are one way of broadly determining when a Clash will take place.

時 Hour	日 Day	月 Month	年 Year
61 onwards	36 - 60	18 - 35	0 - 17

So a Clash between the Year and Month Branch tells us that between a person's teenage and youth years, a momentous event will occur. As your understanding of BaZi increases, you will see that it is possible to pin it down to a precise year, and month. But let's not get ahead of ourselves!

External Clash

An External Clash is sometimes viewed as a dynamic clash because it is influenced by elements that are not within the original Eight Characters in the BaZi. An External Clash is a clash that occurs as a result of certain Branches appearing during certain Annual Pillars or 10-Year Luck Pillars, which have a Clash relationship with the Branches in your BaZi chart.

Since every day in the year has a pillar, along with every month of the year, it is possible to analyse your BaZi very meticulously. However, it is not necessary at this stage to get into such complex analysis. Focusing on Clashes between the Annual Pillar and 10 Year Luck Pillar is more than adequate for you to gain an understanding and appreciation of the obstacles or problems that a Clash will throw up for you.

Here is an example of an External Clash.

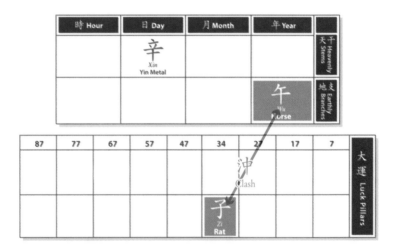

Now, let's see if we can get a clearer picture on this Clash, by decoding it.

Assume that the Wu 午 (Horse) in the Year Branch of the BaZi chart is, after careful analysis, determined to be a negative element. At the age of 34, this person will enter the Zi 子 (Rat) 10-Year Luck Pillar. Now, if you refer to the Six Clashes table, you will see that Zi 子 (Rat) and Wu 午 (Horse) is a Clash. However, this Clash involves a negative element in the chart.

What does this mean? It means that this person goes through a drastic change or event but this drastic change or event brings about a good outcome for the person because, although there is an impact, the result is the removal of a negative element.

Let's drill down and decode the Clash further and understand what area of this person's life will be positively affected by this Clash. Ask yourself, which of the Five Factors (Influence, Resource, Companion, Output, Wealth) is affected by this Clash?

Start by dissecting the two Branches involved in the Clash. Let's take the Zi 子 (Rat) first. The Zi 子 (Rat) contains the hidden stem Gui 癸 Water. Gui 癸 Water, to a Xin 辛 Metal Day Master, is the Output Element. More specifically, it represents the Output Element known as the Eating God. The Eating God star represents ideas, thoughts, cultivation and inventions.

Five Factors:
(Influence, Wealth, Resource, Output, Companion)

Okay, now turn to the other element in the Clash equation - the Wu 午 (Horse). Wu 午 (Horse) contains Ding 丁 Fire as its main Qi. Ding Fire represents the Influence element to a Xin 辛 Metal Day Master. More specifically, it represents the Influence Element known as 7 Killings. This star denotes legal problems, hassles caused by petty people and back-stabbing.

When this Clash takes place, this person would have mastered new skills, knows what they believe in, has confidence in themselves, and can rise above the pettiness that is around them and the problems created by petty individuals around them. As 7 Killings also indicates bodily harm, it also can mean this person, through a skill learnt or acquired, or through action taken, saves their own skin from a dangerous situation.

In advanced study of BaZi, this Clash represents a relationship known as of 'Eating God Controlling 7 Killings'. It denotes rise in power, status and authority after conquering all obstacles and opponents. It is a sign of victory and great stature.

You might have noticed, when we decoded this Clash, that a lot of emphasis was put on the Hidden Stems. The Hidden Stems are in fact, an absolutely essential aspect of decoding a BaZi chart, along with the Ten Gods. Without the Hidden Stems, you're only getting 25% of the picture! And remember, BaZi is a pictorial science. So if you're only seeing 25% of the painting, you're not going to be able to appreciate it in its full glory.

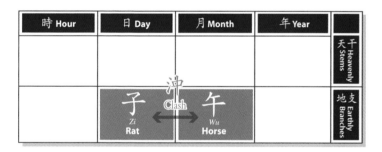

Clash of the Elements: Who wins?

In every Clash, one element will prevail over another. By understanding which element will prevail, we can understand whether the Clash will bring about a positive outcome, or a negative outcome. It will then enable us to take the appropriate steps to deal with the Clash, or embark on precautionary measures. Remember, in BaZi, not taking action is as good as not knowing what is going to happen. Why listen to the weather forecast if you are not going to bother to take an umbrella with you, right?

So how do we decide which element prevails in a Clash? The answer is to look at the Month Branch of the BaZi.

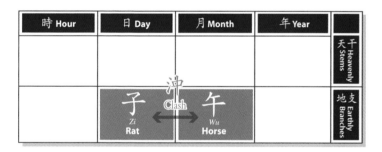

時 Hour	日 Day	月 Month	年 Year	
				天干 Heavenly Stems
	子 *Zi* Rat	午 *Wu* Horse		地支 Earthly Branches

In this BaZi, there is a Clash between the Zi 子 (Rat) and the Wu 午 (Horse). It is a clash between Water and Fire. Now, think back to the Five Elements Cycle, and the Control Cycle. The Five Elements Control Cycle principle is that Water controls Fire by extinguishing it.

As you advance in your study of BaZi, you will develop a more sophisticated appreciation for the Five Element cycle and see that there are subtle differences in the application of the Five Element cycle, as your understanding of the elements grows.

In this case, this BaZi belongs to a person born in the Summer months. The strongest element in the chart is Fire. It is the most prosperous and timely element because it is supported by the month, which is the height of the Fire season. By contrast, the Water element, during the Summer months, is weak and trapped. So, while it is true that Water controls Fire, it is not the case in this BaZi because the Fire element is vibrant and strong and the Water is weak. It is like putting out a bonfire with spit.

Thus in this Clash, we can say that the Zi 子 (Rat) loses out to the Wu 午 (Horse). Now, once we know what Gui 癸 Water represents to the Day Master, we will be able to decode the Clash more completely. However, take a look at the chart. Notice that the Clash involves the Spouse Palace? So, without having completely decoded the Clash, we already know that this Clash involves the Spouse Palace, and affects the spousal relationship. Of course, for an accurate conclusion, the intensity of the Clash, and the nature of the Clash have to be decoded. But, just looking at the Palace location, we already have an inkling of what is going to happen.

Of course, sometimes, the Month does not hold sway over the outcome of a Clash. However, at this level, it is quite safe to use the Month as one indicator and method of determining which Element triumphs in a Clash.

The Meaning of Clashes

Each Clash brings about a unique outcome, depending on the type of Clash, severity, elements involved and Ten Gods. To give you an idea of how Clashes impact on a person, I will explore some simple scenarios and show you how the Clash can be decoded.

As you go through this section, always try to think about what are the Hidden Stems involved in the Clash, and keep in mind which of the Five Factors is being affected.

Loss of Relationship Clash

A Clash with the Branches always involves some emotional impact or response. This is particularly so when the Clash involves the Spouse Palace. If you've forgotten, the Earthly Branch of the Day Pillar is also known as the Spouse Palace.

時 Hour	日 Day	月 Month	年 Year	
				天干 Heavenly Stems
	Spouse Palace			地支 Earthly Branches

Now, it goes without saying that a Clash to the Spouse Palace affects the person's relationship with his/her spouse. Remember in my first book, *The Destiny Code*, I said the Spouse Palace is the 'Untouchable Palace'? We don't like the spouse palace to have a relationship with the other Branches in the BaZi, just like we don't want our spouses to have a relationship with other people!

Of course, it is not necessary to be stressed at every instance the Spouse Palace is involved in a Clash. Remember, we must judge a Clash objectively at all times. We must consider the severity of the Clash, the nature of the problem, and whether it affects a favourable or unfavourable element in the chart.

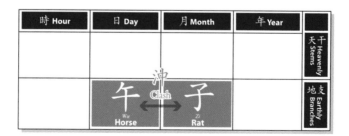

This BaZi chart indicates that a problem is just waiting to pop to the surface for this person, with regard to the relationship with their spouse. By looking at the Age Pillars, we can see that this problem is likely to surface during the person's middle age years.

Since the Clash already exists in the chart, tension is already likely to be present between the person and the spouse. So, tolerance and patience must always be exercised by the person, when it comes to their relationship with their spouse. In particular, this type of clash, involving the Zi 子(Rat) and Wu 午 (Horse) indicates lingering and tiresome, annoying squabbles, and a lack of peace in the person's life.

時 Hour	日 Day	月 Month	年 Year	
				天干 Heavenly Stems
	午 Wu Horse	子 Zi Rat		地支 Earthly Branches

				34				
			沖 Clash					大運 Luck Pillars
			子 Zi Rat					

When the person arrives at the luck pillar where there is a 'Luck Pillar Clash' with the Spouse Palace, and this happens to be around middle age, then this means this Clash is going to take place during that time. The problem will come to the fore at that point in time.

This Clash indicates the likelihood of a very serious change to the relationship. It will be a difficult and challenging time. Now, to know exactly whether the problem is a third party, an attitude problem or a health issue, we must decode this Clash further, applying the Five Factors, or for greater depth, the Ten Gods. Since this is still a Beginners' book, let's just focus on the easy-to-decode aspects first. Decoding this Clash at its most basic level, we can say a serious obstacle to the person's marriage will occur, during their middle age years, that will challenge the marriage significantly.

Loss of Object Clash

A Clash can also indicate a loss of an object or an item. Take a look at the BaZi below.

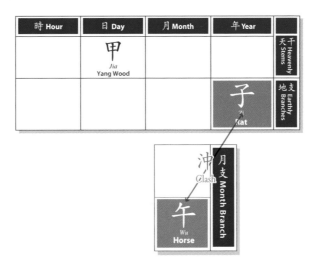

This person lost his passport while on a family holiday. Why did it happen? BaZi can actually give us an answer!

During the month of June, which is the Wu午(Horse) month, this person went on holiday. During that month, there is a Clash between the Month's Branch and the Year Branch of his BaZi. Now, what is affected by this Clash? It affects the Resource Element, specifically, the Direct Resource star of Jia Wood.

Direct Resource star, in the study of BaZi, represents, amongst other things, documents. Direct Resource also represents a person's sense of comfort - as there is a Clash involving the Direct Resource, it indicates discomfort, hassle or unpleasant matters that affect how the person feels. Since the Clash involves the Year Pillar, it denotes extended family is involved. He was on a family holiday.

Now, because the Clash impacts on the Year Pillar, and involves only the Branch of one of the month's in the year (as opposed to an Annual Year Branch or a Luck Pillar Branch) the problem is not a major clash.

Loss of Job Clash

時 Hour	日 Day	月 Month	年 Year	干 Heavenly Stems 天
	庚 *Geng* Yang Metal	丙 *Bing* Yang Fire		
		午 *Wu* Horse		地支 Earthly Branches

Hidden Combo

時 Hour	日 Day	月 Month	沖 Clash 年 Year	干 Heavenly Stems 天
		癸 *Gui* Yin Water		
		亥 *Hai* Pig	子 *Zi* Rat	地支 Earthly Branches

Take a look at this BaZi chart. This person is a Geng 庚 Metal Day Master who lost his job during the Hai 亥 (Pig) month, of a Zi 子 (Rat) year. What happened? The main two elements involved in this equation are Fire and Water. What is Fire to a Geng 庚 Metal person? It is the Influence element. In BaZi, the Influence Element, amongst other things, denotes the boss or superior.

The Clash between the Zi 子 (Rat) and the Wu (Horse) affects the superior because inside the Wu 午 (Horse) is Ding 丁 Fire. Specifically, Ding 丁 Fire represents the Direct Officer star of Geng 庚 Metal. So, the boss is clashed away.

But that is not the only Fire affected. You will notice that this Geng 庚 Day Master has both Bing 丙 Fire and Ding 丁 Fire in the month pillar. Zi 子 (Rat) contains Gui 癸 Water. Gui Water is rainwater or rain clouds, which cover the Bing Fire, diminishing its brightness and brilliance.

With one fell swoop, all the Influence Element in this person's BaZi chart is removed. Hence, the person lost his job during the Hai 亥 (Pig) month.

Now, let's say we want to know if this was caused by the boss or the employee. At a basic elemental level, this problem is caused by a Clash between the Water elements and the Fire elements of the person's chart. What is Water to a Geng 庚 Metal? It is an Output Element. Specifically, in this case, Gui 癸 Water, that is found inside the Zi 子 (Rat), represents the Hurting Officer star. The Hurting Officer star indicates a rebellious nature, going against the order of authority and not toe-ing the line. Thus, this person lost his job because he was outspoken and rebellious and went against his boss. This resulted in this person being ostracised and then forced to resign.

Loss of wealth Clash

Now, a clash can mean the removal of something. When this involves a wealth element, then there's a high chance that the Clash indicates loss of wealth.

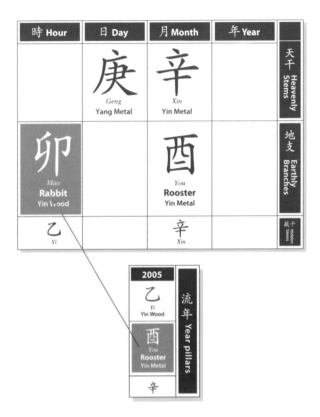

This Geng 庚 Metal Day Master's Wealth element is Yi Wood, which is found inside the Mao 卯 (Rabbit), located at the Hour Branch. This particular Wealth Element is a Direct Wealth star. When the You 酉 (Rooster) appears in 2005, it clashes with the Mao 卯 (Rabbit). Decoded, this Clash means that there is a Clash involving Wealth in 2005.

Now, why does this happen? Look at the BaZi chart - this Geng 庚 Day Master is born in the month of You 酉 (Rooster), which is the season of Autumn. Metal is strong in the Autumn, and Wood is weak. The You 酉 (Rooster) and Mao 卯 (Rabbit) Clash is also present, in weakened form, in this Geng 庚 Day Master's BaZi. The arrival of the You 酉 (Rooster) in 2005 strikes an element which is already weak and has already been affected by a mild Clash within the BaZi. Thus, the Wealth element is easily removed in 2005 and this Geng 庚 Day Master will experience a loss of wealth in 2005.

Moving House Clash

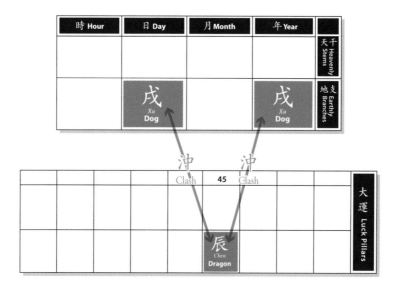

This BaZi chart shows an External Clash between Chen 辰 (Dragon) and Xu 戌 (Dog). If you refer to the chapter on Hidden Stems, you will note that the main Qi in both these Branches is Earth. When Earth and Earth clash, it usually denotes changes to assets or changes involving places.

This Clash involves the Year and the Day Branches of the BaZi. The clash between the Earth elements indicates that it is a change involving the home environment. As the clash involves the Day Branch, which also denotes the person's home or the person themselves, hence we can conclude that this Clash results in the person moving houses.

Now, let's say you don't have a Chen 辰 (Dragon) or Xu 戌 (Dog) in your BaZi chart - does that mean you will never leave the house you are living in? Of course not. I'm simply showing you the most obvious and common possible situations - there are many other circumstances which would prompt movement in a person's life and as you progress along your understanding of BaZi, we will revisit some of these scenarios!

Dealing with a Clash

Now, a simplified approach to a Clash would be to see it as something negative or unfavourable. However, this kind of blanket approach is not correct. A Clash is always uncomfortable and unpleasant, but that does not always mean it is bad or negative. A Clash that removes an unfavourable element in a chart is a good Clash. A Clash that shakes a person out of complacency, or makes them a better person, is not a bad outcome. Sometimes, a Clash brings unfavourable outcomes, but sometimes, it can be a cloud with a silver lining, a lesson or problem or challenge, that brings about a positive lesson.

It is all about how you perceive it. Do you see the situation as a challenge, and rise up, face it and become a better person and a stronger person as a result of the difficulty? Or do you submit and let it take you down and get nowhere? Do you chose to manage the situation with the skills you have, or do you just stand in the middle of the road and wait to get knocked over? Sometimes, we all need a little adversity in life because it is adversity that creates character and adversity that let us see our true strengths and abilities.

Can you cure a Clash?

You may have heard certain New-Age BaZi practitioners (or even goldsmiths or jewellers) saying that wearing certain animal pendants will cure a Clash. The solution to a Clash, according to these practitioners, is to wear a pendant that combines with the offending animal that causes the clash. By doing so, you 'combine away' the clashing animal, thus, saving the day.

		Cure Animal	
子 *Zi* Rat	午 *Wu* Horse	丑 *Chou* Ox	Ox combines with Rat, thereby removing the clash element.
丑 *Chou* Ox	未 *Wei* Goat	午 *Wu* Horse	Horse combines away the goat, therefore saving the Ox.
寅 *Yin* Tiger	申 *Shen* Monkey	巳 *Si* Snake	Snake combines with monkey, therefore saving the Tiger.
卯 *Mao* Rabbit	酉 *You* Rooster	辰 *Chen* Dragon	Because dragon 'combines' with Rooster. So Dragon saves the clash.
辰 *Chen* Dragon	戌 *Xu* Dog	卯 *Mao* Rabbit	Rabbit combines the dog, saving the dog from being clashed by the dragon.
巳 *Si* Snake	亥 *Hai* Pig	寅 *Yin* Tiger	Tiger combines the pig and therefore saving the Snake from the Pig.

Now, I don't deny that wearing a pendant might bring certain psychological influences but do not for a minute be convinced that you have solved the Clash problem! Remember, a Clash in the chart represents an astronomical clash, involving the planets position in relation to your BaZi chart. A pendant is not Kryptonite. It cannot move planets, shift stars and change the impact of the elements.

In BaZi, the cure is always "action." The solution to a problem is to know how you will deal with it when it arrives, or be prepared for its outcomes. You should not be focusing on the things you supposedly to 'wear' for good luck or protection. This is wishful thinking. Rather, it is much wiser to focus on what you must do and what you should avoid doing.

Chapter Six:
Punishment Codes

I was to start this chapter with a story about a person. Let's call him Mr N (for Negativity). We all know a person like Mr N.

Mr N is a nice, amicable and pleasant sort. He's not demanding, doesn't ask for attention and is happy to sit back and let other people do the talking. Mr N has a good job, and he's pretty talented, but he's not exactly the world's most ambitious person. He's happy to just do what he's asked, take the promotion when he's given one and do precisely what is written out in his job description, no more, no less. Mr N is not interested in being better. And even if he was vaguely interested in improving his lot in life, he would never ask for anyone's help. Not because Mr N doesn't want help - he just doesn't see how anyone can help him.

You see, Mr N lives in his own world and it's a very narrow, tunnel-vision world. In that world, no one is nice to anyone. Everyone has an ulterior motive. No one is genuine. In Mr N's world, his situation is always beyond help by anyone because they can never understand his predicament. Mr N is always whining about how no one cares and no one wants to give him a hand.

Does it sound contradictory? Don't be surprised because Mr N, and all his type, are full of contradictions. The glass is always full and yet always empty to them.

Here's Mr N's BaZi:

時 Hour	日 Day	月 Month	年 Year	天干 Heavenly Stems
乙 Yi Yin Wood	戊 Wu Yang Earth	己 Ji Yin Earth	甲 Jia Yang Wood	
卯 Mao Rabbit Yin Wood	申 Shen Monkey Yang Metal	巳 Si Snake Yin Fire	寅 Yin Tiger Yang Wood	地支 Earthly Branches
乙 Yi	戊 Wu 庚 Geng 壬 Ren	庚 Geng 丙 Bing 戊 Wu	戊 Wu 甲 Jia 丙 Bing	藏干 Hidden Stems

90	80	70	60	50	40	30	20	10	大運 Luck Pillars
戊 Wu Yang Earth	丁 Ding Yin Fire	丙 Bing Yang Fire	乙 Yi Yin Wood	甲 Jia Yang Wood	癸 Gui Yin Water	壬 Ren Yang Water	辛 Xin Yin Metal	庚 Geng Yang Metal	
寅 Yin Tiger Yang Wood	丑 Chou Ox Yin Earth	子 Zi Rat Yang Water	亥 Hai Pig Yin Water	戌 Xu Dog Yang Earth	酉 You Rooster Yin Metal	申 Shen Monkey Yang Metal	未 Wei Goat Yin Earth	午 Wu Horse Yang Fire	
戊甲丙	辛己癸	癸	壬甲	丁戊辛	辛	戊庚壬	乙己丁	丁己	

Now, why does Mr N, who is not an unpleasant sort in a sense, have this attitude and problem? It's quite simple - it's to do with the Punishment formations in his BaZi.

時 Hour	日 Day	月 Month	年 Year	
乙 Yi Yin Wood	戊 Wu Yang Earth	己 Ji Yin Earth	甲 Jia Yang Wood	天干 Heavenly Stems
卯 Mao **Rabbit** Yin Wood	申 Shen **Monkey** Yang Metal	巳 Si **Snake** Yin Fire	寅 Yin **Tiger** Yang Wood	地支 Earthly Branches
乙 Yi	戊 庚 壬 Wu Geng Ren	庚 丙 戊 Geng Bing Wu	戊 甲 丙 Wu Jia Bing	藏干 Hidden Stems

Karmic Pricetags

The Punishment Relationship is one of the more complex relationships between the Earthly Branches that can be found in a BaZi chart. The Punishment relationship is often not very well-understood, largely because even some Chinese books on the subject tend to be vague in their explanation of this type of relationship. Most practitioners of BaZi know that a Punishment is something they don't like to see in a chart, but they often do not know for what reason it is unfavourable and how it manifests itself in a person.

Essentially, a Punishment Relationship can be explained as a situation that is caused by something done in the past coming back to haunt you. It is something said or done that comes back to bite you. Think of a Punishment as something that results in instant karma – it is payback for something you have done or didn't do in the past.

Punishment or Xing 刑 is most of the time, psychological in its effect, rather than physical. It almost always relates to how people feel about something in their lives, be it an event, a person or a state of affairs. People with Punishments in their BaZi usually feel permanently unhappy or never satisfied. Happiness never lasts long for them and even when they are in a good mood, they'll find something to make themselves feel unhappy about.

Generally, Punishments are not something that we would like to see in a chart – it is not a good feature to have but of course, it also depends on what is being affected by the Punishment relationship in the BaZi chart and how the Punishment manifests itself. Some punishments are tolerable, while some are more intense. Some make a person supremely pessimistic, like what we have mentioned about Mr N above, while some punishments create consequential events as a result of certain actions, which can be treated as a positive lesson for the future. In severe cases of Punishment formations in the chart – the person faces permanent and long term sadness, unhappiness, dejection or even, depression.

You also want to consider if it is a full Punishment, meaning the full Punishment relationship, which often involves 3 Branches together, appears in the chart, or just a minor punishment which only involves 2 of the 3 Branches in one natal BaZi chart. Of course, the impact of the Punishment depends on whether it is Internal or External Punishment, meaning, the Punishment occurs as a result of the Luck Pillar or Annual Pillar creating a Punishment relationship with the Branches in the BaZi chart.

Dealing with Punishments is often not difficult. Punishments are Cause and Effect situations. It is often a matter of either taking the right action, planning your actions or strategising your responses to certain situations, recognising the area of the problem and developing self-discipline. Once the type of Punishment has been identified and the area or relationship that it involves has been identified, dealing with the situation is not difficult.

The seriousness of Punishments will also greatly depend on whether your favourable or unfavourable elements are involved in the Punishment. If the Punishment involves your favourable elements, the problems are tolerable and not harmful. Conversely, if the Punishment involves your unfavourable elements, the problems would be much more challenging and require more effort to manage.

When it comes to Punishments, the solutions are not always palatable and it is here that often, people find it difficult to make the change. After all, if you are a lifelong smoker, you know what you need to do. You just may not want to do it! It is important to have the mental fortitude and support to do what it takes to overcome the situation and not allow the effects of the Punishment to dictate the situation. Take charge, rather than be taken prisoner, and Punishments are not entirely unmanageable.

Types of Punishment

The first step to decoding Punishments is to IDENTIFY the Punishment. Usually, Punishments involve 3 Earthly Branches but there are some which involve just 2 Earthly Branches. There are four basic types of Punishment relationships that can be found in a BaZi chart:

- Ungrateful Punishment [無恩之刑]
- Bullying Punishment [恃勢之刑]
- Uncivilised Punishment [無禮之刑]
- Self-Punishment [自刑]

Ungrateful Punishment 無恩之刑

Bullying Punishment 恃勢之刑

Uncivilised Punishment 無禮之刑

Self Punishment 自刑

Ungrateful Punishment 無恩之刑

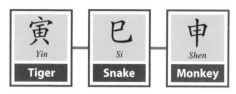

寅	巳	申
Yin	Si	Shen
Tiger	Snake	Monkey

As the name implies, this type of Punishment involves a 'lack of gratitude'. An Ungrateful Punishment refers to situations where you offer someone help, out of the goodness of your heart and without expecting anything in return, but you end up getting into trouble or are on the receiving end of flack as a result of your actions. Individuals on the receiving end of an Ungrateful Punishment may also feel short-changed, or that they have somehow been cheated. In certain special conditions, this formation can make the person volatile and aggressive.

Ungrateful Punishment makes people prone to betrayal although it is not always the case that they are not to blame for the betrayal. You see, people with Ungrateful Punishments see the worse in other people and so sometimes, they create self-fulfilling prophecy situations where their attitude or overly-careful manner causes them to feel betrayed, sometimes, over small matters or brings out the worst in those around them, creating situations where betrayal is inevitable.

Ungrateful Punishments, when present in the BaZi chart, can bring about long-term unhappiness, discontent, pessimism and depression. It is very hard to live life when you only see the negative traits in people or the negativity of situations. It is also hard to live life feeling like there is no one in this world you can trust to help you because you think everyone is out to get you!

Estranged Family Ties

Ungrateful Punishments are also usually not good for family ties. Depending on which Palaces the Punishment Formation effects, it usually weakens the affinity with that relative. In the old BaZi manuscripts, people with the complete Ungrateful Punishment usually have weak affinity with relatives. For example, they do not have harmonious relationship bonds with their parents or siblings, or their parents are divorced and therefore they have a broken family, or they have siblings from different parents (meaning, parent divorced and remarried another person giving birth to half siblings). Needless to say, charts that have the complete Ungrateful Punishment will naturally, in some way, affect the quality of the relationship with the spouse.

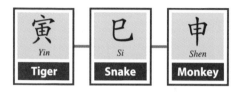

How an Ungrateful Punishment Manifests in a BaZi Chart

The table below shows which Earthly Branches have an Ungrateful Punishment relationship with each other.

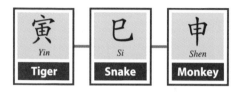

The Ungrateful Punishment relationship only occurs when the Earthly Branches with an Ungrateful Punishment relationship with each other appear side-by-side. It is very important to qualify the Punishment Formation by looking at the positioning of the Branches to see if the Punishment is a complete Formation. In the chart below, all three of the Ungrateful Punishment Earthly Branches are present and are side-by-side. The Punishment Formation is complete and its full effects will be felt by the person.

In the chart below, the Punishments are separated and are technically not complete.

The Yin 寅 (Tiger), Shen 申 (Monkey) and Si 巳 (Snake) are present in the chart. This is the complete Ungrateful Punishment Formation. However, because one of the Branches is separated, the effect is very much reduced.

A person may also 'meet' with an Ungrateful Punishment if the Earthly Branches in their BaZi have an Ungrateful Punishment relationship with the Annual or Luck Pillar.

This example shows just a Yin 寅 (Tiger) and Si 巳 (Snake) Ungrateful Punishment Formation between the Month and Day branches. Clearly, this Punishment is not as severe as having the entire Yin-Shen-Si 寅申巳 (Tiger-Monkey-Snake) complete Punishment Formation.

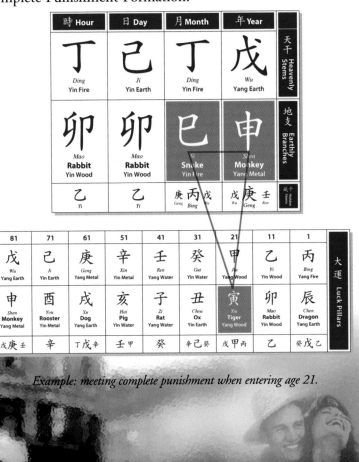

Example: meeting complete punishment when entering age 21.

Another example:

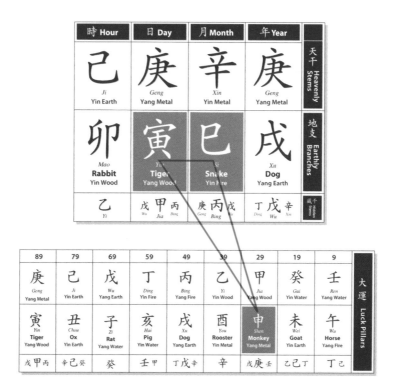

This example shows that the original chart already have a Tiger and Snake Ungrateful Punishment. When the person enters the age of 29, the Ungrateful Punishment is complete.

In the example below, the Ungrateful Punishment Formation is complete in the Ren Shen 壬申 (Water Monkey) year, during the Ji Si 己巳 luck pillar.

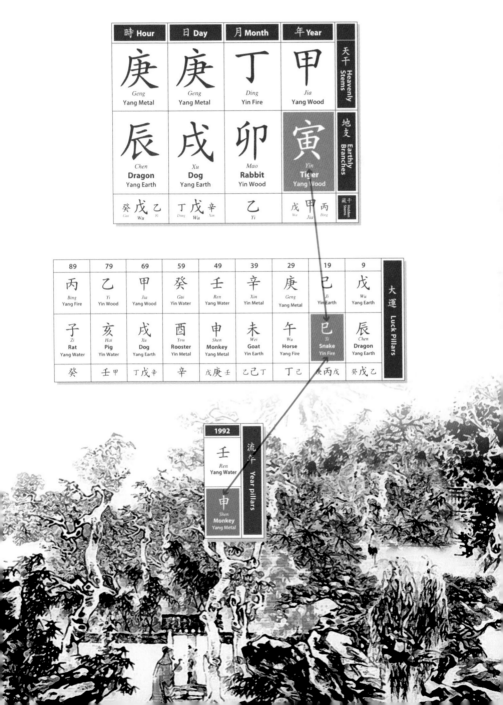

It is important to determine if the Ungrateful Punishment is externalised or internalised. This often dictates whether or not the impact is on the person's relationship with people around them or matters around them or if it affects them psychologically and mentally and has an impact on their character.

Externalised Ungrateful Punishment refers to something done to you, by someone else, which results in you getting into trouble, despite being a good Samaritan in the first place. Internalised Ungrateful Punishment on the other hand, involves the person's perception and thinking of events and relationships around them.

The Meaning of Ungrateful Punishment

What kind of scenarios are examples of Ungrateful Punishment? The common example is the lady who supports her boyfriend or husband through his studies or professional examinations, and then when the boyfriend or husband achieves success or reaches the pinnacle of his career, he breaks-up or divorces his wife for someone else. Another possible scenario is the case of the friend who helps out a good friend during their darkest moments, only to find their friend rebounds and then, takes something away from them, such as perhaps a job.

Dealing with Ungrateful Punishments

People with Internalised Ungrateful Punishment often are very cynical, see the worst in everything, are extremely negative, feel unworthy (although they often do not say this) and frequently think that everything has a catch or everyone is out to get them. They often are paranoid and have inferiority complexes. Their expectations, when they have done something for someone, are usually extremely high, resulting in frequent disappointment or feeling of being short-changed. People with Internalised Ungrateful Punishment often cannot accept that gratitude is not something to be expected.

Of course, the gravity of the Punishment and what is affected by the Punishment must always be considered before we can determine the ultimate effects of the Punishment on the person. An Ungrateful Punishment Formation in the chart does not always mean the person will show a pessimistic outlook or be highly negative in their manner.

It is often very difficult to help individuals with an internalised Ungrateful Punishment because they tend to have a very pessimistic view of the world or offer up many excuses why your suggestions or options are not feasible. Helping them change their perspective and outlook requires both a personal commitment to seeing the world and people in a better light, being more accepting and less angry with their lot in life and often, people around them who are supportive and very positive.

Psychological outlook and mental attitude are crucial to overcoming the inherent problem that having an Ungrateful Punishment in a chart poses. First, there is a need to break out of the comfort zone. Do not be afraid to venture forth boldly into the world and to take your own destiny into your own hands. Secondly, see the positive in everything and when unfavourable or negative things happen, or you experience betrayal or a set back, don't look at it as a reason to be suspicious or distrustful in the future. It is good not to be naïve in life, but at the same time, there is no point living your life as if everyone is out to get you. Negative things happen to everyone but that doesn't mean we stop moving forward and dwell on the unfortunate events in life.

Bullying Punishment 恃勢之刑

A Bullying Punishment refers to situations where a person gets into a situation where they are helpless or without leverage or unable to do anything to defend themselves, and the cause of this misfortune is their own carelessness. Bullying Punishments are usually David v Goliath type situations, but usually without the good ending of the little guy triumphing over the big  guy. Bullying Punishment can also be seen as payback for a mistake or slip-up you have made in the past, which causes you to lose out somehow.

The table below shows which Earthly Branches have a Bullying Punishment relationship with each other.

未	戌	丑
Wei	Xu	Chou
Goat	Dog	Ox

The Bullying Punishment relationship only occurs when the Earthly Branches Wei 未 (Goat), Xu 戌 (Dog) and Chou 丑 (Ox) appear side-by-side, in any order in a chart. If there are only two of the three, it's also considered a Bullying Punishment, however the impact is not so significant and serious.

時 Hour	日 Day	月 Month	年 Year	
辛 *Xin* Yin Metal	癸 *Gui* Yin Water	庚 *Geng* Yang Metal	丁 *Ding* Yin Fire	天干 Heavenly Stems
酉 *You* **Rooster** Yin Metal	丑 *Chou* **Ox** Yin Earth	戌 *Xu* **Dog** Yang Earth	未 *Wei* **Goat** Yin Earth	地支 Earthly Branches
辛 *Xin*	辛 己 癸 *Xin Ji Gui*	丁 戊 辛 *Ding Wu Xin*	乙 己 丁 *Yi Ji Ding*	藏干 Hidden Stems

In this example, the full Bullying Punishment Formation of Chou 丑 (Ox), Xu 戌 (Dog) and Wei 未 (Goat) are present in this chart.

However, a person may also 'meet' with a Bullying Punishment if the Earthly Branches in their BaZi meet with the missing third party that completes the Bullying Punishment formation. For example, the Bullying Punishment relationship is completed by the Annual or Luck Pillar.

In the example below, the person 'meets' with the complete Bullying Punishment when she enters the 38 Years old Luck Pillar.

八字解碼

時 Hour	日 Day	月 Month	年 Year	
戊 *Wu* Yang Earth	辛 *Xin* Yin Metal	乙 *Yi* Yin Wood	乙 *Yi* Yin Wood	天干 Heavenly Stems
戌 *Xu* Dog Yang Earth	未 *Wei* Goat Yin Earth	酉 *You* Rooster Yin Metal	巳 *Si* Snake Yin Fire	地支 Earthly Branches
丁 戊 辛 *Ding Wu Xin*	乙己丁 *Yi Ji Ding*	辛 *Xin*	庚 丙 戊 *Geng Bing Wu*	藏干 Hidden Stems

88	78	68	58	48	38	28	18	8	
甲 *Jia* Yang Wood	癸 *Gui* Yin Water	壬 *Ren* Yang Water	辛 *Xin* Yin Metal	庚 *Geng* Yang Metal	己 *Ji* Yin Earth	戊 *Wu* Yang Earth	丁 *Ding* Yin Fire	丙 *Bing* Yang Fire	大運 Luck Pillars
午 *Wu* Horse Yang Fire	巳 *Si* Snake Yin Fire	辰 *Chen* Dragon Yang Earth	卯 *Mao* Rabbit Yin Wood	寅 *Yin* Tiger Yang Wood	丑 *Chou* Ox Yin Earth	子 *Zi* Rat Yang Water	亥 *Hai* Pig Yin Water	戌 *Xu* Dog Yang Earth	
丁 己	庚 丙 戊	癸 戊 乙	乙	戊 甲 丙	辛 己 癸	癸	壬 甲	丁 戊 辛	

Are you the bully? Or are you being bullied?

A Bullying Punishment can manifest two ways: externally, meaning you are bullied by someone, or internally, meaning, you bully yourself. Now, of course, you might be wondering - how do you 'bully' yourself? How about overburdening yourself with work? Or always giving yourself unnecessary hassles perhaps, because you're just too responsible? Or not being able to say no?

An example of internalised Bullying Punishment is a person who gets pushed around at work or intimidated or harassed at work because they lack qualifications or cannot muster enough courage to speak up. Or is a loner who feels that they are not understood or finds it hard to express their feelings or thoughts verbally. In a marriage, if the woman has a Bullying Punishment in her chart, she may find that if she seeks a divorce from her husband, she does not get spousal support or alimony because of her ignorance, and thus, is put into hard times.

Internalised Bullying Punishment can also manifest in situations where a person makes a promise or gives their word and cannot go back on it, even if they desperately needs to go back on their promise. For example, you promise to sell your car to your girlfriend's brother without profit. Suddenly, you encounter a cash shortfall and someone offers to buy the car off you for a better price. But because it is your girlfriend's brother, you cannot refuse to sell the car to him. This is an internalised Bullying Punishment because the person's hand is forced, due to circumstances of his own making.

What about an external Bullying Punishment? Let's say, a person is being sued and encounters a Bullying Punishment during that year. They may lose a lawsuit because the evidence is against them or the other party, being wealthier, is able to hire a better lawyer. This is an example of an external Bullying Punishment.

Decoding a Bullying Punishment

When looking at a Bullying Punishment, we should determine if it is already present in the chart, or whether it is met in the 10-Year Luck or Annual Pillars, as this will bring about a different type of implication or outcome. It is also important to know which type of Bullying Punishment is involved because each Bullying Punishment relates to different situations or scenarios. We also want to look at the elements involved and the Ten Gods.

The example below provides an illustration of how to decode a Bullying Punishment in a chart.

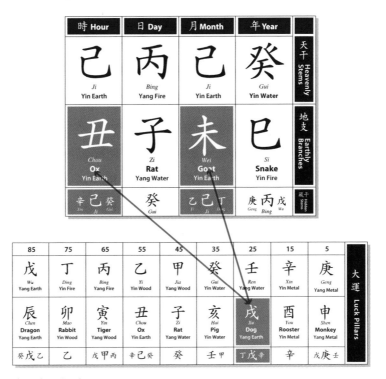

Female 24 July 1953 – 2.30am

This Bing Fire Day Master encounters a complete Bullying Punishment formation at the 10-Year Luck Pillar beginning at the age of 25. The Xu 戌 (Dog) in the 10-Year Luck Pillar completes the formation that is partially present in the chart, in the form of the Wei 未 (Goat) in the Month Branch and the Chou 丑 (Ox) in the Hour Branch. What is the impact of this Bullying Punishment? To know this, we must ask ourselves this question: who or what is being affected?

The Earth Element in this chart is very dominant. Earth represents the Output for Fire and in the case of this Bing Fire Day Master, is the star known as the Hurting Officer star. In the Five Elements cycle, Earth controls Water. Water, specifically Gui Water, to this Bing Fire Lady, is the Husband Star. Since Earth is so strong, Water is weak in this chart.

The arrival of the Bullying Punishment further weakens the Water element so obviously, the spousal relationship is affected during these ten years.

You will also notice that there is already a Harm formation present between the Zi 子 (Rat) and the Wei 未 (Goat) and the Zi 子 (Rat) is also attempting to combine with the Chou 丑 (Ox) branch. Without even knowing what this actually means, it's clear that this woman's marriage, during these 10 years, will be a messy and complicated affair. In real life, this woman lost her fiancée during this 10 Year Luck Pillar.

Standing up to the Bully

When individuals encounter a Bullying Punishment in their chart, they will find they encounter situations where they are often in a weak position or are victimised. And since the Bullying Punishment comprises of the Earthly Branches known as Graveyards (refer to Chapter 2 if you don't remember what this is!), the individuals not only feel beleaguered and under-pressure, but misunderstood and lonely.

Overcoming a Bullying Punishment is much more about mental and psychological attitude than anything else. At times when a person feels under constant pressure, beleaguered and without anyone to turn to, it is not only important to have confidence in oneself at all times, but also, a good support network of people who can help you pull through these difficult times. Positive thinking, staying motivated, and recognising that the situation is to some degree, not your fault is important. As the Graveyard Branches denote loneliness or a feeling of solitude, some people benefit from meditation or spiritual practice.

Ultimately, a Bullying Punishment can still have a good outcome if the elements that are involved in the Punishment are favourable to your chart. Yes, you will experience the problems and challenges, but at the end of the day, you will emerge a stronger, better and more capable person.

Uncivilised Punishment 無禮之刑

In moderate cases, an Uncivilised Punishment refers to a 'bite the hand that feeds you' situation. A person with an Uncivilised Punishment in their chart is disloyal or goes against something that they should be loyal or grateful to. In serious cases, this sort of Punishment can bring about sexual related problems – unhealthy desires (if it is an internal Uncivilised Punishment) or harassment (if it is an external Uncivilised Punishment).

The table below shows which Earthly Branches have an Uncivilised Punishment relationship with each other.

The Uncivilised Punishment relationship only occurs when the Earthly Branches with an Uncivilised Punishment relationship with each other appear side-by-side.

時 Hour	日 Day	月 Month	年 Year	
				天干 Heavenly Stems
	卯 Mao Rabbit ←→	子 Zi Rat		地支 Earthly Branches

However, a person may also 'meet' with an Uncivilised Punishment if the Earthly Branches in their BaZi have a Uncivilised Punishment relationship with the annual or luck pillar.

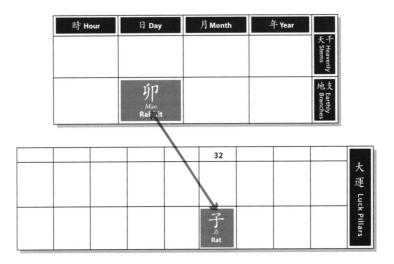

Going Against the Grain

Uncivilised Punishment usually entails some measure of going against something you should not go against, or having to do something that can be construed as 'disloyal'. Let's take a look at an example to get an idea of how an Uncivilised Punishment takes meaning in a chart.

Let's say a person has the Zi 子 and Mao 卯 Uncivilized Punishment in their chart. Zi 子 represents the element of Water, whilst Mao 卯 represents the element of Wood.

八字
解
碼

In the study of the Five Elements, Wood and Water have a Growth relationship – Water grows the Wood. (In case you've forgotten some of the Five Element basics, it's all dealt with in *The Destiny Code*).

Accordingly, Wood should be 'grateful' or 'loyal' to Water, because water is what 'gives life' to Wood. But because it is an Uncivilised Punishment relationship between the two Hidden Branches, Wood is neither 'grateful' nor 'loyal' to the Water, but instead, goes against the Water. Of course, how the relationship or scenario plays out largely depends on what Water and Wood represent in the person's chart and the Ten Gods involved.

If you have a look at the Hidden Branches that have an Uncivilised Punishment Relationship with each other, you will immediately notice that they are all also Peach Blossom stars.

Briefly, Peach Blossom stars are also known as attraction stars and they represent, amongst other things, sex appeal or magnetism.

Hence, an Uncivilised Punishment (involving two negative elements) in a chart can also mean the person is emotionally unstable or not in control of their emotions, and in serious cases, they have uncontrollable sexual desires, are lustful or lascivious. Uncivilised Punishments are one of the reasons that result in a person marrying for sex, for example.

In severe instances, an Uncivilised Punishment in a chart suggests a risk of rape or incest or sexual abuse. Alternatively, the person marries or has a relationship with a spouse or partner who is sexually abusive or physically abusive. In some cases, an Uncivilised Punishment brings about severe personal guilt and/or the inability to face up to something done in the past.

Self-Punishment 自刑

As the name suggests, Self-Punishment involves doing something that you know is wrong, or dumb, or stupid, but doing it anyway. Simple examples of Self-Punishment are smoking despite knowing it carries the risk of lung-cancer or drinking when you know you can't hold your liquor. It can also impact on relationships: a Self-Punishment is usually the cause of a woman or man, dating someone they cannot have, perhaps because that person is married or already attached. Essentially, you do something to yourself that you are conscious, has no benefit, or no positive outcome.

The table below shows which Earthly Branches have a Self-Punishment relationship with each other.

To qualify as a Self-Punishment, the Earthly Branches with a Self-Punishment relationship must be next to each other.

However, a person may also 'meet' with a Self-Punishment if the Earthly Branches in his/her BaZi have a Self-Punishment relationship with the annual or luck pillar.

In the above example, this person meets Self-Punishment twice in his life. Once at 13 – 22 and then the second time when he's 63-72.

Self-Punishment:
Being your own worst enemy

Each set of Self-Punishments has a unique interpretation, in addition to the interpretation afforded by examining the Palaces that they involve, and the Ten Gods involved.

Let's take the example of the Rooster and Rooster Self-Punishment. This Self-Punishment involves two Xin Metal elements and therefore, the Self-Punishment relates to wanting face or recognition, at any price. However, instead of getting recognition or face, the person ends up with egg on their face.

Self-Punishment

In this BaZi, this lady encounters a Self-Punishment when she enters her 16-25 Luck Pillar. Now, we can decode from the chart that the Self-Punishment relates to the Spouse Palace, and that it has something to do with the Companion Element, specifically the Friend star.

It is clear that this Xin 辛 Metal Day Master's negative elements are Water and Metal because the chart is quite strong and does not need any more Metal or Water. This lady had her boyfriend 'stolen' away from her by her best friend and she brought it upon herself because she introduced her best friend to her boyfriend. Now, because the Self-Punishment relates to Xin Metal, it is caused by seeking of face or recognition. This lady wanted her best friend to know what a good catch her boyfriend was and so orchestrated a meeting. The outcome however was that her boyfriend decided her friend was a better bet and dumped her for her best friend!

Dealing with Self-Punishments

Self-Punishment, like the name implies, is a problem caused by the individuals themselves. And they know what the problem is. It is perhaps not pointed out to them. Self-Punishments usually indicate inherent bad habits - retail therapy, chain-smoking, eating food that you're not supposed to eat, procrastination or worrying at work - these are some simple and obvious examples.

Naturally, these are bad habits that essentially can be resolved by either self-discipline, practicing putting your goals or objectives first over gratification or reward or complacency, or simply accepting you have this weakness (like junk food) and not blaming people or the situation when something goes wrong (such as gaining weight!). Of course, it is infinitely more practical and better just to fix the problem. The key to handling Self-Punishments is identifying the problem and then fixing it while it is still manageable. Nip it in the bud and it will be fine.

Chapter Seven:
Harm Codes

	時 Hour	日 Day	月 Month	年 Year	
Heavenly Stems 天干	戊 *Wu* Yang Earth	己 *Ji* Yin Earth	甲 *Jia* Yang Wood	癸 *Gui* Yin Water	
Earthly Branches 地支	辰 *Chen* **Dragon** Yang Earth	未 *Wei* **Goat** Yin Earth	子 *Zi* **Rat** Yang Water	未 *Wei* **Goat** Yin Earth	
Hidden Stems 藏干	癸 *Gui* 戊 *Wu* 乙 *Yi*	乙 *Yi* 己 *Ji* 丁 *Ding*	癸 *Gui*	乙 *Yi* 己 *Ji* 丁 *Ding*	

One of the best ways to learn BaZi is by example. And to illustrate how the Harm relationship affects a person, and how it can manifest, let's take a look at this BaZi. It is a classic story of the Third Party Problem.

This person's college sweetheart was wooed away from him by his best friend. He was so emotionally devastated that he ended up having to repeat his final year at university, due to poor performance in his examinations. In 1972, he met a new girlfriend and got married subsequently. A few years into the marriage, he discovered that his wife was having an extra-marital affair with his best friend at the time. However, he took no action, although his unhappiness over the situation affected his work performance and caused him to lose his job. His relationship with his wife did not improve either. Finally, his wife decided that she would divorce him and she sought half of his personal assets during the divorce proceedings. This man since then has not re-married.

What does his BaZi tell us? The most significant aspect of this BaZi is the presence of a Double Harm Formation.

This is the first Harm. Using the Age Pillars, we can tell that it will happen early in his life, around the teenage years to the early twenties.

時 Hour	日 Day	月 Month	年 Year	
戊	己	甲	癸	天干 Heavenly Stems
Wu Yang Earth	Ji Yin Earth	Jia Yang Wood	Gui Yin Water	
辰	未	子	未	地支 Earthly Branches
Chen Dragon Yang Earth	Wei Goat Yin Earth	Zi Rat Yang Water	Wei Goat Yin Earth	
癸 戊 乙 Gui Wu Yi	乙 己 丁 Yi Ji Ding	癸 Gui	乙 己 丁 Yi Ji Ding	藏干 Hidden Stems

This is the second Harm. Again, using the Age Pillars, we can determine that it will take place during his middle age years. We can also see that in both instances, the type of Harm, which is Wei 未 (Goat) and Zi 子 (Rat) are identical.

Now, why is it that the Harm relates to his spousal relationship? Firstly, the Zi 子 (Rat), represents not only his Wealth Star (which if you recall from *The Destiny Code*, also represents the man's wife), but is also a Peach Blossom star. The Double Harm formation in the BaZi chart clearly affects the Wife Star, and is related to Peach Blossom problems. Because there is a Double Harm formation, the same problem occurred twice in his life.

The problem that this Harm has caused is that the man has become apprehensive, even fearful of marriage. From his BaZi, there is no cause for this concern. Not only are the two Harms a matter of the past, but logically, he should not face this problem later in his life.

Understanding Harms

Now, the little story above would have illustrated to you what a Harm is. From the name 'Harm' itself, it is clear that this type of relationship between the Earthly Branches signifies a situation or scenario or outcome that is negative to the person.

At the most basic level, a Harm creates the feeling of betrayal for the person with a Harm in their BaZi chart. A Harm usually involves feeling that you have received the short end of the stick, or that you have somehow been put in a tormenting or difficult, or sometimes, dangerous situation because of someone else.

Harms are by and large, more unpleasant than Clashes for several reasons: firstly, Harms are frequently emotional in nature, the impact of a Harm usually lingers or takes time to resolve, and thus Harms are usually mentally tormenting. The example above provides a good illustration of the kind of mental torment a Harm can cause. The person in the above example is reluctant to remarry because of the unhappiness caused by the first relationship. It is also very obvious that in both instances of the betrayal, he was significantly affected, to the extent he failed his examinations and could not perform at work.

Secondly, Harms come out of the blue and are often unexpected or unforeseen. You can brace yourself for a Clash most of the time, psychologically, mentally and physically, but a Harm sneaks up on you, and catches you off-guard. And because the Harm lingers, it is worse. Imagine being stabbed in the back by someone you trust and love, and then unable to pull out the knife – that is what a Harm feels like. Again, our story above illustrates this perfectly.

Let me give you an example to illustrate the difference between a Clash and a Harm. A Clash would be a situation where you got hurt in a car accident while driving your own car. A Harm would be a situation where you got hurt in an accident, but you only were in the car because a friend asked you to accompany them on a short drive and they crashed the car.

What are examples of Harms then? A simple example is your best friend finds out that you fancy a certain someone. Your best friend then pursues a relationship with this person. Of course, it doesn't always relate to love and personal relationships. Another example of a Harm is stealing an idea or an invention that you have developed with someone collaboratively. And the 'Stolen Project' Scenario is exactly what our next example is all about.

The Case of the Stolen Project

時 Hour	日 Day	月 Month	年 Year	
乙	乙	戊	丁	天干 Heavenly Stems
Yi Yin Wood	Yi Yin Wood	Wu Yang Earth	Ding Yin Fire	
酉	亥	申	亥	地支 Earthly Branches
You Rooster Yin Metal	Hai Pig Yin Water	Shen Monkey Yang Metal	Hai Pig Yin Water	
辛 Xin	壬 甲 Ren Jia	戊 庚 壬 Wu Geng Ren	壬 甲 Ren Jia	藏干 Hidden Stems

85	75	65	55	45	35	25	15	5	
己	庚	辛	壬	癸	甲	乙	丙	丁	大運 Luck Pillars
Ji Yin Earth	Geng Yang Metal	Xin Yin Metal	Ren Yang Water	Gui Yin Water	Jia Yang Wood	Yi Yin Wood	Bing Yang Fire	Ding Yin Fire	
亥	子	丑	寅	卯	辰	巳	午	未	
Hai Pig Yin Water	Zi Rat Yang Water	Chou Ox Yin Earth	Yin Tiger Yang Wood	Mao Rabbit Yin Wood	Chen Dragon Yang Earth	Si Snake Yin Fire	Wu Horse Yang Fire	Wei Goat Yin Earth	
壬 甲	癸	辛 己 癸	戊 甲 丙	乙	癸 戊 乙	庚 丙 戊	丁 己	乙 己 丁	

This person lost an important project in the year 1984, during the Jia Chen 甲辰 Luck Pillar, which commenced at the age of 35. The project was stolen from right under his nose by his own brother. Why did it happen? In the BaZi, there is a Double Harm Formation, involving the two Hai 亥 (Pig) and the Shen 申 (Monkey) sandwiched between the two Hai 亥 (Pig).

八字
解碼

時 Hour	日 Day	月 Month	年 Year	
乙	乙	戊	丁	天干 Heavenly Stems
Yi / Yin Wood	Yi / Yin Wood	Wu / Yang Earth	Ding / Yin Fire	
酉	亥	申	亥	地支 Earthly Branches
You / Rooster / Yin Metal	Hai / Pig / Yin Water	Shen / Monkey / Yang Metal	Hai / Pig / Yin Water	
辛 Xin	壬 Ren 甲 Jia	戊 Wu 庚 Geng 壬 Ren	壬 Ren 甲 Jia	藏干 Hidden Stems

Revealed!

85	75	65	55	45	35	25	15	5	
己	庚	辛	壬	癸	甲	乙	丙	丁	大運 Luck Pillars
Ji / Yin Earth	Geng / Yang Metal	Xin / Yin Metal	Ren / Yang Water	Gui / Yin Water	Jia / Yang Wood	Yi / Yin Wood	Bing / Yang Fire	Ding / Yin Fire	
亥	子	丑	寅	卯	辰	巳	午	未	
Hai / Pig / Yin Water	Zi / Rat / Yang Water	Chou / Ox / Yin Earth	Yin / Tiger / Yang Wood	Mao / Rabbit / Yin Wood	Chen / Dragon / Yang Earth	Si / Snake / Yin Fire	Wu / Horse / Yang Fire	Wei / Goat / Yin Earth	
壬甲	癸	辛己癸	戊甲丙	乙	癸戊乙	庚丙戊	丁己	乙己丁	

When this man arrived at his 35 Luck Pillar, Jia 甲 Wood, which is hidden inside the Hai 亥 (Pig) Branch, becomes revealed on the stem. In BaZi, when we say something is 'revealed on the stem', that means that it becomes visible and apparent, it appears for all to see. The year 1984 is a Jia Zi 甲 子 year. So, Jia 甲 Wood has well and truly become 'revealed'. Now, to decode the meaning of this, ask yourself: What is Jia 甲 Wood to a Yi 乙 Wood Day Master?

BaZi - The Destiny Code Revealed **181**

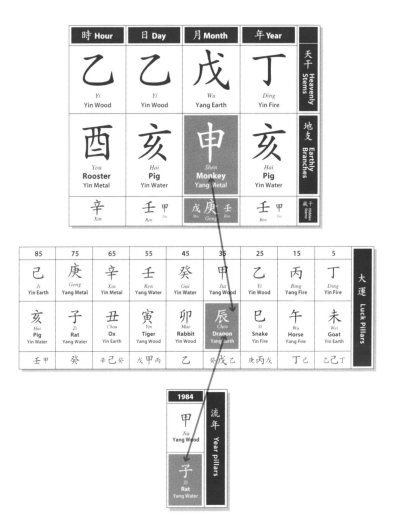

Let's take a look at what else is happening in the BaZi. Notice the Zi 子 (Rat) in the annual pillar of Jia Zi 甲子, is combining with the Chen 辰 (Dragon) in the 35 Luck Pillar? It is also combining with the Shen 申 (Monkey) in the Month Branch of the BaZi. This combination produces Water.

This Yi 乙 Wood Day Master is weak so the combination is a negative one because it produces an element that is unfavourable to the Day Master. You might be thinking now, the combination creates Water – isn't this good for a supposed weak Yi 乙 Wood? Doesn't water 'produce' wood? Not in this case. Why? Because there is already the presence of strong metal in this chart. The chart is born in the Autumn (metal) season and Rooster 酉 (metal) hour. Too much metal and water uproots the plant!

But because the Luck Pillar and the Year Pillar reveals Jia 甲 Wood, the outcome was not unfavourable. This is because Weak Wood meeting Jia 甲 Wood denotes meeting a favourable outcome. The Yi 乙 Wood can receive support from the Jia 甲 Wood. This means, the betrayal happens, but the end result is not unfavourable to the Yi 乙 Wood Day Master.

The project was eventually bogged down with legal disputes and complications and in the end, the sibling who poached the project ended up in serious trouble. Now, you can see it as he was 'betrayed' by his brother, or 'saved' by his brother, right?

Now, these are very common and simple examples of Harms but to be a Harm, there must not only be an emotional impact on the person, but there must also be a loss, be it a financial loss, or an emotional loss.

The Six Harms

The table below shows the Earthly Branches that have a Harm relationship with each other.

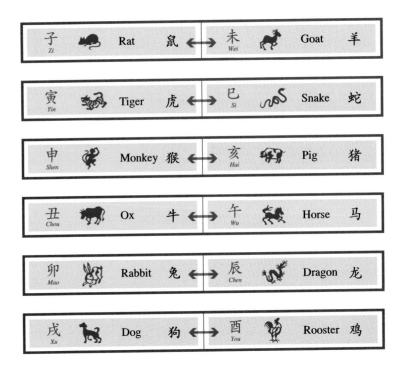

Now, to understand how the Harms are derived, we must first know the Six Combinations and Six Clashes. Why? Because the Harms essentially are derived from studying which elements interfere with or prevent combinations. For example, how is the Shen 申 (Monkey) and Hai 亥 (Pig) Harm derived?

Shen 申 (Monkey) combines with Si 巳 (Snake). Now, what Clashes with Si 巳 (Snake)? Refer back to chapter 5 on Clashes. You'll find that the Hai 亥 (Pig) clashes with the Si 巳 (Snake). The Hai 亥 (Pig) prevents the Si 巳 (Snake) from combining with the Shen 申 (Monkey). That is why the Hai 亥 (Pig) Harms the Shen 申 (Monkey). If you imagine it from a family relationship context, the Shen 申 (Monkey) and Si 巳 (Snake) are like a couple who want to get married. But the mother-in-law does not like the Si 巳 (Snake) and so it causes a rift!

It is for this reason that a Harm is often perceived as a problem caused by a third party or the influence of a third party.

When is a Harm a Harm?

For a Harm relationship to exist between the Earthly Branches in the BaZi chart, the two Earthly Branches with a Harm relationship must appear side by side.

In this BaZi, the Harm is a serious one because the Branches that have a Harm relationship are situated side-by-side in the Month and Day branches of a BaZi chart.

時 Hour	日 Day	月 Month	年 Year	天干 Heavenly Stems
丁	己	壬	辛	
Ding Yin Fire	*Ji* Yin Earth	*Ren* Yang Water	*Xin* Yin Metal	
卯	巳	辰	亥	地支 Earthly Branches
Mao **Rabbit** Yin Wood	*Si* **Snake** Yin Fire	*Chen* **Dragon** Yang Earth	*Hai* **Pig** Yin Water	
乙 *Yi*	庚 丙 戊 *Geng Bing Wu*	癸 戊 乙 *Gui Wu Yi*	壬 甲 *Ren Jia*	藏干 Hidden Stems

Separated

Where there is a separation between the Branches that have a Harm relationship, as in the chart above, the impact of the Harm is reduced significantly. Here, the Chen 辰 (Dragon) is in the Month branch, while the Mao 卯 (Rabbit) is in the Hour pillar, and are separated by the Si 巳 (Snake) in the Day Branch.

External Harms

A person can also meet a Harm relationship when the year pillar or the luck pillar interacts with the Earthly Branches in the BaZi chart.

This person 'meets' a Harm when she enters the 27 Luck Pillar. The Si 巳 (Snake) harms the Yin 寅 (Tiger), which is the Month Branch of her BaZi. So what can we find out about this Harm?

Since the Palace involved is the Month Palace, we can conclude that the Harm involves her parents. Now, let's decode the Harm further by looking at the elements involved. The element involved in the Harm is the Wood element. This lady is a Ji 己 Earth Day Master. Wood represents her Influence element, which you will recall, amongst other things, is the husband or boyfriend star.

Now who is the other player in this Harm? It is the Si 巳 (Snake). Inside the Si 巳 (Snake) is Bing 丙 Fire. Bing 丙 Fire represents the Resource element of the Five Factors. Resource, amongst other things, refers to the mother.

What have we learnt so far about this Harm? It involves a boyfriend or husband star, and the mother. Her parents (and very likely her mother) refused to allow her to get married to the man of her choice, and as a result, she felt betrayed by them.

The Meaning of Harms

All the examples above have illustrated what a Harm is and how a person at the receiving end of a Harm feels. Each type of Harm is unique and carries a distinct interpretation and scenario, in addition to the layer of interpretation carried by the elements and the Ten Gods. I will show you a few examples in the following pages of different types of Harm relationships and how they are decoded from the BaZi charts.

Do remember that when unpleasant things happen to someone, there is never ever one true cause of the problem. Life is complicated, problems are complicated and so, BaZi reflects this complexity. Often in a BaZi chart, more than one activity is going on at the same time and all these work together to create a certain outcome. So bear in mind that in the examples to follow, the problem is not always caused by just the Harm alone, although that is the aspect that we will focus on.

The Tale of A Costly Betrayal

Often when a Harm takes place, people are less fixated about the money, and more by the feeling of betrayal and the emotional disappointment, either in themselves and their own lack of judgement, or in the person who stabbed them in the back. Betrayal is always an unpleasant event but when it is costly, it is almost like a double whammy. Someone stabs you in the back, turns the knife and then, sticks it in deeper, for the road as it were!

Have a look at this BaZi. This gentleman is a Ren 壬 Water Day Master. Let's call him Mr A.

時 Hour	日 Day	月 Month	年 Year	天干 Heavenly Stems
丁 Ding Yin Fire	壬 Ren Yang Water	乙 Yi Yin Wood	甲 Jia Yang Wood	
未 Wei Goat Yin Earth	午 Wu Horse Yang Fire	亥 Hai Pig Yin Water	申 Shen Monkey Yang Metal	地支 Earthly Branches
乙己丁 Yi Ji Ding	丁己 Ding Ji	壬甲 Ren Jia	戊庚壬 Wu Geng Ren	藏干 Hidden Stems

88	78	68	58	48	38	28	18	8	
甲 Jia Yang Wood	癸 Gui Yin Water	壬 Ren Yang Water	辛 Xin Yin Metal	庚 Geng Yang Metal	己 Ji Yin Earth	戊 Wu Yang Earth	丁 Ding Yin Fire	丙 Bing Yang Fire	大運 Luck Pillars
申 Shen Monkey Yang Metal	未 Wei Goat Yin Earth	午 Wu Horse Yang Fire	巳 Si Snake Yin Fire	辰 Chen Dragon Yang Earth	卯 Mao Rabbit Yin Wood	寅 Yin Tiger Yang Wood	丑 Chou Ox Yin Earth	子 Zi Rat Yang Water	
戊庚壬	乙己丁	丁己	庚丙戊	癸戊乙	乙	戊甲丙	辛己癸	癸	

Mr A has a business partner, Mr B. They are both the same age and the best of friends. They started a biscuit producing factory together at the age of 30, after borrowing some money from Mr A's father-in-law. After some tough times, they hit it big. They become one of the biggest biscuit suppliers in Asia.

Their partnership was a good one: Mr A did the marketing. Mr B ran the office, and was in charge of the accounts. Now, like many Asian businessmen, they operated their business together largely on trust. They didn't bother with documentation, especially in relation to who owned various assets in the company. There were no checks and balances in the company to keep everyone honest. Things started to go downhill when it became apparent that Mr B had his hand in the company cookie jar. He had misappropriated company funds for his personal expenditure and the company turned out to be in serious debt and faced a lawsuit.

時 Hour	日 Day	月 Month	年 Year	
	壬 Ren Yang Water			天干 Heavenly Stems
	亥 Hai Pig Yin Water	申 Shen Monkey Yang Metal		地支 Earthly Branches
	壬 Ren 甲 Jia	戊 Wu 庚 Geng 壬 Ren		藏干 Hidden Stems

Let's decode Mr A's BaZi and see how he found himself in this situation. Begin with the basics, which is, the Day Master. Mr A is a Ren 壬 Water Day Master, born in the Winter month of Hai 亥 (Pig). In Winter, the Water element is at its strongest and most prosperous. This Ren 壬 Water Day Master is also rooted in the Shen 申 (Monkey). Recall that inside the Shen 申 (Monkey), there is a Ren 壬 Water in the Hidden Stems. So, this Ren 壬 Water Day Master is strong.

Now, as you will remember from *The Destiny Code*, a strong Day Master's favourable elements are the elements that it controls, the elements that control it and the element that it produces. That means this Day Master likes Fire, Earth and Wood elements. Think about it, which element is the most favourable amongst the trio? In this case, it is Fire. The chart is extremely cold. In fact, it is so cold, the Water is almost frozen! So, we need to thaw the ice a little, and get the water flowing.

Clearly, Metal and Water are unfavourable to this strong Ren 壬 Water Day Master. Water further strengthens the already strong Ren 壬 Water and Metal produces Water which is not needed. In this BaZi, the Water Elements can be found in the Hidden Stems of the Hai 亥 (Pig) and Shen 申 (Monkey).

Notice something very interesting: these are also the two Branches which are in a Harm formation. This is an extremely important signal that the BaZi is giving us - it tells us that this Harm formation is related to these two elements and the Harm's outcome will be negative and unfavourable.

時 Hour	日 Day	月 Month	年 Year	
丁	壬	乙	甲	天干 Heavenly Stems
Ding Yin Fire	Ren Yang Water	Yi Yin Wood	Jia Yang Wood	
未	午	亥	申	地支 Earthly Branches
Wei Goat Yin Earth	Wu Horse Yang Fire	Hai Pig Yin Water	Shen Monkey Yang Metal	
乙 己 丁 Yi Ji Ding	丁 己 Ding Ji	壬 甲 Ren Jia	戊 庚 壬 Wu Geng Ren	藏干 Hidden Stems

To get the full decoded picture, we now need to ask ourselves: What is Water and Metal to a Ren 壬 Water Day Master? Hai 亥 (Pig) is Water, and represents the Companion Element. Shen 申 (Monkey) is Metal and represents the Resource Element.

In the study of BaZi, when Resource star is negative, it indicates carelessness, oversight, complacency, and taking things for granted. Resource is also the star that feeds the Self Element, and thus, denotes information and input. So, when Resource creates a problem, it causes issues as a result of complacency, ignorance, carelessness or taking for granted matters related to information and things you should know.

The Harm adds a new dimension to the nature of this problem that Mr A will face. This is because the Harm relationship is between the Resource and Companion elements. Accordingly, as a result of his own complacency and taking for granted the situation, Mr A's partner, Mr B, took him for a ride, disappointed him and betrayed the trust placed in him by Mr A.

But our story does not end there. Now, from the BaZi chart, we can tell that Mr A is likely to experience a betrayal involving a friend or business partner. As it is an Internal Harm, it is essentially a betrayal waiting to happen. So, the question is WHEN?

Since the Harm is between the Year and Month pillar, and using the Age Pillars, we might deduce that it happens early in life. But remember my story? It took 30 years for the problem to surface. Why is that?

In BaZi, general principles usually have exceptions. And this is a chart that illustrates the point very well.

We have established that the most important element in this chart is Fire. It is not just the Day Master that craves warmth in this chart - the Hai 亥 (Pig) and Shen 申 (Monkey) elements also want warmth. And where is this all-important element located? In the Day and Hour Branch and Stem respectively.

時 Hour	日 Day	月 Month	年 Year	
丁 *Ding* **Yin Fire**	壬 *Ren* **Yang Water**	乙 *Yi* **Yin Wood**	甲 *Jia* **Yang Wood**	天干 Heavenly Stems
未 *Wei* **Goat** Yin Earth	午 *Wu* **Horse** Yang Fire	亥 *Hai* **Pig** Yin Water	申 *Shen* **Monkey** Yang Metal	地支 Earthly Branches
乙 己 丁 *Yi* *Ji* *Ding*	丁 己 *Ding* *Ji*	壬 甲 *Ren* *Jia*	戊 庚 壬 *Wu* *Geng* *Ren*	藏干 Hidden Stems

Take a look at the Luck Pillars. Mr A goes through Fire Luck in his middle age years.

時 Hour	日 Day	月 Month	年 Year	
丁 Ding Yin Fire	壬 Ren Yang Water	乙 Yi Yin Wood	甲 Jia Yang Wood	Heavenly Stems
未 Wei **Goat** Yin Earth	午 Wu **Horse** Yang Fire	亥 Hai **Pig** Yin Water	申 Shen **Monkey** Yang Metal	Earthly Branches
乙 己 丁 Yi Ji Ding	丁 己 Ding Ji	壬 甲 Ren Jia	戊 庚 壬 Wu Geng Ren	Hidden Stems

88	78	68	58	48	38	28	18	8	
甲 Jia Yang Wood	癸 Gui Yin Water	壬 Ren Yang Water	辛 Xin Yin Metal	庚 Geng Yang Metal	己 Ji Yin Earth	戊 Wu Yang Earth	丁 Ding Yin Fire	丙 Bing Yang Fire	Luck Pillars
申 Shen **Monkey** Yang Metal	未 Wei **Goat** Yin Earth	午 Wu **Horse** Yang Fire	巳 Si **Snake** Yin Fire	辰 Chen **Dragon** Yang Earth	卯 Mao **Rabbit** Yin Wood	寅 Yin **Tiger** Yang Wood	丑 Chou **Ox** Yin Earth	子 Zi **Rat** Yang Water	
戊庚壬	乙己丁	丁己	庚丙戊	癸戊乙	乙	戊甲丙	辛己癸	癸	

You're probably thinking - okay, this all doesn't make sense. Fire is supposed to be his favourable element. But when he goes through Fire Luck, he gets this nasty Harm. What gives?

Going through what BaZi practitioners call 'good luck' does not mean it is all sunshine and happy days. But because your Luck Pillars are favourable, chances are that outcomes will be favourable for you. It doesn't mean you don't have to go through any nasty experience. But it does mean that after the bitter medicine, the illness actually goes away and you feel better. It also means that while the Harm happens, it's not as unpleasant as it could be.

So how does the story of Mr A and his cookie-jar dipping partner Mr B end?

The Si 巳 (Snake) luck pillar (58-67) sees Si 巳 (Snake) combine with the Shen 申 (Monkey). At the same time Hai 亥 (Pig) clashes with Si 巳 (Snake). The situation produces a combination and a clash at the same time. As a result, there is a catch 22 or dilemma situation. Let's decode it further. The Companion Element, Hai 亥 (Pig), is clashing with the Si 巳 (Snake), which is the Wealth Element. Meanwhile, Shen 申 (Monkey) and Si 巳 (Snake) combine and transform into Water, an unfavourable element for this already strong Ren 壬 Day Master!

The transformation of Si 巳 (Snake) Fire element into Water Element is like someone trying to 'transfer' Wealth. Why? Si 巳 is Fire element. Fire is this chart's Wealth star. In this scenario, it is 'trying' to become Water element, a Companion element!

Still, because the Si 巳 (Snake) remains a favourable element for this Chart as a whole, a good resolution is likely in 2006. So after the parties sat down and talked and resolved their issues, the problem went away.

八字
解碼

Forever the Backstabbed

時 Hour	日 Day	月 Month	年 Year	
戊	乙	辛	戊	天干 Heavenly Stems
Wu Yang Earth	*Yi* Yin Wood	*Xin* Yin Metal	*Wu* Yang Earth	
寅	未	酉	戌	地支 Earthly Branches
Yin Tiger Yang Wood	*Wei* Goat Yin Earth	*You* Rooster Yin Metal	*Xu* Dog Yang Earth	
戊 甲 丙 *Wu* *Jia* *Bing*	乙 己 丁 *Yi* *Ji* *Ding*	辛 *Xin*	丁 戊 辛 *Ding* *Wu* *Xin*	藏干 Hidden Stems

88	78	68	58	48	38	28	18	8	
庚	己	戊	丁	丙	乙	甲	癸	壬	大運 Luck Pillars
Geng Yang Metal	*Ji* Yin Earth	*Wu* Yang Earth	*Ding* Yin Fire	*Bing* Yang Fire	*Yi* Yin Wood	*Jia* Yang Wood	*Gui* Yin Water	*Ren* Yang Water	
午	巳	辰	卯	寅	丑	子	亥	戌	
Wu Horse Yang Fire	*Si* Snake Yin Fire	*Chen* Dragon Yang Earth	*Mao* Rabbit Yin Wood	*Yin* Tiger Yang Wood	*Chou* Ox Yin Earth	*Zi* Rat Yang Water	*Hai* Pig Yin Water	*Xu* Dog Yang Earth	
丁己	庚丙戊	癸戊乙	乙	戊甲丙	辛己癸	癸	壬甲	丁戊辛	

This gentleman is a Yi 乙 Wood Day Master and for as long as he can remember, has been surrounded by petty people all his life. His colleagues are mean to him, his boss dislikes him, and even his dog at home seems to give him no respect. Why is that?

This Yi 乙 Wood Day master was born in the season of Autumn. In Autumn, Metal is strong and Wood is weak. There are some minor roots in the Wei 未 (Goat) and Yin 寅 (Tiger) but it is barely enough to keep the Yi Wood alive.

The Harm formation is located between the Year and Month Pillar, between the You 酉 (Rooster) and the Xu 戌 (Dog).

Clearly, the strongest element in this chart is 辛 Metal, since it penetrates from the You 酉 (Rooster) through to the Stem in the Month pillar. So this gentleman's negative element is extremely strong and prosperous 辛 Metal, to a Yi 乙 Wood Day Master, is known as 7 Killings. 7 Killings is one of the two types of Influence Elements. When 7 Killings is a negative star, it represents petty people, backstabbing, situations turning tables on you, impossible to handle ultimatums and extreme stress.

This 7 Killings star is extremely close to the Day Master, indicating that the people who are petty and who give him problems are always close to him. It is also found in his Parents Palace, indicating that some of the people who are mean and petty to him, are his own relatives!

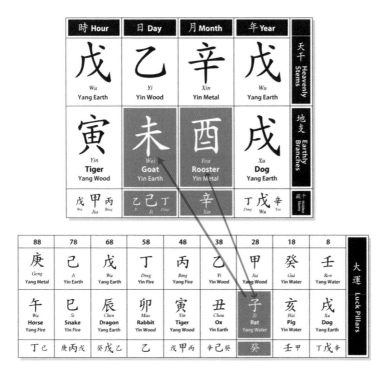

八字解碼

The Double Whammy arrives in 1990, during the Jia Zi 甲 子 Luck Pillar. Can you see the Double Harm in the chart? There is the Harm between the You 酉 (Rooster) and Xu 戌 (Dog) and with the Jia Zi 甲子 luck pillar, a Harm between the Zi 子 (Rat) and the Wei 未 (Goat). Zi 子 (Rat) contains Gui 癸 Water. Gui 癸 Water represents the Resource element for a Yi 乙 Wood Day Master. Accordingly, his thinking and mental state were affected. Obviously disheartened by what he felt to be overwhelming problems in life, this gentleman suffered from a bout of depression.

His relatives, instead of being supportive, bombarded him with belittling comments, nasty remarks and practically called him useless. The Zi 子 (Rat) also Harms the Wei 未 (Goat). As this is a Harm involving the spouse palace, the Harm also affected his relationship with his wife.

Of course, there is also a Destruction relationship between the Zi 子 (Rat) and the You 酉 (Rooster). That aggravated the problem and naturally drove him to drink. But let's focus on the Harm for now.

Dealing with Harms

A Harm often takes us by surprise but it is only able to do that, often, because the person is careless or complacent or took something for granted. It is often the case that a Harm occurs because the person has either been irresponsible, slacking off or is simply kept out of the loop with regard to certain information that is important.

The best way to handle a Harm is to be careful. Cross every T. Dot every 'i'. It is important to be detail-orientated, and be very careful with all matters, big or small, during periods of time when there is a Harm to your BaZi.

But by far, the most important method of dealing with Harms is not to assume that it is always bad. A wave in the ocean can sweep a boat back to shore, but it can also propel the boat forward. When someone throws rocks at your paperboat, they may not be trying to ruin your boat, but be creating waves to help your boat sail.

Sometimes, a Harm will feel like a betrayal, but it carries an important lesson at the end and may even be a dark cloud with a silver lining. Once the feeling has passed, you'll wonder, what all the fuss was about in the first place.

In BaZi, the correct philosophy and approach to Harms is to try to learn the lesson and move on with your life, wiser and more experienced. Being paralysed by what has happened is to not benefit from the situation. Take the lesson to heart, pick yourself up, and the next time the same situation comes along, know that you will be able to make the right decision.

八字解碼

Chapter Eight:
Destruction Codes

Another type of the relationships the elements can have with each other in a BaZi chart is the Destruction relationship. In Chinese, the term is 'Po 破' – like many Chinese words, an exacting precise definition is a bit difficult. 'Destruction' is the technical term that I have chosen for this relationship because a Destruction in a BaZi usually indicates the presence of behaviour or relationships or outcomes that are damaging in nature to the person.

A Destruction in a chart indicates the likelihood of situations or scenarios which make a person feel like they are backed into a corner or their hand is forced or that person is forced by circumstances to take certain action that they do not want to take but have to. It can also result in a person finding themselves in situations in which they are ill-equipped to deal with but have no choice but to face up to.

For example, a person who is forced to work in a factory out of economic necessity and then as a result of a freak accident, loses a finger or is injured physically. Or a person who cannot drink or doesn't like drinking but because of the nature of the job, which requires socialising and entertaining clients, has to consume alcohol. As a result, that person ends up with liver damage or gets sick because of constant alcohol consumption.

Traditionally, a Destruction is associated with a negative outcome for the person. However, this viewpoint is not my approach to BaZi and is not, I believe, the right approach either for today's world. In the old days, there was no such thing as 'no pain, no gain'. Today, in the age of self-help and Neuro-Linguistic Programming (NLP), bitter experiences or bad experiences are often seen as 'empowering', or something that gives the person a new direction of growth and development and used as an impetus for change. A bitter pill is sometimes what is needed to shake a person out of a situation and make them get to the next level.

If a person needs to throw out the old (not always an easy or simple matter) in order to bring in the new, a Destruction is not a bad event. 'Constructive Destruction' is seen as a positive development in the corporate world these days. The operative word of course is constructive. Hence, these days, the approach to Destructions is to advise clients to build upon what has happened to them, or look for a lesson in the event, and to rebuild in a new direction.

Also, while Destructions do have, at the time of occurrence, a negative impact, the intensity of the Destruction must be taken into account before one concludes that it has a definitively nasty impact on the person. The strength of the Destruction and the Branches that have a Destruction relationship must be considered.

Accordingly, when we are looking at a BaZi chart, we never assume that anything negative always means an unfavourable outcome. Sometimes, negative is good, or just what the doctor ordered.

Now, just because a certain Earthly Branch has a destructive relationship with another, that does not mean that a person who is born in the year of the Rat, should not marry a person born in the year of the Rooster or avoid being friends with people who are born in the Rooster year. It does not mean they will have a 'destructive' marriage or relationship. This kind of extrapolation of the Earthly Branches relationship is not just wrong, it is simply not BaZi!

八字
解碼

The Code of Destructive Behaviour

The presence of a Destruction relationship in a BaZi can result in a person engaging in vices or habits that are bad for their health (ie: smoking, drinking, drugs) or their relationships or mental/psychological state. Sometimes, a Destruction causes a person to be broken psychologically, their illusions or dreams shattered. A Destruction relationship can also manifest as a form of constant dissatisfaction. If the Destruction is serious, these people are pathological whiners who have plenty to complain about but don't seem to want to take the action that is needed to change their lot in life.

Most of us probably know someone who is like this – you know, the good friend who thinks they deserve more money from their job but doesn't want to put in more hours. They always have a reason why they shouldn't do something or are always justifying why a particular course of action is not suitable for them. As the conversation progresses, it soon becomes apparent that this person finds every option or suggestion unpalatable.

Another example is the artistic creative person who longs to pursue their artistic dreams but is yet deterred by the slog or suffering that an artistic career might entail. Yet this person is unhappy and feels the world is depriving them of an opportunity to pursue their dreams or let the world know how talented they are.

How Destructions Appear in a BaZi Chart

The table below shows which Earthly Branches have a Destruction relationship with each other.

子 *Zi* Rat	←— Destroy —→	酉 *You* Rooster
申 *Shen* Monkey	←— Destroy —→	巳 *Si* Snake
辰 *Chen* Dragon	←— Destroy —→	丑 *Chou* Ox
午 *Wu* Horse	←— Destroy —→	卯 *Mao* Rabbit
寅 *Yin* Tiger	←— Destroy —→	亥 *Hai* Pig
戌 *Xu* Dog	←— Destroy —→	未 *Wei* Goat

The Earthly Branches that have a Destruction relationship with each other MUST BE next to each other in the BaZi in order to be considered a Destruction in the BaZi. If the two Branches skip a pillar, this is not considered a Destruction.

時 Hour	日 Day	月 Month	年 Year	天干 Heavenly Stems
		子 *Zi* Rat	酉 *You* Rooster	地支 Earthly Branches

Example of real destruction

No destruction relationship

At the basic level, there are two ways a Destruction can manifest in BaZi. As a Static Destruction (which happens between two Earthly Branches located side-by-side IN the BaZi chart) or as a Dynamic Destruction (which happens when Earthly Branch in the BaZi chart has a Destruction relationship with an Earthly Branch in the year or 10-Year Luck Pillar).

Another form in which the Destruction relationship can manifest is through the 10-Year Luck Pillars, known as the Dynamic Destruction. Look at the example below:

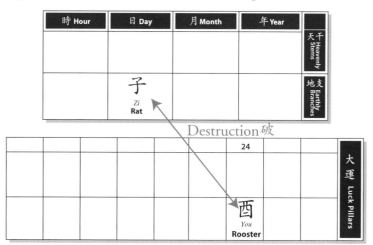

In this example, there is a Destruction relationship between the Day Earthly Branch of the person's BaZi and the person's 10-Year Luck Pillar, beginning at the age of 24. The Earthly Branch of the Day Pillar is also the Spouse Palace in the study of BaZi. We can conclude from this example that the

Destruction relationship relates to the Spouse Palace, since one of the components of the Destruction relationship is located in the Spouse Palace. So what is the likely outcome?

Generally, we can say that during this particular 10-Year block, the person will experience misunderstandings with their spouse that will drive them to a bad habit or cause problems within the household. However, this Destruction may prove to be a positive development in this person's life. A new beginning is on the horizon for this person and if this person uses this opportunity to reflect on their bad habits and make a decisive choice to change for the better, this person may find during this 10-Year period, they may make many positive changes to their life and gain greater happiness or personal satisfaction.

When the Destruction already exists in your chart, it's known as a Static Destruction. So for example, you may have a Destruction relationship between the Earthly Branches located in your Year and Month pillar, or a Destruction relationship between the Earthly Branches located in your Month and Day pillar, or you have a Destruction relationship between the Earthly Branches located in your Day and Hour pillar.

When the Destruction relationship is between the Year and Month Earthly Branches, like in the example below, then this indicates the destructive event or behaviour occurs during childhood or youth years.

時 Hour	日 Day	月 Month	年 Year	
				天干 Heavenly Stems
		← →		地支 Earthly Branches

Destruction between Year and Month

If the Destruction relationship is between the Month and Day Earthly Branches, then the problem will crop up during the person's youth or during middle age.

時 Hour	日 Day	月 Month	年 Year	
				天干 Heavenly Stems
	←——————→			地支 Earthly Branches

Destruction between Month and Day

If the Destruction relationship appears between the Day and Hour Earthly Branches, then the Destruction usually involves destructive events or behaviour occurring during old age, or involving the person's spouse or children.

時 Hour	日 Day	月 Month	年 Year	
				天干 Heavenly Stems
←——————→				地支 Earthly Branches

Destruction between Day and Hour

The meaning of Destruction

Each type of Destruction relationship carries a unique meaning or implication and usually results in a very specific kind of situation or scenario. For example, if someone has a Zi-You 子酉 (Rat-Rooster) Destruction relationship in their BaZi, this means the Destruction is related to alcohol or alcohol abuse. Individuals with this type of Destruction in their chart may be people who often resort to Dutch courage to get things done as they have an inferiority complex. Or they may drown their sorrows in alcohol rather than face up to their problems. Or they handle the stress of their job through drinking.

Rat vs Rooster (子-酉)

A Zi-You 子酉 (Rat-Rooster) Destruction may also bring about ostracism or exile for the person, usually as a result of an alcoholic habit or sexual peccadilloes. Or in some case scenarios, depending on the severity of the Destruction, the Destruction may cause serious depression.

Of course, to get a more precise picture, we need to incorporate into the reading what is known as the Ten Gods 十神. But for now, just recognise that certain types of Destructions can be associated with specific types of negative behaviour.

Let's see how certain types of Destructive behaviour can show up in a BaZi chart and how they can be interpreted.

Below, is an example of a chart with a Zi-You 子酉 (Rat-Rooster) Destruction.

Male (18 Dec 1961, 10.30pm hour)

時 Hour	日 Day	月 Month	年 Year	
丁	乙	庚	辛	天干 Heavenly Stems
Ding Yin Fire	Yi Yin Wood	Geng Yang Metal	Xin Yin Metal	
亥	酉	子	丑	地支 Earthly Branches
Hai Pig Yin Water	You Rooster Yin Metal	Zi Rat Yang Water	Chou Ox Yin Earth	
壬 甲	辛	癸	辛 己 癸	藏干 Hidden Stems
Ren Jia	Xin	Gui	Xin Ji Gui	

84	74	64	54	44	34	24	14	4	
辛	壬	癸	甲	乙	丙	丁	戊	己	大運 Luck Pillars
Xin Yin Metal	Ren Yang Water	Gui Yin Water	Jia Yang Wood	Yi Yin Wood	Bing Yang Fire	Ding Yin Fire	Wu Yang Earth	Ji Yin Earth	
卯	辰	巳	午	未	申	酉	戌	亥	
Mao Rabbit Yin Wood	Chen Dragon Yang Earth	Si Snake Yin Fire	Wu Horse Yang Fire	Wei Goat Yin Earth	Shen Monkey Yang Metal	You Rooster Yin Metal	Xu Dog Yang Earth	Hai Pig Yin Water	
乙	癸戊乙	庚丙戊	丁己	乙己丁	戊庚壬	辛	丁戊辛	壬甲	

This Yi 乙 Day Master's chart has a Zi-You 子酉 (Rat-Rooster) Destruction present in the chart. Not surprisingly, this person is an alcoholic. Now, what is the reason this person hit the bottle?

This BaZi chart is very cold - notice that all the Branches are either Winter season Branches (the Chou 丑, Hai 亥 and Zi 子) or Autumn season Branches (the You 酉). Although there is a Ding 丁 Fire present in this chart, at the Hour, it is not strong enough to warm the chart. Fire, in the study of the Five Elements, is what brings passion and happiness to a person's chart. As the chart is cold and the Fire is weak, and there is preponderance of Water and Metal elements in the chart (remember the BaZi saying, Metal and Water makes a person emotional 金水多情), this person is easily depressed and is emotionally unstable. For that reason, the person hits the bottle.

In the Ding You 丁酉 (Fire Rooster) luck pillar, alcoholism becomes a severe problem. Why? The You 酉 (Rooster) contains Xin 辛 Metal. Xin 辛 Metal is this Yi 乙 Wood Day Master's 7 Killings star. (7 Killings is one of the two manifestations of the Influence Element). 7 Killings represents courage and bravery, when the 7 Killings star is exerting its positive qualities. But in this chart, it is negative and thus manifests its negative qualities, which are irrationality, aggression, rash behaviour and anxiety.

84	74	64	54	44	34	24	14	4	
辛 *Xin* Yin Metal	壬 *Ren* Yang Water	癸 *Gui* Yin Water	甲 *Jia* Yang Wood	乙 *Yi* Yin Wood	丙 *Bing* Yang Fire	丁 *Ding* Yin Fire	戊 *Wu* Yang Earth	己 *Ji* Yin Earth	大運
卯 *Mao* Rabbit Yin Wood	辰 *Chen* Dragon Yang Earth	巳 *Si* Snake Yin Fire	午 *Wu* Horse Yang Fire	未 *Wei* Goat Yin Earth	申 *Shen* Monkey Yang Metal	酉 *You* Rooster Yin Metal	戌 *Xu* Dog Yang Earth	亥 *Hai* Pig Yin Water	Luck Pillars
乙	癸戊乙	庚丙戊	丁己	乙己丁	戊庚壬	辛	丁戊辛	壬甲	

Now, notice that the You 酉 (Rooster) from the Luck Pillar, which contains the Xin Metal 7 Killings, is in a Destruction relationship with the Zi 子 (Rat). The Zi 子 (Rat) contains Gui 癸 Water, which is the Indirect Resource star for this Yi 乙 Wood Day Master. The Indirect Resource star governs how a person feels, the person's comfort level and sensitivity. You will also notice that the You 酉 (Rooster) is also in a Self-Punishment relationship with the You 酉 (Rooster) in the Spouse Palace.

So, having worked out the 'technical' parts, what can we conclude? Clearly, the Ding You 丁酉 Luck Pillar affects the person's relationship with the Spouse. Since it is a Self-Punishment, and that Self-Punishment relates to 7 Killings, we can conclude that the cause of the problem is this person's own (hence the Self in the Self-Punishment) irrational or aggressive behaviour. This behaviour then caused the relationship to go sour and the person then became further depressed. Since the Indirect Resource star is also affected, we can conclude that this person's alcoholism is also linked to self-esteem problems.

Horse vs Rabbit (午-卯)

Another type of Destruction that carries a specific Destructive behaviour is the Wu-Mao 午卯 (Horse-Rabbit) Destruction. The Wu-Mao 午卯 (Horse-Rabbit) Destruction refers to having to do something that results in the persons turning their back on their past, their family or their principles.

It usually refers to the presence of a Catch-22 type situation for the person. For example, your father is a butcher and you are able to get an education and go to university thanks to your father's work as a butcher. But when you come out from university, now armed with a respectable degree and enter the workplace, you are embarrassed by the fact that your father works as a butcher.

In other cases, a Wu-Mao 午卯 (Horse-Rabbit) Destruction can also basically denote bad experiences with friends or a violation of trust between friends. I usually find this advice works well with people under the negative influence of this Destruction: "just because someone doesn't love you the way you want them to, doesn't mean they don't love you with all they have" .

Again, the severity of this Destruction must be weighted by the overall BaZi assessment. Sometimes, the destruction's effects are minor and even negligible.

The Combination-Destruction Relationship

There are also two Earthly Branches which have Combination-Destruction relationships. This means that the Earthly Branches have both a Combination and a Destruction relationship. The table below shows the two Combination-Destruction relationships that are possible between Earthly Branches.

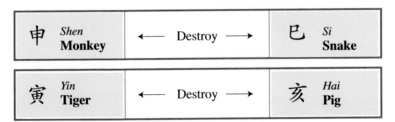

| 申 *Shen* Monkey | ← Destroy → | 巳 *Si* Snake |
| 寅 *Yin* Tiger | ← Destroy → | 亥 *Hai* Pig |

Combination-Destructions usually involve situations or scenarios or relationships where things go from good to bad, or bad to good. For example, the relationship begins all rosy and on a good footing but then ends in bad blood.

For example, a person collaborates with someone else, in the hope of achieving something for the betterment of both but ends up on the bad side of their partner instead, despite that person's noble efforts. Or a person is trapped or put in a difficult situation or sometimes, even outright conned or taken for a ride, as a result of a joint-venture or partnership with someone.

Depending on the circumstances, the Destruction aspect of the Combination-Destruction relationship may be active or inactive. For example, if a BaZi contains the Yin-Hai 寅亥 (Tiger-Pig) Combination Destruction, if the Combination between Tiger and Pig is successful in transforming into Wood, then the Destruction meaning is often not considered. However, if the combination is not successful, then the Destruction must be considered in the reading.

Let's have a look at an example of a Combination-Destruction relationship to understand how it impacts on a person.

Male: Born 12 November 1986 . Horse Hour.

時 Hour	日 Day	月 Month	年 Year	
壬	庚	己	丙	天干 Heavenly Stems
Ren Yang Water	*Geng* Yang Metal	*Ji* Yin Earth	*Bing* Yang Fire	
午	申	亥	寅	地支 Earthly Branches
Wu **Horse** Yang Fire	*Shen* **Monkey** Yang Metal	*Hai* **Pig** Yin Water	*Yin* **Tiger** Yang Wood	
丁己 *Ding Ji*	戊庚壬 *Wu Geng Ren*	壬甲 *Ren Jia*	戊甲丙 *Wu Jia Bing*	藏干 Hidden Stems

88	78	68	58	48	38	28	18	8	
戊	丁	丙	乙	甲	癸	壬	辛	庚	大運 Luck Pillars
Wu Yang Earth	*Ding* Yin Fire	*Bing* Yang Fire	*Yi* Yin Wood	*Jia* Yang Wood	*Gui* Yin Water	*Ren* Yang Water	*Xin* Yin Metal	*Geng* Yang Metal	
申	未	午	巳	辰	卯	寅	丑	子	
Shen **Monkey** Yang Metal	*Wei* **Goat** Yin Earth	*Wu* **Horse** Yang Fire	*Si* **Snake** Yin Fire	*Chen* **Dragon** Yang Earth	*Mao* **Rabbit** Yin Wood	*Yin* **Tiger** Yang Wood	*Chou* **Ox** Yin Earth	*Zi* **Rat** Yang Water	
戊庚壬	乙己丁	丁己	庚丙戊	癸戊乙	乙	戊甲丙	辛己癸	癸	

This Geng 庚 Metal Day Master has a Combination-Destruction present between the Year and Month Pillars. This person has a difficult relationship with his father, who is divorced from his mother. He was sent away to live with his grandparents at an early age and his father rarely came to see him.

Through the Palaces, we can see that the Hai 亥 (Pig) in the Month Palace and Yin 寅 (Tiger) in the Year Palace are in a Combination-Destruction relationship. Now, as you will have already noticed from all the previous examples, you need to dig deep in order to find out what is really going on in the BaZi. So let's take a closer look at the Yin 寅 (Tiger).

Inside the Yin 寅 (Tiger), there is Jia 甲 Wood. In the study of the Ten Gods 十神, Jia 甲 Wood, to a Geng 庚 Metal Day Master, is the Indirect Wealth star. Amongst other things, the Indirect Wealth star, to a man, represents his Father. The Yin 寅 (Tiger) combines with the Hai 亥 (Pig) in the Month Branch, which is the Parents Palace. So the father is supposed to take care of him.

But, the Destruction aspect of the Combination-Destruction relationship creates problems here. And because the Combination aspect of the Combination-Destruction relationship does not successfully transform into Wood in the BaZi chart itself, and the first two 10-Year Luck Pillars are also not conducive to the Combination component, the Destruction aspect of the relationship comes into play.

In this case, the Destruction relationship impacts on the Father star, and thus, involves the relationship with the Father. This person is upset with his father because he feels his father did not live up to his responsibilities as a father and he is disappointed with his father. The preference for the grandparents is due to the presence of Bing 丙 Fire in the Year Pillar. This element is integral towards maintaining the chart's warmth and keeping it comfortable. Hence, he is happier living with his grandparents.

The Devastation of Clash and Destruction

In some BaZi charts, a Destruction formation can appear together with a Clash. The typical formation for this sort of occurrence is the presence of the Wu-Mao 午卯 (Horse-Rabbit) Destruction in tandem with the Zi-You 子酉 (Rat-Rooster) Destruction. This sort of formation usually indicates problems of a sexual nature, for example, sexual abuse or sexual assault or problems caused by sex. Why? Because when such a line-up is present in the Earthly Branches of a BaZi, all the Peach Blossom stars are present in the chart and Peach Blossom stars typically govern matters relating to attraction and sexuality. The formation is particularly troubling if the stars that are affected are negative elements.

The example below is an illustration of why a Clash and Destruction formation in a chart is highly unfavourable.

Female, 18 March 1954 at 12.30am

時 Hour	日 Day	月 Month	年 Year	
壬	癸	丁	甲	天干 Heavenly Stems
Ren Yang Water	*Gui* Yin Water	*Ding* Yin Fire	*Jia* Yang Wood	
子	酉	卯	午	地支 Earthly Branches
Zi **Rat** Yang Water	*You* **Rooster** Yin Metal	*Mao* **Rabbit** Yin Wood	*Wu* **Horse** Yang Fire	
癸 *Gui*	辛 *Xin*	乙 *Yi*	丁 己 *Ding*	藏干 Hidden Stems

84	74	64	54	44	34	24	14	4	
戊	己	庚	辛	壬	癸	甲	乙	丙	大運 Luck Pillars
Wu Yang Earth	*Ji* Yin Earth	*Geng* Yang Metal	*Xin* Yin Metal	*Ren* Yang Water	*Gui* Yin Water	*Jia* Yang Wood	*Yi* Yin Wood	*Bing* Yang Fire	
午	未	申	酉	戌	亥	子	丑	寅	
Wu Horse Yang Fire	*Wei* Goat Yin Earth	*Shen* Monkey Yang Metal	*You* Rooster Yin Metal	*Xu* Dog Yang Earth	*Hai* Pig Yin Water	*Zi* Rat Yang Water	*Chou* Ox Yin Earth	*Yin* Tiger Yang Wood	
丁己	乙己丁	戊庚壬	辛	丁戊辛	壬甲	癸	辛己癸	戊甲丙	

This lady was raped by her male friend after she became drunk. As a result of the encounter, she became pregnant. She chose to abort the child and did not seek legal redress because the man apologised to her. Following that event, she has experienced problems with her marriage and relationships.

What does the BaZi chart tell us? First, there is a Wu-Mao 午 卯 (Horse-Rabbit) Destruction and it affects the Month and Year Branches. This tells us her family is not a happy one. Her mother is what we call a second wife in the Asian context. In the west, the woman is a mistress. She is ashamed of this aspect of her life.

The Day Branch and Hour Branch show a Destruction formation involving the Zi-You 子酉 (Rat-Rooster). This tells us that there are problems with children and denotes a regrettable event involving children (such as an abortion.) Remember earlier I talked about how a Destruction frequently involves a person feeling backed into a corner or forced to take certain actions due to circumstances? Destructions usually involve a person having to handle something which that person is ill-equipped to deal with but has no choice but to face up to. In this woman's case, she had to handle the pregnancy because it was the result of something she didn't want to happen.

You will notice that there is also a Clash in her chart, between the Mao 卯 and You 酉 (Rabbit and Rooster). This affects the Spouse Palace and hence, her marriage has issues. But that's not the only reason why her marriage has problems. Remember, in BaZi, we don't arrive at our conclusion based on one observation, but several observations that support the same conclusion.

In addition to the Clash with the Spouse Palace, this lady's chart reveals no true Husband Star. This Gui 癸 Water lady's true Husband Star, known as the Direct Officer star, is Wu 戊 Earth. Now, you will see that the entire chart does not have any Wu 戊 Earth in it. So this Gui 癸 Water has to use Ji 己 Earth, which is the 7 Killings Star. The only Ji 己 Earth she has is inside the Wu 午 (Horse). This 7 Killings is 'destroyed' by the Wu 午-Mao 卯 (Horse-Rabbit) Destruction. What does this mean? It means that she has a distorted view of men, because of something that happened to her - an event or a relationship in the past.

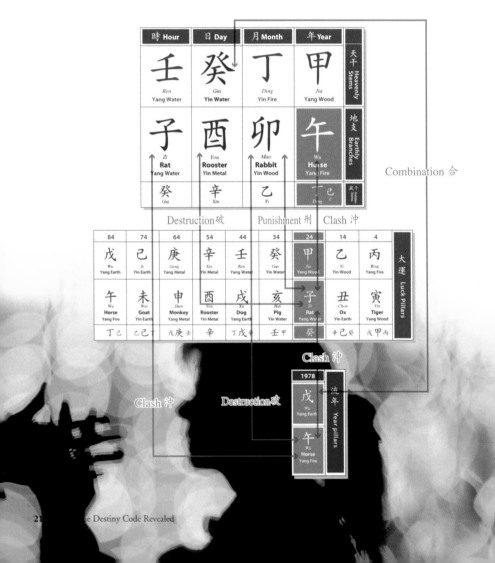

The date the rape incident took place in 1978, was in the year of Wu Wu 戊午 (Earth Horse), during the Jia Zi 甲子 (Wood Rat) 10 year Luck Pillar. During that year, the Zi 子 (Rat) in the Annual Pillar, clashes with the Wu 午 (Horse) present in the Year Branch of her BaZi chart. The 7 Killings star is being clashed! The clash involves the Zi 子 (Rat) which contains Gui 癸 Water. Gui 癸 Water is the Companion element to this Gui 癸 Water Day Master. The Clash indicates a forcible attempt by a friend to be her boyfriend.

The Zi 子 (Rat) also creates an Uncivilised Punishment formation with the Mao 卯 (Rabbit) in the Month Pillar. Rape is one example of an Uncivilised Punishment. The Zi 子 (Rat) also creates a Destruction with the You 酉 (Rooster) in her Day Branch. That tells us that alcohol is the cause of the problem. 1978 is the year of Wu Wu 戊午, which indicates the Husband Star has arrived, and Wu 戊 combines with the Gui 癸 Day Master. So on the surface, it appears to be a husband appearing but in fact, in the Earthly Branches, something very different is manifesting!

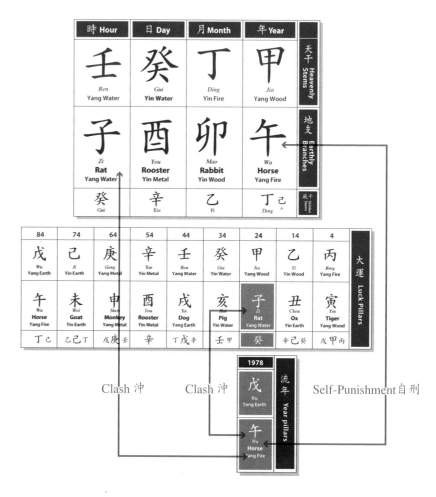

八字解碼

Clash 沖   Clash 沖   Self-Punishment 自刑

1978, the year of Wu Wu 戊午 (Earth Horse) also clashes with the Zi 子 (Rat) in the Hour Branch, denoting an activity that takes place suddenly, in the blink of an eye almost. The Wu 午 (Horse) is also in a Self-Punishment formation with the Wu 午 (Horse) in the Year Branch. That tells us that the 'boyfriend' (7 Killings star) committed an activity that he regretted. The Wu 午 (Horse) in the Annual Pillar is also in a Destruction relationship with the Mao 卯 (Rabbit) in the Month Pillar, indicating a psychologically traumatic event occurred that year.

I have all four Peach Blossom Stars! Should I be worried?

Just because you have all the Peach Blossom stars (Zi 子 (Rat), Wu 午 (Horse), Mao 卯 (Rabbit), You 酉 (Rooster) present in your chart does not mean you are going to experience what this lady encountered. Nor does it mean that if you have all the Peach Blossom stars, you are destined to be a prostitute or gigolo, a common but incorrect assumption frequently made. Each chart is unique and the placement of the Peach Blossom stars (which palace, in what relationship with the other Earthly Branches on the left and right) matters. If we tweak the chart above and change the position of the Year and Month pillars, like below:

It's a big difference in the interpretation! All the four Peach Blossom stars are present but in a different order, the impact is different. There still is a Wu-Mao 午卯 (Horse-Rabbit) Destruction but there is no clash with the Spouse Palace. That means that while an unpleasant event may take place, it does not have an impact on her marriage or future relationships.

When the chart is tweaked this way, the Ji 己 Earth, which is the 7 Killings star, is now a strong and better quality star and does not have a contaminating effect on the Gui 癸 Water Day Master. When the Year and Month branches are swapped, notice that the luck pillars have also changed. The Zi-Wu 子午 (Rat-Horse) Clash is now likely to only happen in her 60s.

What does this exercise tell us? First, that we should never assume anything when it comes to BaZi. Each chart should be read individually, and analysed individually. Of course, in BaZi, we do use some modelling, in the form of structures, to derive conclusions but these are always conclusions that have to be supported by more than one finding in the chart. Hence, the golden rule when it comes to reading a BaZi chart is to never assume that one chart, that bears a passing resemblance to another chart, will experience the same events or outcomes.

Dealing with Destruction

Invariably, individuals with a Destruction relationship in their BaZi can end up being extremely frustrated people who blame everyone but themselves for their lot in life. They are unwilling to help themselves but yet unable to be satisfied with what they have either. The saying 'Heaven helps those who help themselves' clearly does not apply to these people!

But there are also some instances where a Destruction can bring a good outcome – the person is broken and scrapes the bottom of the barrel, but as a result of the experience, that person bounces back, bigger and better, so to speak. They go through a life-changing or very drastic situation but come back from it changed, for the better. A Destruction can signal a positive change, from old to new, or the removal of a bad habit. In that respect, a Destruction in a BaZi is not always detrimental. Most of the time, it can also bring about positive outcomes.

The key to dealing with a Destruction in your BaZi chart is not to whine about it but to ask yourself, what you have gotten out of the experience, miserable as it may be. Find the lesson, find the problem and then make your breakthrough. A Destruction pillar ultimately is like closing a chapter on one part of your life and moving on to a new chapter. Seize the opportunity for a fresh start, and let go of the past. Listen to the message that your BaZi is giving you and move on!

八字解碼

Chapter Nine:
Earthly Branch Relationships in Action

From the start of this book, I have always talked about how the best way to learn BaZi is from examples. I note that students usually find it easier to 'learn by osmosis' many of the Earthly Branch relationships when they have some fun with the examples. So that's what we have in this chapter - real life examples, and how the Earthly Branch relationships reflect the events that happened in their lives.

I have used some famous living and some no-longer-with-us personalities in this chapter. The purpose is not to speculate on the events in their lives, but to show you how these events are explained through BaZi and so you can research on your own, how these people handled the situation and whether or not they did the right thing, based on their BaZi.

They say history affords the best lesson in life, since it does repeat itself. Looking at the momentous events in a famous person's life is the easiest way to learn BaZi because usually these personalities have their lives extensively documented (the downside to being famous!) and you can find out a lot about them on the Internet. Now, all you have to do is look at the BaZi and match it to the events, outcomes and personalities!

In some instances, the outcomes were negative but this is because the wrong action was taken or no action was taken. Hence, this harks back to the point about BaZi - knowing is one thing, but doing the right thing is just as important.

By this chapter, the key basics of understanding BaZi have all been covered. By this stage, you know how to identify the Day Master and know a little about the individual Day Masters. You have knowledge of all the Earthly Branch relationships and the Heavenly Stem relationships, and how to analyse them. From this point on, your knowledge and accuracy with BaZi analysis should start to improve.

As you read through this chapter, you will notice I make increasing reference to the 10 Gods 十神 technique and reduce my usage of the more basic terminology. The 10 Gods will be extensively covered in my next book but you should get an appetiser of this technique in this chapter and see how it adds yet another powerful dimension to decoding a Destiny Chart.

Three Harmony Combinations and Clash

時 Hour	日 Day	月 Month	年 Year	
日元 DM 壬 *Ren* **Yang Water**	偏印 IR 庚 *Geng* **Yang Metal**	食神 EG 甲 *Jia* **Yang Wood**		天干 Heavenly Stems
寅 *Yin* **Tiger** Yang Wood	午 *Wu* **Horse** Yang Fire	辰 *Chen* **Dragon** Yang Earth		地支 Earthly Branches
戊 甲 丙 Wu Jia Bing	丁 己 Ding Ji	癸 戊 乙 Gui Wu Yi		藏干 Hidden Stems

85	75	65	55	45	35	25	15	5	
官 DO 己 *Ji* Yin Earth	殺 7K 戊 *Wu* Yang Earth	財 DW 丁 *Ding* Yin Fire	才 IW 丙 *Bing* Yang Fire	偏 HO 乙 *Yi* Yin Wood	食 EG 甲 *Jia* Yang Wood	劫 RW 癸 *Gui* Yin Water	比 F 壬 *Ren* Yang Water	印 DR 辛 *Xin* Yin Metal	大運 Luck Pillars
卯 *Mao* Rabbit Yin Wood	寅 *Yin* Tiger Yang Wood	丑 *Chou* Ox Yin Earth	子 *Zi* Rat Yang Water	亥 *Hai* Pig Yin Water	戌 *Xu* Dog Yang Earth	酉 *You* Rooster Yin Metal	申 *Shen* Monkey Yang Metal	未 *Wei* Goat Yin Earth	
乙	戊甲丙	辛己癸	癸	壬甲	丁戊辛	辛	戊庚壬	乙己丁	

Unless you've been living on the moon for the last 5 years, you would have heard of Mr Dan Brown, or his book, the *Da Vinci Code*. I do not have Mr Brown's complete chart as we do not know the hour of birth but that's okay. We can still analyse it based on the first three pillars.

So what does Mr Dan Brown's BaZi tell us about him and why is it he could become a famous and extremely successful author?

Mr Brown's chart is a structure known as *Shi Shen Pei Yin Ge* 食神配印格 or Output matches Resource Structure. In BaZi, structures are an important method to appreciate the beauty of a chart and see its true qualities. It is considered an advanced concept so at this point, just appreciate that there are such things as 'special structures' in BaZi and they add a new dimension of interpretation to a chart. The *Shi Shen Pei Yin Ge* structure is a special one that indicates a talent and ability to bring ideas into reality.

A more basic analysis would be this: the Eating God star 食神, represented by the Jia 甲 Wood element is extremely strong, having roots in the Chen辰 (Dragon) and Yin 寅 (Tiger) branches of the BaZi. Eating God, in case you do not know, is one of the Output elements. Jia 甲 Wood is also considered ideal for authors, especially when it is also the Eating God star. At a basic level of BaZi, Eating God represents, amongst other things, a person's output or what they create. Individuals with Eating God also tend to be people who are behind the scenes or who work unseen, such as an author.

Now to be a successful author, you cannot just be able to write (otherwise, everyone out there who wrote would be a successful novelist). You have to have unique ideas, a special insight into the world, or great imagination and inspiration. In the study of BaZi, the Resource star relates to knowledge, inspiration, ideas and the star known as Indirect Resource 偏印 relates to unconventional ideas, unique perspectives and unorthodox thinking. All the qualities needed for someone planning to write a novel full of codes, brain cracking puzzles, tricky anagrams and the mystery of the century!

In truly unique and special BaZi charts, the elements all work together and play off each other. We call this the interdependence of elements. In Mr Brown's Destiny Code, there is a perfect use of the Eating God star (represented by Jia 甲 Wood) because it is made useful by the Indirect Resource star (represented by Geng 庚 Metal). Wood is chopped by Metal and made useful. So his writing is supported by good ideas.

His Indirect Resource star in turn is of good quality because of the Ding 丁 Fire found in the Wu 午 (Horse), located in the Month Branch of his BaZi.

時 Hour	日 Day	月 Month	年 Year	
日元 DM 壬	偏印 IR 庚	食神 EG 甲		天干 Heavenly Stems
Ren Yang Water	→ Geng Yang Metal	Jia Yang Wood		
寅	午	辰		地支 Earthly Branches
Yin Tiger Yang Wood	Wu Horse Yang Fire	Chen Dragon Yang Earth		
戊 甲 丙 Wu Jia Bing	→ 丁 己 Ding Ji	癸 戊 乙 Gui Wu Yi		藏干 Hidden Stems

85	75	65	55	45	35	25	15	5	
官 DO 己	殺 7K 戊	財 DW 丁	才 IW 丙	偏 HO 乙	食 EG 甲	劫 RW 癸	比 F 壬	印 DR 辛	大運 Luck Pillars
Ji Yin Earth	Wu Yang Earth	Ding Yin Fire	Bing Yang Fire	Yi Yin Wood	Jia Yang Wood	Gui Yin Water	Ren Yang Water	Xin Yin Metal	
卯 Mao Rabbit Yin Wood	寅 Yin Tiger Yang Wood	丑 Chou Ox Yin Earth	子 Zi Rat Yang Water	亥 Hai Pig Yin Water	戌 Xu Dog Yang Earth	酉 You Rooster Yin Metal	申 Shen Monkey Yang Metal	未 Wei Goat Yin Earth	
乙	戊甲丙	辛己癸	癸	壬甲	丁戊辛	辛	戊庚壬	乙己丁	

This Ding 丁 Fire forges and makes useful the Geng 庚 Metal. Ding 丁 Fire is the Direct Wealth star 正財 for Mr Brown's chart. Direct Wealth, amongst other things, represents putting one's nose to the grindstone, working hard and also is the Wife star 妻星 for a man.

Of course, there are many authors out there - not all of them are worth an estimated USD250 million. So does Mr Brown's chart reveal his wealth potential? Yes. In the BaZi classic Di Tian Sui 滴天髓, a verse states: "How do you know if a person is rich? Because he's born in the Door of Wealth 何知其人富,財氣通門戶".

Mr Brown's Wealth is represented by the element of Fire in his chart. The Month Branch of Mr Brown's BaZi, the Wu 午 (Horse) is a strong Wealth star. Inside the Yin 寅 (Tiger) is also a Wealth star, an Indirect Wealth star, that is in Growth (Chang Sheng 長生). Mr Brown's Indirect Wealth star is Bing 丙 Fire or the fire of the sunlight, indicating his Wealth potential from book royalties, like the fire of the sun, is infinite!

So, it can be said that in this BaZi, the individual has the potential and capacity to become a successful and wealthy author, and the Wife star is useful, helpful and of great significance.

The Man Behind the Code

Mr Brown met his wife in 1993 and married her in 1997. In a newspaper article by the Observer, he is quoted as saying she is his 'inspiration' and she has a big mention in his books and CDs (yes, before he wrote books, he wrote music, which is also an Eating God star activity). When he decided to become an author, his wife helped him get his first book deal, organised book signing for his first book, did his PR, got him onto talk shows and helped him do a great deal of research into the historical and art references for the *Da Vinci Code*.

He also has stated in numerous interviews that his routine consists of getting up at 4am and banging out the words in his loft. Talk about putting your nose to the grindstone!

His book is a best-seller although some reviewers complained about his awkward writing. Again the explanation is in the BaZi. Mr Brown's Eating God star is represented by the element of Jia 甲 Wood. Jia 甲 Wood, in BaZi, is represented by tall trees. Trees grow only one way and are straightforward and to the point, remember? Hence, Mr Brown's fuss-free get-to-the-point writing. It doesn't have to be beautiful to the ears, as long as you get the point!

When Combo means USD250 million

At the 35 Luck Pillar of Jia Xu 甲戌 the Xu 戌 (Dog) completes the Three Harmony Combination of Yin 寅 (Tiger), Wu 午 (Horse) and Xu 戌 (Dog). With the arrival of the Xu 戌 (Dog) the fire frame combination is complete. Refer to Chapter 4 on Combinations to quickly refresh your memory on this combination.

Fire is the Wealth Element to this Ren 壬 Water Day Master. In Dan Brown's case, the Yin-Wu-Xu 寅午戌 combination brought him an income of US250 million (estimated as of 2006). Not bad, right?

Here, most people might be thinking: I have this combo in my chart - how come I don't have US250 million spare change in my account? You might have noticed that I didn't discuss the strength of the Day Master in the earlier sections.

This Ren 壬 Water Day Master is weak in the BaZi chart itself, but as it proceeds through the Metal Pillars, it is strengthened. Xu 戌 (Dog) is part of the season of Metal, remember? So this Ren 壬 Water Day Master is not weak any more. Also, Xu 戌 (Dog) contains Metal, so his Geng 庚 Metal Indirect Resource star is now rooted and strong. Resource is what strengthens and feeds the Day Master, remember? This strengthened Geng 庚 Metal Indirect Resource now adds to the strength of the Day Master.

時 Hour	日 Day	月 Month	年 Year	
	日元 DM 壬 Ren Yang Water	偏印 IR 庚 Geng Yang Metal	食神 EG 甲 Jia Yang Wood	天干 Heavenly Stems
	寅 Yin Tiger Yang Wood	午 Wu Horse Yang Fire	辰 Chen Dragon Yang Earth	地支 Earthly Branches
	戊 Wu 甲 Jia 丙 Bing	丁 Ding 己 Ji	癸 Gui 戊 Wu 乙 Yi	藏干 Hidden Stems

85	75	65	55	45	35	25	15	5	
官 DO 己 Ji Yin Earth	殺 7K 戊 Wu Yang Earth	財 DW 丁 Ding Yin Fire	才 IW 丙 Bing Yang Fire	傷 HO 乙 Yi Yin Wood	食 EG 甲 Jia Yang Wood	劫 RW 癸 Gui Yin Water	比 F 壬 Ren Yang Water	印 DR 辛 Xin Yin Metal	大運 Luck Pillars
卯 Mao Rabbit Yin Wood	寅 Yin Tiger Yang Wood	丑 Chou Ox Yin Earth	子 Zi Rat Yang Water	亥 Hai Pig Yin Water	戌 Xu Dog Yang Earth	酉 You Rooster Yin Metal	申 Shen Monkey Yang Metal	未 Wei Goat Yin Earth	
乙	戊甲丙	辛己癸	癸	壬甲	丁戊辛	辛	戊庚壬	乙己丁	

Metal Luck

八字解碼

Clash - not always a bad thing!

Now, you will notice that there is a Clash between the Xu 戌 (Dog) and the Chen 辰 (Dragon) which releases Water from the storage. This is quite an advanced concept but because my purpose in this chapter is to expose you to some of the more sophisticated concepts in BaZi, I have decided to include it in here.

時 Hour	日 Day	月 Month	年 Year	
日元 DM 壬 *Ren* Yang Water	偏印 IR 庚 *Geng* Yang Metal	食神 EG 甲 *Jia* Yang Wood		天干 Heavenly Stems
寅 *Yin* **Tiger** Yang Wood	午 *Wu* **Horse** Yang Fire	辰 *Chen* **Dragon** Yang Earth		地支 Earthly Branches
戊 甲 丙 *Wu Jia Bing*	丁 己 *Ding Ji*	癸 戊 乙 *Gui Wu Yi*		藏干 Hidden Stems

Clash 沖

85	75	65	55	45	35	25	15	5	
官 DO 己 *Ji* Yin Earth	殺 7K 戊 *Wu* Yang Earth	財 DW 丁 *Ding* Yin Fire	才 IW 丙 *Bing* Yang Fire	傷 HO 乙 *Yi* Yin Wood	食 EG 甲 *Jia* Yang Wood	劫 RW 癸 *Gui* Yin Water	比 F 壬 *Ren* Yang Water	印 DR 辛 *Xin* Yin Metal	大運 Luck Pillars
卯 *Mao* **Rabbit** Yin Wood	寅 *Yin* **Tiger** Yang Wood	丑 *Chou* **Ox** Yin Earth	子 *Zi* **Rat** Yang Water	亥 *Hai* **Pig** Yin Water	戌 *Xu* **Dog** Yang Earth	酉 *You* **Rooster** Yin Metal	申 *Shen* **Monkey** Yang Metal	未 *Wei* **Goat** Yin Earth	
乙	戊甲丙	辛己癸	癸	壬甲	丁戊辛	辛	戊庚壬	乙己丁	

The Clash in this case is a favourable Clash because it releases a favourable element, which is Water. In fact, the Clash releases Gui 癸 Water, which is the Rob Wealth star. Now, Rob Wealth 劫財 means many things but if you are a famous celebrity, author or actor, Rob Wealth usually means your fans.

You might note that the element being clashed is Wu 戊 Earth, which is the 7 Killings star 七殺 of this Ren 壬 Water Day Master. In case you have forgotten, 7 Killings is part of the Influence Star group. As you will know, Mr Brown was sued for plagiarism in 2005 by two authors claiming the Da Vinci Code plagiarised their work and demanding a slice of his royalties. The 7 Killings star 七殺, amongst other things, refers to lawsuits and legal action.

7 Killings belongs to the Influence Stars group. Rob Wealth is one of the Companion Stars.

The Rob Wealth star 劫財, as its name literally suggests, indicates also individuals who are trying to 'rob your wealth'. Now, I don't mean real robbery of the knife and gun kind. Rob Wealth, in a nice way, means sharing your money. In a bad way, cashing in on your success. But because Gui 癸 Water is favourable, its favourable aspects (the fans) comes forth, rather than the unfavourable aspects (people trying to cash in on your success!). During this Luck Pillar, he got

sued and the people suing him were trying to cash in on his success but because the pillar is favourable to him and the element clashed out is favourable to him, his opponents were vanquished.

Combo - not always good!

Whenever I talk about this chart in class, students are often puzzled as to why Mr Brown had to wait till 35 to see success as a writer. After all, the logic is that since he is a weak Ren 壬 Water, entering the You 酉 (Rooster) Luck Pillar at 25 would have seen things improve since Metal strengthens Water.

Superficially that would seem to be the case. But remember how I always say we have to look at what is going on underneath? If you look at what is happening in the Earthly Branches, you will understand why he only got his break in the 35 Luck Pillar.

時 Hour	日 Day	月 Month	年 Year	
日元 DM 壬 *Ren* Yang Water	偏印 IR 庚 *Geng* Yang Metal	食神 EG 甲 *Jia* Yang Wood		天干 Heavenly Stems
寅 *Yin* Tiger Yang Wood	午 *Wu* Horse Yang Fire	辰 *Chen* Dragon Yang Earth		地支 Earthly Branches
戊 *Wu* 甲 *Jia* 丙 *Bing*	丁 *Ding* 己 *Ji*	癸 *Gui* 戊 *Wu* 乙 *Yi*		藏干 Hidden Stems

Combination合

85	75	65	55	45	35	25	15	5	
官 DO 己 *Ji* Yin Earth	殺 7K 戊 *Wu* Yang Earth	財 DW 丁 *Ding* Yin Fire	才 IW 丙 *Bing* Yang Fire	傷 HO 乙 *Yi* Yin Wood	食 EG 甲 *Jia* Yang Wood	劫 RW 癸 *Gui* Yin Water	比 RW 壬 *Ren* Yang Water	印 DR 辛 *Xin* Yin Metal	大運 Luck Pillars
卯 *Mao* Rabbit Yin Wood	寅 *Yin* Tiger Yang Wood	丑 *Chou* Ox Yin Earth	子 *Zi* Rat Yang Water	亥 *Hai* Pig Yin Water	戌 *Xu* Dog Yang Earth	酉 *You* Rooster Yin Metal	申 *Shen* Monkey Yang Metal	未 *Wei* Goat Yin Earth	
乙	戊甲丙	辛己癸	癸	壬甲	丁戊辛	辛	戊庚壬	乙己丁	

The You 酉 (Rooster) is combining with the Chen 辰 (Dragon) but this combination is unsuccessful because of the season of the chart, which is Wu 午 (Horse) or the height of Summer. The Fire is too strong and the Metal transformation does not take place, as the strong Fire counters the Metal. So it looks good, but in fact, is not good. In Chinese we have a saying - looks good but does not taste nice. That is the case here.

So what is affected by the combination? Chen 辰 (Dragon) contains the roots of the Wood and Gui 癸 (Yin Water). These two elements are integral to both the Ren 壬 Water Day Master and his Jia 甲 Wood Eating God star. His Output is affected and lacks quality. The Ren 壬 Water Day Master finds support is withdrawn because the Gui 癸 Water, which is lending strength to the Ren 壬 Water Day Master is gone. No Gui 癸 Water also means no Rob Wealth 劫財 - no adoring fans to love your work and buy your books!

Differentiating Structure from Description

I received a phone call from a local reader of my articles who happens to be a BaZi enthusiast. An abridged version of Mr Dan Brown's analysis had appeared in a leading Malaysian daily. He disagreed with my analysis and said Mr Brown's chart was a Cai Duo Shen Ruo Ge 財多身弱格 (Wealth Strong Self Weak) structure. He also said that the Jia 甲 Wood in this chart, which is the Eating God star 食神, is dead because it is wood in Wu 午 (Horse) month. So it should be unfavourable to this chart.

"Cai Duo Shen Ruo 財多身弱" is not a "structure". It is merely a description of the Day Master being very weak as a result of too many wealth elements in the chart. The Eating God star is seated on Chen 辰 (Dragon), it is not seated on Wu 午 (Horse). Jia Chen 甲辰 pillar, in advanced BaZi, is considered beautiful, high quality, solid wood. Furthermore, the Gui 癸 Water in the Chen 辰 (Dragon) helps to pacify the heat of the summer season.

Mr Brown is a world famous author - Eating God star is the author star. If this Eating God star is really dead or rotten, how on earth did Mr Brown become a world famous author with a best-seller? Also, this Ren 壬 Water Day Master is strictly speaking NOT that weak. A weak Day Master would not be able to control the Wealth element, which is Fire and would certainly not be able to bank every penny of that US250 million royalty fortune.

I encourage students to debate and discuss BaZi but conclusions must always be supported by a reason and logical deduction. You can't slap a label on a chart and then conclude your analysis. Equally, to debate BaZi, the fundamentals must be the same. Talking BaZi to what I call 'new age' BaZi practitioners is difficult because they are not using the same basics and fundamentals as classical BaZi practitioners. Once we were on the same plane, the gentleman caller realised his analysis was off-the-mark and we had a lot of fun chatting about BaZi these days.

Bullying Punishment

時 Hour	日 Day	月 Month	年 Year	
傷官 HO 丙	日元 DM 乙	劫財 RW 甲	七殺 7K 辛	天干 Heavenly Stems
Bing Yang Fire	Yi Yin Wood	Jia Yang Wood	Xin Yin Metal	
戌	未	午	丑	地支 Earthly Branches
Xu Dog Yang Earth	Wei Goat Yin Earth	Wu Horse Yang Fire	Chou Ox Yin Earth	
丁 戊 辛 Ding Wu Xin	乙 己 丁 Yi Ji Ding	丁 己 Ding Ji	辛 己 癸 Xin Ji Gui	藏干 Hidden Stems

82	72	62	52	42	32	22	12	2	
P IR 癸	印 DR 壬	殺 7K 辛	官 DO 庚	才 IW 己	財 DW 戊	食 EG 丁	傷 HO 丙	比 F 乙	大運 Luck Pillars
Gui Yin Water	Ren Yang Water	Xin Yin Metal	Geng Yang Metal	Ji Yin Earth	Wu Yang Earth	Ding Yin Fire	Bing Yang Fire	Yi Yin Wood	
卯 Mao Rabbit Yin Wood	寅 Yin Tiger Yang Wood	丑 Chou Ox Yin Earth	子 Zi Rat Yang Water	亥 Hai Pig Yin Water	戌 Xu Dog Yang Earth	酉 You Rooster Yin Metal	申 Shen Monkey Yang Metal	未 Wei Goat Yin Earth	
乙	戊 甲 丙	辛 己 癸	癸	壬 甲	丁 戊 辛	辛	戊 庚 壬	己 己 丁	

Let's begin with the technical analysis of this chart first, then we move on to the interpretation of the technicalities.

This Yi 乙 Wood Day Master is a weak Yi 乙 Wood, being born in Wu 午 (Horse) month, the height of Summer. In the middle of Summer, it's hot so this Yi 乙 Wood obviously needs Water. Now, superficially, this chart doesn't seem to have any Water but that's the sort of assumption that is made by people who don't know what Hidden Stems are. If you look inside the Chou 丑 (Ox), you will notice that the Gui 癸 Water is stashed away there. This Gui 癸 Water is not weak - it is supported by the Xin 辛 Metal above and it is extremely important to this Yi 乙 Wood Day Master.

Chou
Ox
Yin Earth

辛 己 癸
Xin Ji Gui

The Chou 丑 (Ox) is important for this chart for two reasons: firstly, because it contains the needed Gui 癸 Water to help this Yi 乙 Wood grow and secondly, Chou 丑 (Ox) contains wet Ji 己 Earth, which is ideal to grow the Yi 乙 Wood also.

The third component needed for Yi 乙 Wood to grow is Bing 丙 Fire. Yi 乙 Wood is the beautiful flower and without sunlight, how can we appreciate the flowers when they are blooming? This Yi 乙 Wood has a Bing 丙 Fire in the Hour pillar. Bing 丙 Fire is the Output star of this Yi 乙 Wood. In the advanced study of BaZi, it is known as the Hurting Officer star 傷官 of Yi 乙 Wood. The Hurting Officer star indicates creative and artistic talents, and a person who enjoys being in the limelight.

The Hurting Officer star is typically the star of a performer, someone who wants to be seen, and who plays to the gallery. When you put the picture together, this chart tells us that this lady is very attractive and good-looking, who loves to be in the spotlight and center of attention.

I'm sure you're very curious now who this lady is but we will get there! Read on...

Let's turn all that technical analysis into practical information. This lady is a Yi 乙 Wood Day Master. From Chapter 2, you will remember that Yi 乙 Wood is soft twines, ivy, beautiful flowers and grass. Yi 乙 Wood people are usually also very good at 'growing on other people' and can be manipulative (but of course, not always in a bad way). Yi 乙 Wood people are usually very good at playing coy. Combined with the Hurting Officer star in the Hour pillar, and you have someone who is a star, in every sense of the word.

We know that this Yi 乙 Wood needs Water, specifically Gui 癸 Water. Gui 癸 Water, to this Yi 乙 Wood Day Master, is known as the Indirect Resource star 偏印. It represents amongst other things, the mother, and also, charitable activities and endeavours. Accordingly, we can say that this person is very close to her mother and, is also very involved in charity.

Now, at a higher level of BaZi, one looks to appreciate not just the BaZi as a whole, but differentiate the grade and quality of each pillar.

If you look at this BaZi, you will notice that the Year Pillar is an extremely good pillar. This tells us that her family background is good, especially the grandfather. It also tells us that her husband is someone important, and who has a good name. Yes, you can use a person's BaZi to find out more about their relatives too.

This chart uses Xin 辛 Metal as the Husband Star because there is no true Husband Star, which is supposed to be Geng Metal for this Yi Wood Day Master. So the 7 Killings Star 七殺, Xin 辛 Metal, is read as the Husband Star. If you look at the Xin 辛 Metal in this chart, it is seated on Chou 丑 (Ox) and it is a very steady Xin 辛 Metal, supported by the Earth in the Chou 丑 (Ox).

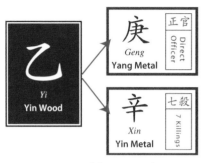

At this point, we know that Gui 癸 Water is important to this Yi Wood Day Master. Without the Gui Water, this Yi 乙 Wood will be a shrivelled up cactus. So the Chou 丑 (Ox) Earthly Branch as a whole is very important to this Yi 乙 Wood. You can say that the Chou 丑 (Ox) controls this Yi 乙 Wood's water supply if you like.

Who is Chou 丑 (Ox) to her? Inside Chou 丑 (Ox) is the Ji 己 Earth hidden stem.

Ji 己 Earth is the Resource star 印星 of Xin 辛 Metal. Remember how I said Resource, amongst other things, represents the mother? If Ji 己 Earth is the 'mother' of Xin 辛 Metal, and Xin 辛 Metal is the husband of the Yi 乙 Wood, this means Ji 己 Earth is the mother-in-law of this Yi 乙 Wood Day Master. So, the mother-in-law is a powerful figure in this Yi 乙 Wood Day Master's life.

Despite the fact that this chart has Gui 癸 Water, this Yi 乙 Wood Day Master is an unhappy person who's life is pressured and taxed, particularly by the mother-in-law, who 'controls' the most vital and needed element of this chart.

Who is the person you might be wondering?

This is the chart of the late Diana Frances Mountbatten-Windsor, better known as Diana, Princess of Wales, and former wife of the heir to the British throne, Prince Charles.

Diana was the daughter of an Earl, so she had an aristocratic background and was clearly no commoner. Her husband, obviously, is from an exceptionally good family, being of royal blood. All this, we can determine from the Year Pillar alone in her chart.

The Hurting Officer star in her chart tells us why she was an eloquent speaker, and explains her passion for dancing and singing talent. This Yi 乙 Wood flourished under the glare of the photograph flashes and media attention - during her lifetime, Diana appeared on the cover of People magazine more times than any other individual and was said to be the most photographed person in the world. She has also been described as the most famous person in the world. From the moment she became the wife of Prince Charles, till her death, and beyond, she remained an icon and an enduring celebrity.

Her charitable endeavours are well-documented, particularly in the field of AIDS, the homeless and landmines, although she had also lent her name to many other causes during her time as Princess of Wales. And of course, her powerful mother-in-law is none other than the Queen of England, Elizabeth II.

八字
解碼

Some Day My Prince Will Come - The Combination

Diana met Charles in 1977, a Ding Si 丁巳 Year. At that time, she was in the luck pillar of Bing Shen 丙申.

82	72	62	52	42	32	22	12	2	
IR 癸 Gui Yin Water	DR 壬 Ren Yang Water	辛 Xin Yin Metal	DO 庚 Geng Yang Metal	RW 己 Ji Yin Earth	DW 戊 Wu Yang Earth	EG 丁 Ding Yin Fire	HO 丙 Bing Yang Fire	F 乙 Yi Yin Wood	大運 Luck Pillars
卯 Mao Rabbit Yin Wood	寅 Yin Tiger Yang Wood	丑 Chou Ox Yin Earth	子 Zi Rat Yang Water	亥 Hai Pig Yin Water	戌 Xu Dog Yang Earth	酉 You Rooster Yin Metal	申 Shen Monkey Yang Metal	未 Wei Goat Yin Earth	
乙	戊甲丙	辛己癸	癸	壬甲	丁戊辛	辛	戊庚壬	乙己丁	

1972 壬子	1973 癸丑	1974 甲寅	1975 乙卯	1976 丙辰	1977 丁巳	1978 戊午	1979 己未	1980 庚申	1981 辛酉	流年 Year pillars

Shen 申 (Monkey) and Si 巳 (Snake) is a combination but remember when it comes to combinations, what matters is whether or not the combination produces a favourable element and if it actually takes place. This combination does produce a favourable element, Water, but unfortunately, it is not a real combination because the combination doesn't produce in this case. The season of birth, which is Wu 午 (Horse) does not support the combination. What does that mean? It suggests that her relationship with Charles might not have been 'true love'.

She married Charles in 1981, which is the year of Xin You 辛酉. The Husband Star protrudes to the Stem and becomes prominent that year. In 1982, she became Her Royal Highness the Princess of Wales, ranking third after the Queen Mother and the Queen.

She also entered the luck pillar of Ding You 丁酉. This Luck Pillar is a formation known as *Eating God Controlling Seven Killings Formation* (Shi Shen Zhi Sha 食神制殺) and heralds power and authority. It was also during this period that Diana experienced post-partum depression, after the birth of Prince William in 1982. The You 酉 (Rooster) in the ten year luck pillar is in a Harm Formation with the Xu 戌 (Dog) in the BaZi chart. The Xu 戌 (Dog) is located in the children's palace, hence the depression is related to childbirth.

	時 Hour	日 Day	月 Month	年 Year	
	傷官 HO 丙 Bing Yang Fire	日元 DM 乙 Yi Yin Wood	劫財 RW 甲 Jia Yang Wood	七殺 7K 辛 Xin Yin Metal	天干 Heavenly Stems
	戌 Xu Dog Yang Earth	未 Wei Goat Yin Earth	午 Wu Horse Yang Fire	丑 Chou Ox Yin Earth	地支 Earthly Branches
	丁 戊 辛 Ding Wu Xin	乙 己 丁 Yi Ji Ding	丁 己 Ding Ji	辛 己 癸 Xin Ji Gui	藏干 Hidden Stems

Harm 害

82	72	62	52	42	32	22	12	2	
IR 癸 Gui Yin Water	DR 壬 Ren Yang Water	7K 辛 Xin Yin Metal	DO 庚 Geng Yang Metal	IW 己 Ji Yin Earth	DW 戊 Wu Yang Earth	EG 丁 Ding Yin Fire	HO 丙 Bing Yang Fire	F 乙 Yi Yin Wood	大運 Luck Pillars
卯 Mao Rabbit Yin Wood	寅 Yin Tiger Yang Wood	丑 Chou Ox Yin Earth	子 Zi Rat Yang Water	亥 Hai Pig Yin Water	戌 Xu Dog Yang Earth	酉 You Rooster Yin Metal	申 Shen Monkey Yang Metal	未 Wei Goat Yin Earth	
乙	戊甲丙	辛己癸	癸	壬甲	丁戊辛	辛	戊庚壬	乙己丁	

Once Diana exited the Ding You 丁酉 pillar, her separation and divorce from Charles took place in 1992, during the Wu Xu 戊戌 luck pillar. Xu 戌 (Dog) is the Direct Wealth 正財 star of Yi 乙 Wood and this is a very strong Direct Wealth luck pillar - the figure has never been confirmed but Diana is said to have received an extremely substantial lump sum settlement from Charles (reputed to be 17 million pounds).

This chart also has a very strong Peach Blossom star, the Wu 午 (Horse). But this Peach Blossom star is negative, and it harms the Chou 丑 (Ox) in the Year Pillar and it combines the Wei (Goat) in the Day Branch. Wu 午 (Horse) harms the Chou 丑 (Ox) - who is Chou 丑 (Ox)? It is the mother-in-law and the Royal Family. So, her attractiveness (remember, Peach Blossom is what gives you popularity and magnetism) annoyed the Royal Family.

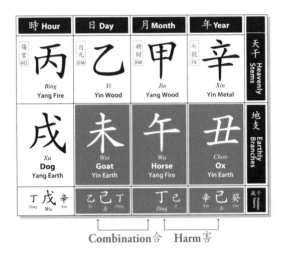

Combination合   Harm害

The Peach Blossom star combines with the Spouse Palace, indicating that her Peach Blossom interferes with the relationship with the spouse. It is a known fact that Diana was vastly more popular than her husband and this caused some dissatisfaction.

Here's something interesting about the Husband Star in this chart. We can also ascertain from this chart that the husband has a choice of spouse: he can choose between an extremely good looking wife or a relatively less attractive one, and both potential wives come from moneyed backgrounds. Jia 甲 Wood is the Rob Wealth star, or competitor, of this Yi 乙 Wood. Both the Jia 甲 and Yi 乙 Wood are seated on Wealth stars, hence we know that the husband has a choice between two ladies who come from rich families. Diana was the daughter of an Earl. Camilla Parker-Bowles was the daughter of a wine merchant. Now side-by-side, the Yi 乙 is obviously more attractive than the Jia 甲, especially since this Jia 甲 Wood, in BaZi terms, is charred, dead and older looking! But on the other hand, it is closer to the Xin 辛 Metal Husband Star!

This is an advanced reading technique I teach in my classes called the *Shifting Palace Method.* Using this method, you can learn more about another person who is related to the person whose Destiny Chart is being decoded including their personality, innate nature, even how they will look!

The Death of a Princess -
a case of Punishment Formation

Diana died in Paris in 1997, the year of Ding Chou 丁丑. Take a look at her 10 year Luck Pillar during that year - it is Wu Xu 戊戌. She has a complete Bullying Punishment of Chou 丑 (Ox), Xu 戌 (Dog) and Wei 未 (Goat).

According to the official account, she was chased by the paparazzi - being hounded and feeling you have nowhere to go but one way is a form of Bullying Punishment. Where did she meet with the car accident? Inside a tunnel - inside the Earth. If you look at the Earthly Branches involved in the Bullying Punishment, you will notice that they all have Earth in the Hidden Stems.

Combination and Ungrateful Punishment

八字解碼

時 Hour	日 Day	月 Month	年 Year	
壬 Ren Yang Water (偏官 7K)	辛 Xin Yin Metal (日元 DM)	壬 Ren Yang Water (傷官 HO)	壬 Ren Yang Water (傷官 HO)	天干 Heavenly Stems
辰 Chen Dragon Yang Earth	卯 Mao Rabbit Yin Wood	寅 Yin Tiger Yang Wood	寅 Yin Tiger Yang Wood	地支 Earthly Branches
癸 戊 乙	乙 Yi	戊 甲 丙 Wu Jia Bing	戊 甲 丙 Wu Jia Bing	藏干 Hidden Stems

84	74	64	54	44	34	24	14	4	
辛 Xin Yin Metal (比 F)	庚 Geng Yang Metal (劫 RW)	己 Ji Yin Earth (卩 IR)	戊 Wu Yang Earth (卩 DR)	丁 Ding Yin Fire (殺 7K)	丙 Bing Yang Fire (官 DO)	乙 Yi Yin Wood (才 RW)	甲 Jia Yang Wood (財 DW)	癸 Gui Yin Water (食 EG)	大運 Luck Pillars
亥 Hai Pig Yin Water	戌 Xu Dog Yang Earth	酉 You Rooster Yin Metal	申 Shen Monkey Yang Metal	未 Wei Goat Yin Earth	午 Wu Horse Yang Fire	巳 Si Snake Yin Fire	辰 Chen Dragon Yang Earth	卯 Mao Rabbit Yin Wood	
壬 甲	丁 戊 辛	辛	戊 庚 壬	乙 己 丁	丁 己	庚 丙 戊	癸 戊 乙	乙	

This chart belongs to the famous Australian naturalist Steve Irwin, known internationally as the 'Crocodile Hunter', who was killed in 2006, after being stung in the chest by a stingray. This BaZi's first three pillars are accurate but the hour is not. However, I believe that the Dragon Hour (7am-9am) may be the correct hour in this case because of Irwin's personality and career, which suggest that his chart is a special formation known as *Triple Ren with Xin*, as described in Yuan Hai Zi Ping 淵海子平, a classical text on BaZi. In the old days, this special formation belongs to individuals with outstanding performance skills - to opera singers for example. It is the chart of a person who is a consummate performer.

八字
解
碼

Structures in BaZi are an important methodology in understanding and analysing BaZi and will be covered extensively in my later books. Now, to some people, this looks like a Follow the Leader Structure 從格. Briefly, a Follow the Leader structure is where the Day Master conforms to one particular element in the BaZi due to its overwhelming strength. This is an incorrect assessment of this BaZi. Firstly, if that was the case, then Steve Irwin would have hated his job as 'Crocodile Hunter'. And I think it is obvious to anyone who has seen his show that he loved what he did and was extremely passionate about what he did. Secondly, a Follow the Leader formation always manifests as a person doing something which he does not like to do but has to do as he has to conform to the strongest element. Also, if the chart is really a Follow the Leader chart, then Irwin would probably have written nature books rather than made documentaries, since Wood is the publishing business in the study of the 5 Elements.

So, what does Steve Irwin's BaZi tell us? Let's first go with the basics - the Day Master.

Steve Irwin's Day Master is Xin 辛 Metal. Xin 辛 Metal is jewellery metal or small metal - you can picture this as your Cartier rings, your Swiss Army knives or your Rolex watches. It is beautiful, elegant, and to be admired. Xin 辛 Metal Day Masters love attention, love to perform and love to be the center of the attraction. Hence, Irwin was destined to be a showman - be it feeding crocodiles at Australia Zoo, the zoo his family owned, or making crazy nature documentaries, courtesy of Animal Planet.

In his Month Stem and Year Stem, there is Ren 壬 Water. In BaZi, Ren 壬 Water (an Output element of this Xin 辛 Metal) is the Hurting Officer star. This is an excellent formation as the Xin 辛 Metal needs to be washed by the Ren 壬 Water in order to be polished, shiny and beautiful.

In BaZi, Xin 辛 Metal is the most talkative of the Day Masters. A good Xin 辛 Metal talks a mile to a minute and always has something to say or an opinion to express. This is because Xin 辛 Metal loves to produce Water. Have you ever turned on a tap? The water just pours out and runs and runs. If you have ever watched 'Crocodile Hunter', you will notice the hyper-articulate nature of Steve Irwin. Also, Xin 辛 Metal using Hurting Officer denotes going against the order or prevailing status quo of the day. Irwin paved the way for nature documentaries that were energetic and adventurous, and a whole new form of entertainment. His style was vastly different from the prevailing approach to nature documentaries.

Why was he attracted to crocodiles? In BaZi, Jia 甲 Wood can also refer to 'armour'. The crocodile is a creature with an armour. As for the penchant for handling snakes, Si 巳 (Snake), Yin 寅 (Tiger) and Shen 申 (Monkey), along with Hai 亥 (Pig) are part of the same group of Earthly Branches. The Si 巳 (Snake), Yin 寅 (Tiger), Shen 申 (Monkey) and Hai 亥 (Pig) are also all associated with danger and hazardous activities - doubtlessly, it is clear that catching crocs and handling snakes are hazardous.

This Xin 辛 Metal Day Master is born in the season of Wood. Wood is the Wealth Element of a Xin 辛 Metal Day Master. However, the wood inside the Yin 寅 (Tiger) is Jia 甲 Wood. Jia 甲 Wood is strong, solid tree trunks. Now, imagine a small penknife trying to chop down a redwood tree. This Xin 辛 Metal Day Master has to work very hard in order to achieve success. I don't think anyone can doubt that wrestling crocodiles, handling poisonous reptiles and picking up snakes are hard or at the very least, extremely difficult work.

時 Hour	日 Day	月 Month	年 Year	天干 Heavenly Stems
傷官 HO 壬 *Ren* Yang Water	日元 DM 辛 *Xin* Yin Metal	傷官 HO 壬 *Ren* Yang Water	傷官 HO 壬 *Ren* Yang Water	
辰 *Chen* Dragon Yang Earth	卯 *Mao* Rabbit Yin Wood	寅 *Yin* Tiger Yang Wood	寅 *Yin* Tiger Yang Wood	地支 Earthly Branches
癸 戊 乙 *Gui Wu Yi*	乙 *Yi*	戊 甲 丙 *Wu Jia Bing*	戊 甲 丙 *Wu Jia Bing*	藏干 Hidden Stems

Wood is very strong in this chart as there is the Yin 寅 (Tiger) and Mao 卯 (Rabbit) present, which is 2 out of 3 of the Branches from the season of Spring, when Wood is strongest. If Irwin was born in the Dragon Hour, then he had the entire Directional Combination for the season of Wood. Hence, he was attracted to matters of nature. Wood, in the study of the Five Elements, represents benevolence, growth and nurturing. Irwin also had a foundation called Wildlife Warriors, devoted to the conservation of animals. Some people questioned his motivations in setting up the charity but it's very clear from his chart that his intentions were genuine and honest. Also,

Wood is a negative element for this Xin 辛 Metal Day Master and so by giving away his money to charity, Irwin was doing the right thing, BaZi-wise.

What about personal relationships? What does Irwin's BaZi tell us about that?

Wood (both Yi 乙 Wood and Jia 甲 Wood), besides representing the Wealth Star of Xin Metal, also represents, for a man, the Wife Star. Irwin met his wife, Terri, during the Luck Pillar of Yi Si 乙巳. Yi 乙 Wood, which is soft twines and ivy, is much easier to 'cut' compared to Jia 甲 Wood. Hence, Irwin met his wife during this luck pillar.

Si 巳 (Snake) is a Travelling (Sky Horse) Star. Within Si 巳 (Snake) is Bing 丙 Fire. Fire represents the South Direction. How did Irwin meet his wife? When she travelled to Australia

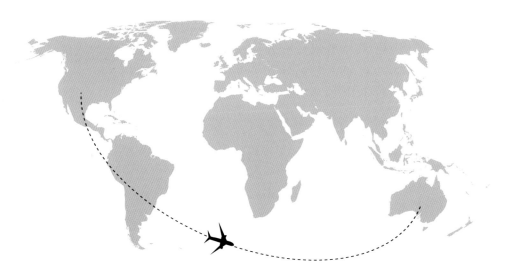

from the US! The Yi乙 Wood comes with Bing丙 Fire inside the Snake. Bing 丙 Fire represents the Direct Officer star for a Xin 辛 Metal Day Master and denotes fame and status. Irwin filmed the first episode of Crocodile Hunter during his honeymoon with his wife! From the BaZi, clearly, she was instrumental to his becoming famous!

It was however only in his next Luck Pillar, Bing Wu 丙午, that Irwin became truly famous around the world. Firstly, the Wu午 (Horse) and the Yin寅 (Tiger) form half a Three Harmony Fire Frame combination. Secondly, Fire, to a Xin辛 Metal Day Master, is Officer Luck, and signals fame and glory. As the sun blazes over this Xin Metal, surrounded by the Ren壬 Water, the Xin辛 Metal's beauty is revealed to the world. Imagine a beautiful ring, glistening and sparkling under the sea water, illuminated by the sun. This is how we can 'picture' Steve Irwin's BaZi during this Luck Pillar.

The Tragic Event

How do we derive the tragic occurrence of his death from Irwin's BaZi? Firstly, he had just changed Luck Pillars, into the Luck Pillar of Ding Wei 丁未. The Ding 丁 combines with all the Ren 壬 in his chart, and successfully transforms into Wood. The element most integral to his chart's success is removed and the element that is most negative to the chart is now enhanced.

The Wei 未 (Goat) combines with the Mao 卯 (Rabbit) Branch. In BaZi language, we say the feet of the Day Master is combined away. This indicates movement away from home and negative events happening since Wei 未 and Mao 卯 is a half combination that also produces Wood. So the negative element is now appearing in a double whammy formation in the BaZi.

時 Hour	日 Day	月 Month	年 Year	
傷官 HO 壬 Ren Yang Water	日元 DM 辛 Xin Yin Metal	傷官 HO 壬 Ren Yang Water	傷官 HO 壬 Ren Yang Water	天干 Heavenly Stems
辰 Chen Dragon Yang Earth	卯 Mao Rabbit Yin Wood	寅 Yin Tiger Yang Wood	寅 Yin Tiger Yang Wood	地支 Earthly Branches
癸 Gui 戊 Wu 乙 Yi	乙 Yi	戊 Wu 甲 Jia 丙 Bing	戊 Wu 甲 Jia 丙 Bing	藏干 Hidden Stems

亥 Hai Pig Yin Water 壬 甲 (Sea)

84	74	64	54	44	34	24	14	4	
比 F 辛 Xin Yin Metal	劫 RW 庚 Geng Yang Metal	P R 己 Ji Yin Earth	印 DR 戊 Wu Yang Earth	殺 7K 丁 Ding Yin Fire	官 DO 丙 Bing Yang Fire	才 RW 乙 Yi Yin Wood	財 DW 甲 Jia Yang Wood	食 EG 癸 Gui Yin Water	大運 Luck Pillars
亥 Hai Pig Yin Water	戌 Xu Dog Yang Earth	酉 You Rooster Yin Metal	申 Shen Monkey Yang Metal	未 Wei Goat Yin Earth	午 Wu Horse Yang Fire	巳 Si Snake Yin Fire	辰 Chen Dragon Yang Earth	卯 Mao Rabbit Yin Wood	
壬 甲	丁 戊 辛	辛	戊 庚 壬	乙 己 丁	丁 己	庚 丙 戊	癸 戊 乙	乙	

Wei未 (Goat) and Mao卯 (Rabbit) are two Branches in a Three Harmony Combination and the third animal Branch in the Combination is Hai亥 (Pig). Inside Hai亥 (Pig) is Ren壬. Ren壬 Water is sea water and the water of great lakes and rivers. As the Hai-Mao-Wei 亥卯未 combination is obviously negative (producing Wood) and the third component to complete the combination is the Hai亥 (Pig), which contains Ren壬, clearly, any activity involving the sea is potentially dangerous.

Why did the event happen this year? This is the year of Bing Xu 丙戌. In BaZi, Xu 戌 (Dog) is one of the four graveyards. When an element is 'in the graveyard' it is old and worn, the Qi is weak and can sometimes in extreme cases, denote death. In Xu 戌 (Dog), Xin Metal is in the graveyard. Bing Xu also creates a formation known as *Heaven and Earth Combine* with Day Master, and there is a *Fan Yin* formation with his Year and Month pillars.

The Fu Yin Formation 伏吟 is another advanced BaZi concept - I mention it here because it is integral to understanding why the events happened the way they did, so don't worry if you don't quite know what it is.

A Fu Yin 伏吟 is not an event we like to see in a BaZi since it denotes a sudden event that causes tears. In short, this entire BaZi is affected by the Year's elements. The day the tragic event took place was a Bing Shen 丙申 day in a Bing Shen 丙申 month - again, the Ren Yin 壬寅 in the Month and Year pillars are in a Fu Yin 伏吟 Formation with that day.

時 Hour	日 Day	月 Month	年 Year	
癸	丙	丙	丙	天干 Heavenly Stems
Gui Yin Water	*Bing* Yang Fire	*Bing* Yang Fire	*Bing* Yang Fire	
巳	申	申	戌	地支 Earthly Branches
Si Snake Yin Fire	*Shen* Monkey Yang Metal	*Shen* Monkey Yang Metal	*Xu* Dog Yang Earth	
庚 丙 戊 *Geng Bing Wu*	戊 庚 壬 *Wu Geng Ren*	戊 庚 壬 *Wu Geng Ren*	丁 戊 辛 *Ding Wu Xin*	藏干 Hidden Stems

Why a sting ray? The Jia 甲 wood in Hai 亥 represents the barb. Also, all creatures found in the sea are regarded as being associated with Ren 壬 Water or

Hai 亥 (Pig) Earthly Branch. In the advanced technique of BaZi known as "*Chou Xiang Fa* 抽像法" (*Pictorial Method*) the Ren 壬 Water has a long horizontal middle stroke when written in Chinese. Both Jia 甲 and Ren 壬 characters have the ideographic symbolism of a barb or tail and look like a stingray.

Ding 丁 Fire, in the study of BaZi, represents the heart and in this Luck Pillar, it is combined away by the Ren 壬 Water. The heart is clearly affected in any incident - in this case, the barb pierced his heart. I believe there may have been more than one stingray present during the accident because Ren 壬 and Yin 寅 (with the Jia 甲 inside) strongly suggests two or more creatures.

時 Hour	日 Day	月 Month	年 Year	
壬 Ren Yang Water	辛 Xin Yin Metal	壬 Ren Yang Water	壬 Ren Yang Water	天干 Heavenly Stems
辰 Chen Dragon Yang Earth	卯 Mao Rabbit Yin Wood	寅 Yin Tiger Yang Wood	寅 Yin Tiger Yang Wood	地支 Earthly Branches
癸 Gui 戊 Wu 乙	乙 Yi	戊 Wu 甲 Jia 丙 Bing	戊 Wu 甲 Jia 丙 Bing	藏干 Hidden Stems

Combination 合

84	74	64	54	44	34	24	14	4	
比 F 辛 Xin Yin Metal	劫 RW 庚 Geng Yang Metal	P IR 己 Ji Yin Earth	印 DR 戊 Wu Yang Earth	殺 7K 丁 Ding Yin Fire	官 DO 丙 Bing Yang Fire	才 IW 乙 Yi Yin Wood	財 DW 甲 Jia Yang Wood	食 EG 癸 Gui Yin Water	大運 Luck Pillars
亥 Hai Pig Yin Water	戌 Xu Dog Yang Earth	酉 You Rooster Yin Metal	申 Shen Monkey Yang Metal	未 Wei Goat Yin Earth	午 Wu Horse Yang Fire	巳 Si Snake Yin Fire	辰 Chen Dragon Yang Earth	卯 Mao Rabbit Yin Wood	
壬 甲	丁 戊 辛	辛	戊 庚 壬	乙 己 丁	丁 己	庚 丙 戊	癸 戊 乙	乙	

Finally, the Shen 申 (Monkey) of the day and month of the event, and the fact that he was in the sea (Hai 亥) and filming a documentary (a fire type activity since it relates to entertainment) means he has the complete set of Punishments on that day, and specifically an Ungrateful Punishment between the Shen 申 (Monkey) and the Yin 寅 (Tiger).

Remember in Chapter 7, I talked about the meaning of Ungrateful Punishment? An Ungrateful Punishment involves doing good for someone but getting no gratitude in return. Irwin was killed by one of the creatures that he had devoted his life to protecting, a classic illustration of an Ungrateful Punishment.

In BaZi, a person's luck continues, even though the person is no longer with us in this world. Steve Irwin's name, and his contributions to conservation, will live on and be remembered for a long time. This is because the Ding Wei 丁未 Luck Pillar is still a very strong pillar of Fire, which brings fame and good name to the Xin 辛 Metal Day Master. So Irwin will not fade from the media and public's minds so quickly.

八字
解碼

COMBINATION-DESTRUCTION

時 Hour	日 Day	月 Month	年 Year	
正印 DR **乙** Yi Yin Wood	日元 DM **丙** Bing Yang Fire	傷官 HO **己** Ji Yin Earth	食神 EG **戊** Wu Yang Earth	天干 Heavenly Stems
未 Wei **Goat** Yin Earth	**寅** Yin **Tiger** Yang Wood	**未** Wei **Goat** Yin Earth	**午** Wu **Horse** Yang Fire	地支 Earthly Branches
乙 Yi 己 Ji 丁 Ding	戊 Wu 甲 Jia 丙 Bing	乙 Yi 己 Ji 丁 Ding	丁 Ding 己 Ji	藏干 Hidden Stems

This is the BaZi chart of the famous South African Nobel Prize Laureate Nelson Mandela. I had the privilege of meeting him in 1999 when I was in South Africa for a seminar.

The first thing you will notice about this chart is that it has no Water and Metal, not even in the Hidden Stems. Fire is also extremely strong in this chart - structurally, it has a *Follow Prosperous Structure*, which immediately tells us that this chart is special and so has to be read with regard to its unique nature.

The conventional assumption is that a chart like this needs Water and accordingly, Water must be the favourable element, with Metal as a secondary favoured element. This is a very superficial way of looking at a BaZi chart. Special charts should be considered with regard to their special nature and structure. This chart does not particularly need Water, but favours Water for balance. (There is a difference between 'need' and 'favouring' an element). So the person will be attracted to politics, which is the Influence element for a Bing丙 Fire Day Master but is not motivated by power (Water element) or money (Wealth element) in his deeds. That is how we translate 'favours water but does not need water' in a practical sense.

Earth is extremely strong and dominant in this chart. In the study of the BaZi 10 Gods 十神, Earth element, specifically Ji己 Earth, to a Bing丙 Fire Day Master, is the Hurting Officer star 傷官. The Hurting Officer star 傷官 wants to change the rules, challenge the norms, create new order. Fire is also very strong in this chart, so we can see that he desires change for his own people. Hence, Mandela became a key figure in the challenge against apartheid in South Africa.

Now let's take a look at his pillars.

87	77	67	57	47	37	27	17	7	
食 EG 戊 Wu Yang Earth	劫 RW 丁 Ding Yin Fire	比 F 丙 Bing Yang Fire	印 DR 乙 Yi Yin Wood	P IR 甲 Jia Yang Wood	官 DO 癸 Gui Yin Water	殺 7K 壬 Ren Yang Water	財 DW 辛 Xin Yin Metal	才 IW 庚 Geng Yang Metal	大運 Luck Pillars
辰 Chen Dragon Yang Earth	卯 Mao Rabbit Yin Wood	寅 Yin Tiger Yang Wood	丑 Chou Ox Yin Earth	子 Zi Rat Yang Water	亥 Hai Pig Yin Water	戌 Xu Dog Yang Earth	酉 You Rooster Yin Metal	申 Shen Monkey Yang Metal	
癸戊乙	乙	戊甲丙	辛己癸	癸	壬甲	丁戊辛	辛	戊庚壬	

————Water————

2004 甲申	1994 甲戌	1984 甲子	1974 甲寅	1964 甲辰	1954 甲午	1944 甲申	1934 甲戌	1924 甲子	
2005 乙酉	1995 乙亥	1985 乙丑	1975 乙卯	1965 乙巳	1955 乙未	1945 乙酉	1935 乙亥	1925 乙丑	流年 Year pillars
2006 丙戌	1996 丙子	1986 丙寅	1976 丙辰	1966 丙午	1956 丙申	1946 丙戌	1936 丙子	1926 丙寅	
2007 丁亥	1997 丁丑	1987 丁卯	1977 丁巳	1967 丁未	1957 丁酉	1947 丁亥	1937 丁丑	1927 丁卯	
2008 戊子	1998 戊寅	1988 戊辰	1978 戊午	1968 戊申	1958 戊戌	1948 戊子	1938 戊寅	1928 戊辰	
2009 己丑	1999 己卯	1989 己巳	1979 己未	1969 己酉	1959 己亥	1949 己丑	1939 己卯	1929 己巳	
2010 庚寅	2000 庚辰	1990 庚午	1980 庚申	1970 庚戌	1960 庚子	1950 庚寅	1940 庚辰	1930 庚午	
2011 辛卯	2001 辛巳	1991 辛未	1981 辛酉	1971 辛亥	1961 辛丑	1951 辛卯	1941 辛巳	1931 辛未	
2012 壬辰	2002 壬午	1992 壬申	1982 壬戌	1972 壬子	1962 壬寅	1952 壬辰	1942 壬午	1932 壬申	
2013 癸巳	2003 癸未	1993 癸酉	1983 癸亥	1973 癸丑	1963 癸卯	1953 癸巳	1943 癸未	1933 癸酉	

It would be assumed that since this chart favours Water, the Water Pillars would be good for him. In Gui Hai 癸亥 Luck Pillar, Mandela did indeed become active in politics, but it did not bring him power and glory - instead, he ended up being imprisoned in 1962. For the next 27 years, almost the entire duration of his Water Luck Pillars, Mandela was in prison. Mandela survived the imprisonment because the structure of his chart did not break, with the introduction of Water, because his chart did not originally have Water.

What does this mean? If you look at the original chart, there isn't a single drop of Water in the chart. This means that the Day Master is not accustomed to this element. So when the element appears in the Luck Pillars, something which is an alien experience or uncomfortable experience must be endured.

So let's see why he ended up in prison, using the knowledge you have already learnt in the previous chapters and from the previous book. The year he was sent to jail was 1962, the Ren Yin 壬寅 year, in a Gui Hai 癸亥 Luck Pillar. There is a Combination-Destruction present but the transformation into Wood is not successful, thus the destruction manifests. This is a double-destruction because there is a Combination-Destruction between the Luck Pillar and the Annual Pillar, and between the Luck Pillar and the Day Branch of the BaZi.

Now, the Hai 亥 (Pig) and the Wei 未 (Goat) create a Half Combination and pushes up a Mao 卯 (Rabbit). This is a concept known as '*Silent Push*' and is an advanced approach to Three Harmony Combinations. Don't worry too much if you don't know how it works - just note at this point that there is an 'invisible' Mao 卯 (Rabbit). Mao 卯 (Rabbit) is the Direct Resource of this Bing 丙 Fire Day Master and also refers to support and noble people. Because it is invisible, it denotes that there are people who support him, but who cannot be public in their support or publicly help him. Also, during this year and Luck Pillar, all the Branches are affected and are in movement, which is usually an indication of problems in a BaZi.

Mandela was released in 1990 - by this point, he had entered the Bing Yin 丙寅 Luck Pillars. There is a half Three Harmony Fire Frame combination between the Wu 午 (Horse) in the annual pillar and the Yin 寅 (Tiger) in the Luck Pillar. The Fire is strong and supporters are plentiful.

87	77	67	57	47	37	27	17	7	
食 EG 戊 Wu Yang Earth	劫 RW 丁 Ding Yin Fire	比 F 丙 Bing Yang Fire	印 DR 乙 Yi Yin Wood	P IR 甲 Jia Yang Wood	官 DO 癸 Gui Yin Water	殺 7K 壬 Ren Yang Water	財 DW 辛 Xin Yin Metal	才 IW 庚 Geng Yang Metal	大運 Luck Pillars
辰 Chen Dragon Yang Earth	卯 Mao Rabbit Yin Wood	寅 Yin Tiger Yang Wood	丑 Chou Ox Yin Earth	子 Zi Rat Yang Water	亥 Hai Pig Yin Water	戌 Xu Dog Yang Earth	酉 You Rooster Yin Metal	申 Shen Monkey Yang Metal	
癸戊乙	乙	戊甲丙	辛己癸	癸	壬甲	丁戊辛	辛	戊庚壬	

Got married   *Released from prison*

In 1998, Mandela married his third wife, a 50 year old companion. By this point, he is in the Ding Mao 丁卯 Luck Pillar, a personal Peach Blossom luck pillar for him, as he is born in the Wu 午 (Horse) year. This is good Peach Blossom! If someone still wants you at 80, it's a good thing! His wedding was attended by over 2,000 people including many celebrities and world politicians - they are represented by the Ding 丁 Fire or Rob Wealth star, in the Luck Pillar. The Mao 卯 (Rabbit) in the Earthly Branch of the Luck Pillar also indicates true support and a strong reputation and good name, at this point in his life.

Combinations

時 Hour	日 Day	月 Month	年 Year	
正財 DW	日元 DM	食神 EG	正印 DR	天干 Heavenly Stems
辛	丙	戊	乙	
Xin Yin Metal	Bing Yang Fire	Wu Yang Earth	Yi Yin Wood	
卯	辰	寅	未	地支 Earthly Branches
Mao **Rabbit** Yin Wood	Chen **Dragon** Yang Earth	Yin **Tiger** Yang Wood	Wei **Goat** Yin Earth	
乙 Yi	癸 戊 乙 Gui Wu Yi	戊 甲 丙 Wu Jia Bing	乙 己 丁 Yi Ji Ding	藏干 Hidden Stems

In all the previous examples, I talked about the technical analysis aspects of the chart - the strength of the Day Master, the clashes and the combinations and relationships between the Branches. That is one way to study a BaZi. Another approach, which is more sophisticated and which is practiced at the highest levels of BaZi, is to see the 'picture' that the BaZi paints. Appreciating a BaZi at its highest level involves being able to visualise the BaZi, almost like a painting and to see if what it shows is a beautiful picture.

The chart above is the BaZi of Steve Jobs, the founder of Apple Computers. It is a beautiful chart - the Bing 丙 Fire Day Master here is just right, not too hot, not too blazing. That is the beauty of this chart. Many people assume that Bing 丙 Fire must be hot to be a good Bing 丙 Fire. Intensity of Fire is the consideration when it comes to Ding 丁 Fire, but not Bing 丙 Fire. When it comes to Bing 丙 Fire, we want it to be bright but not the kind that hurts your eyes. We want it to be warm, but not hot that it sears your skin.

時 Hour	日 Day	月 Month	年 Year	天干 Heavenly Stems
正印 DW 辛 *Xin* Yin Metal	日元 DM 丙 *Bing* Yang Fire	食神 EG 戊 *Wu* Yang Earth	正印 DR 乙 *Yi* Yin Wood	
卯 *Mao* **Rabbit** Yin Wood	辰 *Chen* **Dragon** Yang Earth	寅 *Yin* **Tiger** Yang Wood	未 *Wei* **Goat** Yin Earth	地支 Earthly Branches
乙 *Yi*	癸 *Gui* 戊 *Wu* 乙 *Yi*	戊 *Wu* 甲 *Jia* 丙 *Bing*	乙 *Yi* 己 *Ji* 丁 *Ding*	藏干 Hidden Stems

Picture a gentle and warming sun, shining over a lush forest as represented by the full season of Spring that is present in the chart through the Directional Combination of Yin 寅 (Tiger), Chen 辰 (Dragon) and Mao 卯 (Rabbit) - that is the picture this BaZi paints. This person's purpose in life is to change the world, to grow and nurture new ideas, to illuminate. Money is not the foremost thing on this person's mind because whilst there is Wealth in the chart, it is not rooted and hence, is not what drives this person. But because the Bing 丙 Fire Day Master combines with Wealth, making money is easy for Steve Jobs. Indeed, Steve Jobs displayed entrepreneurial prowess very early in life, despite his hippy nature.

Now, let us take a look at some of the important events in his life, and how they correspond to the luck pillars in his BaZi.

87	77	67	57	47	37	27	17	7	
傷 HO 己 Ji Yin Earth	才 IW 庚 Geng Yang Metal	財 DW 辛 Xin Yin Metal	殺 7K 壬 Ren Yang Water	官 DO 癸 Gui Yin Water	卩 IR 甲 Jia Yang Wood	印 DR 乙 Yi Yin Wood	比 F 丙 Bing Yang Fire	劫 RW 丁 Ding Yin Fire	大運 Luck Pillars
巳 Si Snake Yin Fire	午 Wu Horse Yang Fire	未 Wei Goat Yin Earth	申 Shen Monkey Yang Metal	酉 You Rooster Yin Metal	戌 Xu Dog Yang Earth	亥 Hai Pig Yin Water	子 Zi Rat Yang Water	丑 Chou Ox Yin Earth	
庚丙戊	丁己	乙己丁	戊庚壬	辛	丁戊辛	壬甲	癸	辛己癸	

1976

丙 Bing Yang Fire

辰 Chen Dragon Yang Earth

流年 Year Pillars

Half-Combo

Apple Computers was founded in 1976, which is the year of Bing Chen 丙辰, during the Bing Zi 丙子 Luck Pillar. Zi 子 (Rat) is his *Death and Emptiness - Death and Emptiness* 空亡 is an advanced concept that I will introduce in my subsequent books but for the purposes of this chart, the interpretation tells us that during these years, the person lacks personal direction and discipline.

Indeed, in the run up years to 1976, Jobs dropped out of college, hung out with hippies, and travelled to India in search of personal enlightenment. A combination however can relieve Emptiness and in 1976, the Chen 辰 (Dragon) combines with the Zi 子 (Rat) to relieve the emptiness - there is a sense of realisation and direction. Also, the year of Bing Chen 丙辰 sees the arrival of another Bing 丙 Fire or Companion element - it was in 1976 that Jobs founded Apple with his friend, Steve Wozniak.

Apple went IPO in 1983, as Jobs entered his Yi Hai 乙
亥 Luck Pillars. The Hai 亥 (Pig) completes the
Hai-Mao-Wei 亥卯未 (Pig-Rabbit-Goat) Three
Harmony Combination, creating a Wood Frame.
This denotes support, good connections, good
network and also, paper money, since Wood is a
Resource star to this Bing 丙 Fire Day Master. Stock
options and paper documents are part of the Resource
Star. However, the Hai 亥 (Pig) also creates a Combination-
Destruction with the Tiger, denoting that during this period,
there is a potential time-bomb problem waiting to happen
that involves the goodwill he enjoys or his support.

In 1985, Steve Jobs was pushed out of the company he founded. 1985 was a Yi Chou乙丑 year - Chou丑 (Ox) and Wei未 (Goat) clash, breaking the Hai-Mao-Wei亥卯未 combo. Joint-ventures and partnerships bring about problems and the destruction is caused by excessive aggression and recklessness leading to a loss of goodwill - when he was pushed out of Apple, Jobs had embarked on an ambitious project, the Macintosh XL that was eating into cash but showing few returns. Chou 丑 (Ox) and Yin 寅 (Tiger) is also a Hidden Combination amongst the two Hidden Stems, an advanced Combination concept. This points to the plotting and orchestration that had been said to be going on behind the scenes that led to his ouster.

It was only in 1996, in a new luck pillar of Jia Xu甲戌, that Steve Jobs returned to Apple. 1996 is the year of Bing Zi 丙子. Zi子 is a Direct Officer star for Bing丙 Fire indicating a change in business environment, a new lifestyle or  = Companion Element 比劫 concept and of course, authority and power. The Xu戌 (Dog) and the Yin寅 (Tiger) is a half Three Harmony Fire Frame combination, and the Xu 戌 (Dog) and Mao卯 (Rabbit) is a combination that also produces Fire. All these combinations produce the elements he likes and signals a return to the company in the midst of adoration since Fire is his Companion element. This is the period of rebirth and new growth for Jobs as Jia甲 Wood in the Luck Pillars, seeing Bing丙 Fire is a favourable formation in advanced BaZi.

While Jobs made many notable changes to Apple, he is most famous for reviving Apple's fortunes through the iPod MP3 player. The announcement of the iPod coincided with the change in Luck Pillars, into the Gui You癸酉 Luck Pillar. Now, in this chart, Bing丙 combines with Xin辛 and Xin辛

八字
解
碼

is this Bing 丙 Fire Day Master's Wealth element. An iPod, translated into BaZi terms, is Xin 辛 Metal - Xin 辛, amongst other things, refers to cute, small little things. In the study of the Five Elements, Metal is white, not yellow. Naturally, the iPod was first released in white. This BaZi also tells us why Jobs named his company Apple - the spring season dominates this chart, hence the preference for a name related to fruit. Also, cutting an apple, can be pictorially translated into BaZi as 'Xin 辛 cutting Mao 卯' - look at the Hour Pillar of Job's chart - it is Xin Mao 辛卯.

Chapter Ten
Practical BaZi Analysis

By this stage, you will have at your fingertips, a wealth of information and techniques that you can apply to a Destiny Chart. The last nine chapters of this book have focused on theoretical and technical information about elemental relationships between the Heavenly Stems and Earthly Branches. I have explained the key relationships - Combinations, Clashes, Harms, Destructions and Punishments and also through examples, explained how these elemental relationships are decoded.

So, in this chapter, let's get practical.

My classes and seminars on BaZi around the world are attended by people from all walks of life and backgrounds. There are individuals who are there because they are looking at developing an alternative career as Destiny Analysts (extremely lucrative in the West), there are individuals who are there to further their interest in Chinese Metaphysics, there are corporate people who are interested in empowering themselves through an understanding of BaZi and using it for business purposes and individuals who are attending because they are interested in using BaZi to better understand themselves.

They all want one thing when they come to a class: the ability to utilise the information they have learnt in a practical context. It's one thing to be able to handle the technical analysis. But at the end of the day, what does it all mean?

The key to this, as I tell my students, is a proper format of reading. You need to approach a BaZi in a systematic

fashion. Professional BaZi consultants can switch in and out of different perspectives on a BaZi but at the beginner's level, this can sometimes be confusing and complicated. So, the trick is to go with a format and be guided on how to decode the BaZi.

And that is what I am going to show you here - a simple format, that beginners to decoding Destiny Charts can utilise. Of course, as your understanding of BaZi grows, I will show you more sophisticated formats and techniques to approach BaZi in a systematic manner.

Now, for some 'trade secrets' on decoding Destiny Charts.

The most important thing about approaching a Destiny Chart is not to rush yourself or panic when there's something you do not understand or cannot decipher at first glance. The moment you hit the panic button, your brain will freeze up and you probably won't even be able to recite the Five Element cycle if asked to. If you do freeze up, put the chart aside for a minute, and then come back to it.

Always focus on the question at hand and look for the answer there. Many beginners often make the mistake of trying to derive the encyclopaedia of their life, or a person's life, by looking at the BaZi. At the highest level, yes, the BaZi can be perceived as a single image or pictorial depiction. But at the beginner's level, focus on one question, one answer at a time. Even in a professional Bazi consult, clients will be asked to list their questions. The purpose is to make the session productive and also, ensure the client focuses on their issues, not the issues which the consultant deems important. So remember, ask yourself, what is the question, and then seek out the answer. At the end of this section, I'll share with you some techniques for analysing certain issues, such as relationships and career.

To help you along, I've included some forms where you can work out the information pertaining to your own personal Destiny Chart. It's helpful to use your own chart first to practice - you after all, know yourself better than anyone else! Then as you feel more confident with your analysis, work on the charts of the people you know - friends, colleagues and family members - to build up your confidence.

So, let's start decoding!

PART ONE: The Basic Analysis

Step 1: Plot the BaZi

Using the technique outlined in my first book, *The Destiny Code*, plot your BaZi, the 10-Year Luck Pillars and the Age Limits out. If you want to be fast, use the online calculator at **www.joeyyap.com**.

The example I will be using for this section is the Destiny Chart of a male born 1st October 2006 at 7.45am.

Click here

* This is a screen capture of www.joeyyap.com website as of Oct 2006. As the site may be updated, the link position may change. Please contact us directly if you cannot see the link.

Step 2: Identify the Day Master

Using a red pen, circle the Day Master. The Day Master is the Heavenly Stem of the Day you were born.

A person born 1st October 2006 at 7.45am, has a Gui 癸 Water Day Master

Day Master

Step 3: Analyse the Basic Personality of the person

Using the information from Chapter 2, you will already be able to engage in some analysis of the person's basic innate personality, by looking at this person's Day Master. So for example, for this Gui 癸 Water Day Master, we can say this person is someone who is always on the move and cannot sit still. Water is always moving so this person is impatient for results and does things quickly and with great urgency. This person is not suited for a job behind a desk but should be in a job that enables a lot of movement or travel. See - you're already analysing the BaZi, and that's just from the Day Master!

Step 4: Determine if the Day Master is Strong or Weak

This technique has been explained in Chapter Six of *The Destiny Code*. Briefly, if your Day Master is born in season, then the Day Master is considered prosperous or strong. If the Day Master is not born in season, then it is considered weak. In case you have forgotten, the key to determining if a Day Master is strong or weak, is usually the Month Branch.

時 Hour	日 Day	月 Month	年 Year	
丙	癸	丁	丙	天干 Heavenly Stems
Bing Yang Fire	Gui Yin Water	Ding Yin Fire	Bing Yang Fire	
辰	亥	酉	戌	地支 Earthly Branches
Chen Dragon Yang Earth	Hai Pig Yin Water	You Rooster Yin Metal	Xu Dog Yang Earth	
癸 戊 乙 Gui Wu Yi	壬 甲 Ren Jia	辛 Xin	丁 戊 辛 Ding Wu Xin	藏干 Hidden Stems

Again, using the example of the BaZi of a person born 1st October 2006, 7.45am, this person is Gui 癸 Water born in You 酉 (Rooster) month. You 酉 (Rooster) is the Autumn season, which is part of the season of Metal. However, as Metal produces Water in the 5 Element cycle, this Gui 癸 Water is not prosperous, but is strong.

死 Dead	囚 Trap	休 Weak	相 Strong	旺 Prosperous	Strength / Season
土 Earth	金 Metal	水 Water	火 Fire	木 Wood	春 Spring
金 Metal	水 Water	木 Wood	土 Earth	火 Fire	夏 Summer
木 Wood	火 Fire	土 Earth	水 Water	金 Metal	秋 Autumn
火 Fire	土 Earth	金 Metal	木 Wood	水 Water	冬 Winter

Step 5: Determine the Favourable and Unfavourable Elements of the Day Master

Once you know whether or not the Day Master is strong or weak, you will be able to ascertain the Favourable and Unfavourable Elements of the Day Master. In case you've forgotten, here is a quick recap:

Strong Day Master	
Favours	**Dislikes**
• Controlling another element • Being Controlled by another element • Producing another element	• The same element • The element that produces the Day Master

Weak Day Master	
Favours	**Dislikes**
• The same element • The element that produces the Day Master	• Controlling another element • Being Controlled by another element • Producing another element

Okay, now, at this stage, you need to know what Resource 印星, Influence 官殺, Wealth 財星, Companion 比劫 and Output 食傷 elements are for the Day Master. In case you've forgotten, I've reproduced the table here for you:

Day Master	木 Wood 甲 乙 *Jia Yi*	金 Metal 庚 辛 *Geng Xin*	水 Water 壬 癸 *Ren Gui*	土 Earth 戊 己 *Wu Ji*	火 Fire 丙 丁 *Bing Ding*
Wealth Element 財星	Earth	Wood	Fire	Water	Metal
Output Element 食傷	Fire	Water	Wood	Metal	Earth
Influence Element 官殺	Metal	Fire	Earth	Wood	Water
Resource Element 印星	Water	Earth	Metal	Fire	Wood
Companion Element 比劫	Wood	Metal	Water	Earth	Fire

So, let's apply the information to the sample Destiny Chart below.

時 Hour	日 Day	月 Month	年 Year	
丙 *Bing* **Yang Fire**	癸 *Gui* **Yin Water**	丁 *Ding* **Yin Fire**	丙 *Bing* **Yang Fire**	天干 Heavenly Stems
辰 *Chen* **Dragon** Yang Earth	亥 *Hai* **Pig** Yin Water	酉 *You* **Rooster** Yin Metal	戌 *Xu* **Dog** Yang Earth	地支 Earthly Branches
癸 戊 乙 *Gui Wu Yi*	壬 甲 *Ren Jia*	辛 *Xin*	丁 戊 辛 *Ding Wu Xin*	藏干 Hidden Stems

The Day Master is:

Strong	✓
Weak	

My Day Master Favours:

Five Factors	Element	✓ : Favours ✗ : Does not favour
Resource	Metal	✗
Influence	Earth	✓
Wealth	Fire	✓
Companion	Water	✗
Output	Wood	✓

Step 6: Look at the Luck Pillars

Now, take a look at the luck pillars. Using the red pen, mark out the seasons. So for example, Hai 亥 (Pig), Zi 子 (Rat) and Chou 丑 (Ox) are the season of Water. So put a bracketed line under these three pillars and write 'water'. Do the same for all the other seasons, as I have done with the example below.

62	52	42	32	22	12	2	
甲 *Jia* Yang Wood	癸 *Gui* Yin Water	壬 *Ren* Yang Water	辛 *Xin* Yin Metal	庚 *Geng* Yang Metal	己 *Ji* Yin Earth	戊 *Wu* Yang Earth	大運 Luck Pillars
辰 *Chen* Dragon Yang Earth	卯 *Mao* Rabbit Yin Wood	寅 *Yin* Tiger Yang Wood	丑 *Chou* Ox Yin Earth	子 *Zi* Rat Yang Water	亥 *Hai* Pig Yin Water	戌 *Xu* Dog Yang Earth	
癸戊乙	乙	戊甲丙	辛己癸	癸	壬甲	丁戊辛	

Wood   Water

Step 7: Identify the Favourable and Unfavourable Luck Periods

By looking at the Favourable and Unfavourable Elements, you can ascertain when a person will go through favourable luck periods, and unfavourable luck periods. So in the case of our Gui 癸 Day Master, as he favours Wood, Earth and Fire, so we can say that when he arrives at Wood Luck, which is the season of Spring, beginning with the Ren Yin 壬寅 Luck Pillar, then his favourable luck period commences. Prior to that, his Luck Pillars were not favourable.

Okay, now, try it with your own chart using the blank sheet I have prepared for you at the back of this section.

PART TWO:
Incorporating in the Relationships Codes

After you've handled Part One as described above, you're ready to use the new codes that you've learnt in this book. Again, use back the form that I've included in the back of the book for this part of the analysis.

Step 1: Identify the Elemental Relationships in the chart

Check all the Earthly Branches and identify which Earthly Branches have any relationship with each other and then circle these Branches and make a note of the relationship.

So, in our example above, there is a Harm Relationship between the You 酉 (Rooster) in the Month Branch and the Xu 戌 (Dog) in the Year Branch.

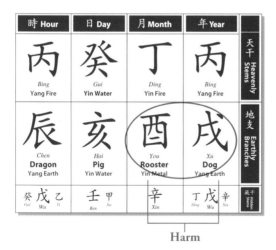

To make it easy and fast for you to identify the elemental relationships between the Earthly Branches, I've included a little 'cheat sheet' for you. How do you use this 'cheat sheet'? Find the Earthly Branches on the right hand side of the table, and see what kind of relationships they have with other Branches, which is located on the top of the table.

So for example, what relationship does the You 酉 (Rooster) Earthly Branch have with the Branches left and right of it in the BaZi, which are Xu 戌 (Dog) in the Year Branch, and Hai 亥 (Pig) in the Day Branch? Remember, a Clash, Combination, Harm, Punishment or Destruction has to be side-by-side in order to take effect.

亥 *Hai* Pig	戌 *Xu* Dog	酉 *You* Rooster	申 *Shen* Monkey	未 *Wei* Goat	午 *Wu* Horse	巳 *Si* Snake	辰 *Chen* Dragon	卯 *Mao* Rabbit	寅 *Yin* Tiger	丑 *Chou* Ox	子 *Zi* Rat	
害 Harm	刑 Punishment			三合 3 Combination	合 Combination	沖 Clash		三合 3 Combination	破 Destruction			酉 *You* Rooster

As you can see from the extract of the table, You 酉 (Rooster) has a Harm relationship with the Xu 戌 (Dog) but no elemental relationship with the Hai 亥 (Pig).

Using the cheat sheet, check the Destiny Chart for all possible relationships - Clash, Combination, Harm, Punishment and Destruction and mark these on the sheet I've provided. Don't worry if it looks messy. The main point is to identify the relationships.

Joey Yap's 12 Earthly Branches Relationships Table

十二地支刑沖破害三合六合表

亥 Hai Pig	戌 Xu Dog	酉 You Rooster	申 Shen Monkey	未 Wei Goat	午 Wu Horse	巳 Si Snake	辰 Chen Dragon	卯 Mao Rabbit	寅 Yin Tiger	丑 Chou Ox	子 Zi Rat	
		破 Destruction	三合 3 Combination	害 Harm	沖 Clash		三合 3 Combination	刑 Punishment		合 Combination		**子 Zi Rat**
	刑 Punishment	三合 3 Combination		刑沖 Punishment Clash	害 Harm	三合 3 Combination	破 Destruction				合 Combination	**丑 Chou Ox**
合破 Combination Destruction	三合 3 Combination		刑沖 Punishment Clash		三合 3 Combination	刑 Punishment 害 Harm						**寅 Yin Tiger**
三合 3 Combination	合 Combination	沖 Clash		三合 3 Combination	破 Destruction		害 Harm				刑 Punishment	**卯 Mao Rabbit**
	沖 Clash	合 Combination	三合 3 Combination				刑 Punishment	害 Harm		破 Destruction	三合 3 Combination	**辰 Chen Dragon**
沖 Clash		三合 3 Combination	破刑合 Combination Punishment Destruction						刑 Punishment 害 Harm	三合 3 Combination		**巳 Si Snake**
	三合 3 Combination			合 Combination	刑 Punishment			破 Destruction	三合 3 Combination	害 Harm	沖 Clash	**午 Wu Horse**
三合 3 Combination	刑破 Punishment Destruction				合 Combination			三合 3 Combination		刑沖 Punishment Clash	害 Harm	**未 Wei Goat**
害 Harm						破刑合 Combination Punishment Destruction	三合 3 Combination		刑沖 Punishment Clash		三合 3 Combination	**申 Shen Monkey**
	害 Harm	刑 Punishment				三合 3 Combination	合 Combination	沖 Clash		三合 3 Combination	破 Destruction	**酉 You Rooster**
		害 Harm		刑破 Punishment Destruction	三合 3 Combination		沖 Clash	合 Combination	三合 3 Combination	刑 Punishment		**戌 Xu Dog**
刑 Punishment			害 Harm	三合 3 Combination		沖 Clash		三合 3 Combination	合破 Combination Destruction			**亥 Hai Pig**

Step 2: Analyse the Relationships via Palaces

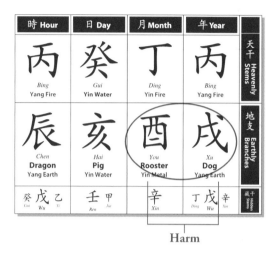

Harm

Look at which Earthly Branch is involved in the Combination, Clash, Harm, Punishment or Destruction and note down the palaces that are involved. If the Year Branch is involved, then the Grandparents Palace is involved. If the Month Branch is involved, then it relates to Parents since that is the Parent's Palace. If the Day Branch is involved, it relates to the Spouse Palace or the person's home. If it is the Hour Branch that is involved, then it relates to their children or employees.

So in our example, the harm is between the Year Branch and Month Branch, involving the Grandparents Palace and the Parents Palace.

時 Hour	日 Day	月 Month	年 Year
Children Palace	Self / Spouse Palace	Parents Palace	Grand Parents Palace

Step 3: Identify the Dynamic Elemental Relationships

Bring the Luck Pillars into play now. Check each of the 10 Year Luck Pillars and highlight using a red pen, which Earthly Branches in the Luck Pillars have a relationship with the Earthly Branches in the BaZi.

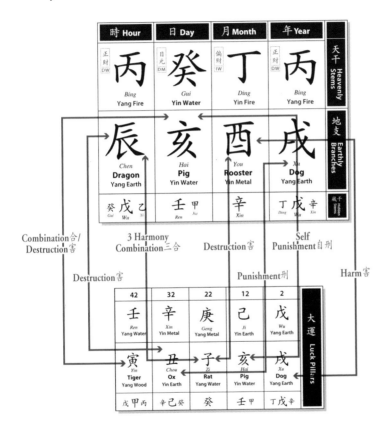

As we can see from this example, there is a Harm relationship between the Xu 戌 (Dog) and You 酉 (Rooster) during the first luck pillar aged 2-11. There is a Self-Punishment between the Hai 亥 (Pig) Luck Pillar aged 12 and Hai 亥 (Pig) in the Day Branch. In the Geng Zi 庚子 Luck Pillar, there is a Half Combination with the Chen 辰 (Dragon) and a Destruction with the You 酉 (Rooster).

In the Xin Chou 辛丑 Luck Pillar, there is half a Bullying Punishment with Chou 丑 (Ox) in the Luck Pillar and Xu 戌 (Dog) in the Year Branch and a Destruction between the Chou 丑 (Ox) and the Chen 辰 (Dragon) in the Hour Branch.

Step 4: Analyse the Dynamic Relationships via Palaces

Let's now decode the technical analysis by using the Palaces. In the Ji Hai 己亥 Luck Pillar, as the Self-Punishment involves the Day Branch, we can conclude that it involves the person's home or a person at home. If you add the layer of the Five Factors, you can see that involves the Companion element. This indicates that it has to do with a sibling or a relative.

The Geng Zi 庚子 Luck Pillar that creates a Destruction that involves the Month Branch. As this involves the Parent's Palace, we can say that the Destructive relationship is the result of either something happening to the parents or involving the person's superior, since the Parent's Palace also denotes boss or superior. Also, as it is the specific Zi-You 子酉 (Rat-Rooster) destruction, we can say this person has a tendency to drink or abuse alcohol, as a result of work pressure or problems at home.

八字解碼

Name: _____

Date of Birth: _____

Time of Birth: _____ Gender : Male / Female

時 Hour	日 Day	月 Month	年 Year	
				天干 Heavenly Stems
				地支 Earthly Branches
				藏干 Hidden Stems

								大運 Luck Pillars

The Day Master is:

Strong	
Weak	

My Day Master Favours :

Five Factors	Element	✓ : Favours ✗ : Does not favour
Resource		
Influence		
Wealth		
Companion		
Output		

八字
解
碼

The Four Aspects of Life - Tips for Analysing Career, Wealth, Relationships and Health

Most of the time, when people get stuck with analysing a Destiny Chart, it is because they're not focusing on what I call the Four Aspects: career, wealth, relationships and health. So when you are looking at a Destiny chart, having worked out all the technical issues, you are ready to examine the chart from these four aspects.

Career Analysis

Let's take career first. When will a person's career be in flight, and when will it be stagnant? For this, the Luck Pillars afford the best answer. If a person is going through favourable luck pillars, then it is usually a period of time when there is career advancement or growth and progress. By contrast, during unfavourable luck pillars, it is hard to make any advancement up the corporate ladder. You may climb, but find you slip back.

If you are very familiar with the Five Factors, you need to look at whether or not those luck pillars are supportive of the Output element, or go against it due to Clash, Destruction, Punishment or Harm. This is because the Output element governs what a person produces, their accomplishments, their achievements and their ability to perform on the job. If the Output element is affected in the Luck Pillars, then career is definitely going to be affected.

If the Influence element is favourable and the person goes through Influence Luck pillars, then this indicates a period of promotion, status and power. There will be opportunities for the person to leap up the ranks quickly and rapidly during this period.

Wealth Analysis

For Wealth Analysis, typically the question, at least for Asians is straightforward: *When will I get rich?*

The easiest way to look at this is to check when the person goes through Wealth Luck or the season of their wealth. So if you are a Geng 庚 Metal Day Master, and you go through Wood Luck in your Luck Pillars, then you are going through Wealth Luck and that is the time when things will improve financially and afford opportunities to make money. However, this is only if Wealth is a favourable element. Remember, if wealth is unfavourable, then going through wealth luck will make the person have money problems or this person will make money but it gets them into trouble.

If there is any kind of elemental relationship affecting the Wealth element in the chart - a Clash, Harm, Destruction or Punishment for example, then these are periods when wealth brings problems, or in an attempt to get rich, the person gets into trouble because of the means in which they are used to attempt to acquire wealth. A Clash, Harm, Destruction or Punishment that involves the Wealth element also denotes a loss of wealth during that time. Hence, those are periods to advise the person to remain conservative with money and to avoid risky endeavours or investments.

八字
解碼

Relationship Analysis

This is a little tricky because the spouse star differs for women and men. Again, the easiest way to determine when a person has luck with the opposite sex is to check the Luck Pillars. If the man is going through Wealth Luck, it's not just money he's making, but honeys he is attracting too! So a Gui 癸 Water male, going through Fire Luck in his Luck Pillars, is doing well financially and will probably find it easy to find a girlfriend or spouse during that period.

For a lady, you want to see the Influence element appearing on Stem or for the lady to go through Influence Luck Pillars or see the Influence Element in the Earthly Branches. So for example, a Jia 甲 Wood lady, going through Metal Luck, will find it easier to meet a Significant Other or prospective Spouse.

The caveat of course is whether or not the Spouse Palace is affected during those luck pillars, and whether or not the Influence element (in the case of a lady) or Wealth element (in the case of a man) is favourable or unfavourable. If the Spouse Palace is affected by clash, harm, destruction or punishment during the period of time favourable to a relationship, the person will get into a relationship but it may not work out or the relationship is just plain bad. If there is no elemental relationship between the luck pillar and the Spouse Palace but the Influence element or Wealth element is unfavourable, then the person meets someone but that person is either not up to expectation or the relationship is unfulfilling.

Health Analysis

In BaZi, health analysis looks to utilise the Five Elements, and favourable and unfavourable elements to determine the person's health weaknesses. A person's unfavourable element is usually the area that will create the most health issues. For example, if your unfavourable element is Fire, then Fire-related health issues such as heart attack, eye problems or acne or a boil.

🔥 **Fire**	Eyes/Heart
⛰️ **Earth**	Skin, flesh, muscles and malignancies of the cells
💧 **Water**	Kidneys, water retention, bloating, oedema
⚙️ **Metal**	Intestines, brain, lungs
🌲 **Wood**	Arteries and veins, limbs, liver

Sometimes, there is more than one negative element and so the health problem is a culmination of two elemental problems. For example, a person with Metal and Water as unfavourable elements, and going through Metal and Water in their Luck Pillars, may find they have pulmonary oedema.

The 10 Gods Code

In my next book, I will be showing you how to incorporate a decoding technique known as the 10 Gods 十神. Most of you would already know something about the 10 Gods, having read *The Destiny Code* and Chapter 9 of this book. It offers a more sophisticated approach to the Five Factors, by incorporating the principle of Yin and Yang into the Five Factors. We'll be going much deeper into this technique and opening a whole new layer of decoding of Destiny Charts. Terms like 7 Killings 七殺, Hurting Officer 傷官, Eating God 食神 and Indirect Resource 偏印 will become second nature to you, as you delve deeper into this technique and your ability to seek and decode out accurate and precise information from a Destiny Chart.

You might be wondering - am I saving the best for the last? In *The Destiny Code*, I talked about how BaZi is a bit like art appreciation. As you develop your skills, and you understand more about what you are looking at, so your ability to appreciate any Destiny Chart and its beauty grows.

The 10 Gods is also a basic technique, along with understanding the different types of elemental relationships. Metaphysics is a unique subject that is inherently basic at its highest level of application, and yet that is an understanding that only materialises when there is depth of knowledge, and appreciation of the application of the basic concepts and ideas at its highest levels. Post the 10 Gods, there are other techniques such as Structures, Special Structures, Auxiliary Stars, Formations and Useful God Principles, all which add more layers to the interpretation of a BaZi.

With each layer of techniques, with each new concept and idea I introduce to you, you will find your appreciation of a BaZi chart (the same one!) changes and grows. New perspectives and insights enter the picture, and your understanding of the person will deepen. So revisit the Destiny Charts that you looked at when you first explored this subject. Get a folder and collect all the Destiny Charts you've drawn up or printed using the online calculator. Keep referring to them as you study this fascinating subject. Go through your own Destiny Chart again. And read through the examples in this book once more. With each time, you will find new clarity, new thoughts and new understanding.

And that, is the challenge, and joy, of BaZi.

THE ULTIMATE BAZI COLLECTION

BaZi – The Destiny Code (Book 1)

This is an ideal introductory book on BaZi or Four Pillars of Destiny, written in an easy-to-read style with helpful illustrations. In this comprehensive book, delve deeper into BaZi beyond the conventional Chinese Astrology readings. Learn about the Ten Heavenly Stems, Twelve Earthly Branches, special relationships between the Five Elements, the technique of plotting a BaZi chart and simple, quick analysis techniques for deciphering your Destiny Code.

BaZi – The Destiny Code Revealed (Book 2)

Elevate the knowledge gained through **BaZi – The Destiny Code** with this comprehensive volume, taking a step further into BaZi chart interpretation through an understanding of the Key Elemental relationships that affect the Heavenly Stems and Earthly Branches.

The Ten Gods
An Introduction to The Ten Gods in BaZi

The Ten Gods are an integral and core component of the study of BaZi. This book presents a one-of-a-kind reference designed to provide a thorough and extensive introduction to the specific subject matter, the Ten Gods in BaZi. It has been written with the novice and intermediate students of BaZi in mind, bringing the necessary understanding for anyone seeking to master BaZi beyond the beginner level.

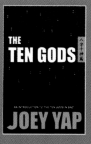

These titles are available at the Mastery Academy Online Store at
www.MasteryAcademy.com/eStore

COMING SOON

Book 3	Book 4	Book 5	Book 6

Complete your BaZi knowledge with **The Power of X** series (Books 3 to 6), a follow-up to **BaZi – The Destiny Code** and **BaZi – The Destiny Code Revealed**.

About Joey Yap

Joey Yap is the founder of the Mastery Academy of Chinese Metaphysics, a global organization devoted to the teaching of Feng Shui, BaZi, Mian Xiang and other Chinese Metaphysics subjects. He is also the Chief Consultant of Joey Yap Consulting Group, an international consulting firm specialising in Feng Shui and Chinese Astrology services and audits.

Joey Yap is the bestselling author of over 60 books on Feng Shui, Chinese Astrology, Face Reading and Yi Jing, many of which have topped the Malaysian and Singaporean MPH bookstores' bestseller lists.

Thousands of students from all around the world have learnt and mastered Classical Feng Shui, Chinese Astrology, and other Chinese Metaphysics subjects through Joey Yap's structured learning programs, books and online training. Joey Yap's courses are currently taught by over 30 instructors worldwide.

Every year Joey Yap conducts his 'Feng Shui and Astrology' seminar to a crowd of more than 3500 people at the Kuala Lumpur Convention Center. He also takes this annual seminar on a world tour to Frankfurt, San Francisco, New York, Toronto, London, Sydney and Singapore.

In addition to being a regular guest on various radio and TV shows, Joey Yap has also written columns for The New Straits Times and The Star - Malaysia's two leading newspapers. He has also been featured in many popular global publications and networks like Time International, Forbes International, the International Herald Tribune and Bloomberg.

He has also hosted his own TV series, 'Discover Feng Shui with Joey Yap', on 8TV, a local Malaysian network in 2005; and 'Walking The Dragons with Joey Yap' on Astro Wah Lai Toi, Malaysia's cable network in 2008.

Joey Yap has worked with HSBC, Bloomberg, Microsoft, Samsung, IBM, HP, Alliance, Great Eastern, Citibank, Standard Chartered, OCBC, SIME UEP, Mah Sing, Auto Bavaria, Volvo, AXA, Singtel, ABN Amro, CIMB, Hong-Leong, Manulife and others.

Author's personal website :**www.joeyyap.com**

Joey Yap on Facebook:

 www.facebook.com/JoeyYapFB

EDUCATION

The Mastery Academy of Chinese Metaphysics:
the first choice for practitioners and aspiring students of the art and science of Chinese Classical Feng Shui and Astrology.

For thousands of years, Eastern knowledge has been passed from one generation to another through the system of discipleship. A venerated master would accept suitable individuals at a young age as his disciples, and informally through the years, pass on his knowledge and skills to them. His disciples in turn, would take on their own disciples, as a means to perpetuate knowledge or skills.

This system served the purpose of restricting the transfer of knowledge to only worthy honourable individuals and ensuring that outsiders or Westerners would not have access to thousands of years of Eastern knowledge, learning and research.

However, the disciple system has also resulted in Chinese Metaphysics and Classical Studies lacking systematic teaching methods. Knowledge garnered over the years has not been accumulated in a concise, systematic manner, but scattered amongst practitioners, each practicing his/her knowledge, art and science, in isolation.

The disciple system, out of place in today's modern world, endangers the advancement of these classical fields that continue to have great relevance and application today.

At the Mastery Academy of Chinese Metaphysics, our Mission is to bring Eastern Classical knowledge in the fields of metaphysics, Feng Shui and Astrology sciences and the arts to the world. These Classical teachings and knowledge, previously shrouded in secrecy and passed on only through the discipleship system, are adapted into structured learning, which can easily be understood, learnt and mastered. Through modern learning methods, these renowned ancient arts, sciences and practices can be perpetuated while facilitating more extensive application and understanding of these classical subjects.

The Mastery Academy espouses an educational philosophy that draws from the best of the East and West. It is the world's premier educational institution for the study of Chinese Metaphysics Studies offering a wide range and variety of courses, ensuring that students have the opportunity to pursue their preferred field of study and enabling existing practitioners and professionals to gain cross-disciplinary knowledge that complements their current field of practice.

Courses at the Mastery Academy have been carefully designed to ensure a comprehensive yet compact syllabus. The modular nature of the courses enables students to immediately begin to put their knowledge into practice while pursuing continued study of their field and complementary fields. Students thus have the benefit of developing and gaining practical experience in tandem with the expansion and advancement of their theoretical knowledge.

Students can also choose from a variety of study options, from a distance learning program, the Homestudy Series, that enables study at one's own pace or intensive foundation courses and compact lecture-based courses, held in various cities around the world by Joey Yap or our licensed instructors. The Mastery Academy's faculty and make-up is international in nature, thus ensuring that prospective students can attend courses at destinations nearest to their country of origin or with a licensed Mastery Academy instructor in their home country.

The Mastery Academy provides 24x7 support to students through its Online Community, with a variety of tools, documents, forums and e-learning materials to help students stay at the forefront of research in their fields and gain invaluable assistance from peers and mentoring from their instructors.

TM

MASTERY ACADEMY
OF CHINESE METAPHYSICS

www.masteryacademy.com

MALAYSIA
19-3, The Boulevard
Mid Valley City
59200 Kuala Lumpur, Malaysia
Tel : +603-2284 8080
Fax : +603-2284 1218
Email : info@masteryacademy.com

Australia, Austria, Canada, China, Croatia, Cyprus, Czech Republic, Denmark, France, Germany, Greece, Hungary, India, Italy, Kazakhstan, Malaysia, Netherlands (Holland), New Zealand, Philippines, Poland, Russian Federation, Singapore, Slovenia, South Africa, Switzerland, Turkey, U.S.A., Ukraine, United Kingdom

JOEY YAP'S
BAZI PROFILING SYSTE~

Unleashing personal potential to achieve peak performa

The Path of Least Resistance to Success

Joey Yap's BaZi Profiling System is designed to help you make the most out o~ protential and other people that matter to you. Using the proven BaZi (Chinese Astr~ system, Joey has simplified the process to analyze your character based on your Date an~ of Birth, at three different levels. These levels function collectively as a means of pro~ categorical descriptions of your inborn personality traits, temperaments, behavioral pa~ suitable roles in life and your Path of Least Resistance to Success!

The fast and easy way to reveal the insights to your personality and career!

• Identify your areas of strength and possible areas of weakness in career and life

• Understand your own preference for personal development , career choices and organization effectiveness

• Capitalise on your natural tendency and strengths and use them to aid your career and your to Success.

• View problems and challenges that come up at work as potential opportunities for greater su~

• Transform your business to achieve peak business performance by developing leaders and eff~ organization

www.baziprofiling.com

Introducing...
The Mastery Academy's E-Learning Center!

The Mastery Academy's goal has always been to share authentic knowledge of Chinese Metaphysics with the whole world.

Nevertheless, we do recognize that distance, time, and hotel and traveling costs – amongst many other factors – could actually hinder people from enrolling for a classroom-based course. But with the advent and amazing advance of IT today, NOT any more!

With this in mind, we have invested heavily in IT, to conceive what is probably the first and only E-Learning Center in the world today that offers a full range of studies in the field of Chinese Metaphysics.

| Convenient | Study from Your Own Home | Easy Enrollment |

The Mastery Academy's E-Learning Center

Now, armed with your trusty computer or laptop, and Internet access, knowledge of classical Feng Shui, BaZi (Destiny Analysis) and Mian Xiang (Face Reading) are but a literal click away!

Study at your own pace, and interact with your Instructor and fellow students worldwide, from anywhere in the world. With our E-Learning Center, knowledge of Chinese Metaphysics is brought DIRECTLY to you in all its clarity – topic-by-topic, and lesson-by-lesson; with illustrated presentations and comprehensive notes expediting your learning curve!

Your education journey through our E-Learning Center may be done via any of the following approaches:

1. Online Courses

There are 3 Programs available: our Online Feng Shui Program, Online BaZi Program, and Online Mian Xiang Program. Each Program consists of several Levels, with each Level consisting of many Lessons in turn. Each Lesson contains a pre-recorded video session on the topic at hand, accompanied by presentation-slides and graphics as well as downloadable tutorial notes that you can print and file for future reference.

Video Lecture

Presentation
Slide

Downloadable
Notes

2. MA Live!

MA Live!, as its name implies, enables LIVE broadcasts of Joey Yap's courses and seminars – right to your computer screen. Students will not only get to see and hear Joey talk on real-time 'live', but also participate and more importantly, TALK to Joey via the MA Live! interface. All the benefits of a live class, minus the hassle of actually having to attend one!

How It Works

1.

Our Live Classes

2.

You at Home

3. Video-On-Demand (VOD)

Get immediate streaming-downloads of the Mastery Academy's wide range of educational DVDs, right on your computer screen. No more shipping costs and waiting time to be incurred!

**Instant VOD
Online**

1.

Choose From Our list
of Available VODs!

2.

Click "Play" on Your PC

Welcome to **www.maelearning.com**; the web portal of our E-Learning Center, and YOUR virtual gateway to Chinese Metaphysics!

Mastery Academy around the world

- Canada
- United States
- Denmark
- United Kingdom
- Czech Republic
- Austria
- Switzerland
- Poland
- Netherlands
- Germany
- France
- Italy
- Slovenia
- Hungary
- Croatia
- Cyprus
- Greece
- Russian Federation
- Ukraine
- Turkey
- Kazakhstan
- India
- China
- Philippines
- Kuala Lumpur
- Malaysia
- Singapore
- Australia
- New Zealand
- South Africa

JOEY YAP CONSULTING GROUP

Joey Yap & Joey Yap Consulting Group

Headed by Joey Yap, Joey Yap Consulting Group (JYCG) is a leading international consulting firm specializing in Feng Shui, Mian Xiang (Face Reading) and BaZi (Destiny Analysis) consulting services worldwide. Joey Yap - an internationally renowned Master Trainer, Consultant, Speaker and best-selling Author - has dedicated his life to the art and science of Chinese Metaphysics.

JYCG has its main office in Kuala Lumpur, and draws upon its diverse reservoir of strength from a group of dedicated and experienced consultants based in more than 30 countries, worldwide.

As the pioneer in blending established, classical Chinese Metaphysics techniques with the latest approach in consultation practices, JYCG has built its reputation on the principles of professionalism and only the highest standards of service. This allows us to retain the cutting edge in delivering Feng Shui and Destiny consultation services to both corporate and personal clients, in a simple and direct manner, without compromising on quality.

Across Industries: Our Portfolio of Clients

Our diverse portfolio of both corporate and individual clients from all around the world bears testimony to our experience and capabilities.

Virtually every industry imaginable has benefited from our services - ranging from academic and financial institutions, real-estate developers and multinational corporations, to those in the leisure and tourism industry. Our services are also engaged by professionals, prominent business personalities, celebrities, high-profile politicians and people from all walks of life.

JOEY YAP CONSULTING GROUP

Name (Mr./Mrs./Ms.):_____

Contact Details

Tel:_____ Fax:_____

Mobile :_____

E-mail:_____

What Type of Consultation Are You Interested In?
☐ Feng Shui   ☐ BaZi   ☐ Date Selection   ☐ Yi Jing

Please tick if applicable:
☐ Are you a Property Developer looking to engage Joey Yap Consulting Group?

☐ Are you a Property Investor looking for tailor-made packages to suit your investment requirements?

Please attach your
name card here.

Thank you for completing this form. Please fax it back to us at:

Malaysia & the rest of the world
Fax : +603-2284 2213   Tel : +603-2284 1213

Feng Shui Consultations

For Residential Properties
- Initial Land/Property Assessment
- Residential Feng Shui Consultations
- Residential Land Selection
- End-to-End Residential Consultation

For Commercial Properties
- Initial Land/Property Assessment
- Commercial Feng Shui Consultations
- Commercial Land Selection
- End-to-End Commercial Consultation

For Property Developers
- End-to-End Consultation
- Post-Consultation Advisory Services
- Panel Feng Shui Consultant

For Property Investors
- Your Personal Feng Shui Consultant
- Tailor-Made Packages

For Memorial Parks & Burial Sites
- Yin House Feng Shui

BaZi Consultations

Personal Destiny Analysis
- Personal Destiny Analysis for Individuals
- Children's BaZi Analysis
- Family BaZi Analysis

Strategic Analysis for Corporate Organizations
- Corporate BaZi Consultations
- BaZi Analysis for Human Resource Management

Entrepreneurs & Business Owners
- BaZi Analysis for Entrepreneurs

Career Pursuits
- BaZi Career Analysis

Relationships
- Marriage and Compatibility Analysis
- Partnership Analysis

For Everyone
- Annual BaZi Forecast
- Your Personal BaZi Coach

Date Selection Consultations

- **Marriage Date Selection**
- **Caesarean Birth Date Selection**
- **House-Moving Date Selection**
- **Renovation & Groundbreaking Dates**

- **Signing of Contracts**
- **Official Openings**
- **Product Launches**

Yi Jing Assessment

A Time-Tested, Accurate Science

• With a history predating 4 millennia, the Yi Jing - or Classic of Change - is one of the oldest Chinese texts surviving today. Its purpose as an oracle, in predicting the outcome of things, is based on the variables of Time, Space and Specific Events.

• A Yi Jing Assessment provides specific answers to any specific questions you may have about a specific event or endeavor. This is something that a Destiny Analysis would not be able to give you.

Basically, what a Yi Jing Assessment does is focus on only ONE aspect or item at a particular point in your life, and give you a calculated prediction of the details that will follow suit, if you undertake a particular action. It gives you an insight into a situation, and what course of action to take in order to arrive at a satisfactory outcome at the end of the day.

Please Contact JYCG for a personalized Yi Jing Assessment!

INVITING US TO YOUR CORPORATE EVENTS

Many reputable organizations and institutions have worked closely with JYCG to build a synergistic business relationship by engaging our team of consultants, led by Joey Yap, as speakers at their corporate events. Our seminars and short talks are always packed with audiences consisting of clients and associates of multinational and public-listed companies as well as key stakeholders of financial institutions.

We tailor our seminars and talks to suit the anticipated or pertinent group of audience. Be it a department, subsidiary, your clients or even the entire corporation, we aim to fit your requirements in delivering the intended message(s).

CHINESE METAPHYSICS REFERENCE SERIES

The Chinese Metaphysics Reference Series is a collection of reference texts, source material, and educational textbooks to be used as supplementary guides by scholars, students, researchers, teachers and practitioners of Chinese Metaphysics.

These comprehensive and structured books provide fast, easy reference to aid in the study and practice of various Chinese Metaphysics subjects including Feng Shui, BaZi, Yi Jing, Zi Wei, Liu Ren, Ze Ri, Ta Yi, Qi Men and Mian Xiang.

The Chinese Metaphysics Compendium

At over 1,000 pages, the *Chinese Metaphysics Compendium* is a unique one-volume reference book that compiles all the formulas relating to Feng Shui, BaZi (Four Pillars of Destiny), Zi Wei (Purple Star Astrology), Yi Jing (I-Ching), Qi Men (Mystical Doorways), Ze Ri (Date Selection), Mian Xiang (Face Reading) and other sources of Chinese Metaphysics.

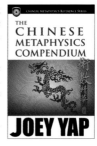

It is presented in the form of easy-to-read tables, diagrams and reference charts, all of which are compiled into one handy book. This first-of-its-kind compendium is presented in both English and the original Chinese, so that none of the meanings and contexts of the technical terminologies are lost.

The only essential and comprehensive reference on Chinese Metaphysics, and an absolute must-have for all students, scholars, and practitioners of Chinese Metaphysics.

The Ten Thousand Year Calendar (Pocket Edition) | The Ten Thousand Year Calendar | Dong Gong Date Selection | The Date Selection Compendium | Plum Blossoms Divination Reference Book | San Yuan Dragon Gate Eight Formations Water Method | Xuan Kong Da Gua Ten Thousand Year Calendar

Bazi Hour Pillar Useful Gods - Wood | Bazi Hour Pillar Useful Gods - Fire | Bazi Hour Pillar Useful Gods - Earth | Bazi Hour Pillar Useful Gods - Metal | Bazi Hour Pillar Useful Gods - Water | Xuan Kong Da Gua Structures Reference Book | Xuan Kong Da Gua 64 Gua Transformation Analysis

Bazi Structures and Structural Useful Gods - Wood | Bazi Structures and Structural Useful Gods - Fire | Bazi Structures and Structural Useful Gods - Earth | Bazi Structures and Structural Useful Gods - Metal | Bazi Structures and Structural Useful Gods - Water | Xuan Kong Purple White Script | Earth Study Discern Truth Second Edition

+603 - 2284 8080

Educational Tools & Software

Xuan Kong Flying Stars Feng Shui Software
The Essential Application for Enthusiasts and Professionals

The Xuan Kong Flying Stars Feng Shui Software is a brand-new application by Joey Yap that will assist you in the practice of Xuan Kong Feng Shui with minimum fuss and maximum effectiveness. Superimpose the Flying Stars charts over your house plans (or those of your clients) to clearly demarcate the 9 Palaces. Use it to help you create fast and sophisticated chart drawings and presentations, as well as to assist professional practitioners in the report-writing process before presenting the final reports for your clients. Students can use it to practice their Xuan Kong Feng Shui skills and knowledge, and it can even be used by designers and architects!

Some of the highlights of the software include:
- Natal Flying Stars
- Monthly Flying Stars
- 81 Flying Stars Combinations
- Dual-View Format
- Annual Flying Stars
- Flying Stars Integration
- 24 Mountains

All charts will be are printable and configurable, and can be saved for future editing. Also, you'll be able to export your charts into most image file formats like jpeg, bmp, and gif.

The Xuan Kong Flying Stars Feng Shui Software can make your Feng Shui practice simpler and more effective, garnering you amazing results with less effort!

Mini Feng Shui Compass

This Mini Feng Shui Compass with the accompanying Companion Booklet written by leading Feng Shui and Chinese Astrology Master Trainer Joey Yap is a must-have for any Feng Shui enthusiast.

The Mini Feng Shui Compass is a self-aligning compass that is not only light at 100gms but also built sturdily to ensure it will be convenient to use anywhere. The rings on the Mini Feng Shui Compass are bi-lingual and incorporate the 24 Mountain Rings that is used in your traditional Luo Pan.

The comprehensive booklet included will guide you in applying the 24 Mountain Directions on your Mini Feng Shui Compass effectively and the 8 Mansions Feng Shui to locate the most auspicious locations within your home, office and surroundings. You can also use the Mini Feng Shui Compass when measuring the direction of your property for the purpose of applying Flying Stars Feng Shui.

Educational Tools & Software

BaZi Ming Pan Software Version 2.0
Professional Four Pillars Calculator for Destiny Analysis

The BaZi Ming Pan Version 2.0 Professional Four Pillars Calculator for Destiny Analysis is the most technically advanced software of its kind in the world today. It allows even those without any knowledge of BaZi to generate their own BaZi Charts, and provides virtually every detail required to undertake a comprehensive Destiny Analysis.

This Professional Four Pillars Calculator allows you to even undertake a day-to-day analysis of your Destiny. What's more, all BaZi Charts generated by this software are fully printable and configurable! Designed for both enthusiasts and professional practitioners, this state-of-the-art software blends details with simplicity, and is capable of generating 4 different types of BaZi charts: **BaZi Professional Charts, BaZi Annual Analysis Charts, BaZi Pillar Analysis Charts and BaZi Family Relationship Charts.**

Additional references, configurable to cater to all levels of BaZi knowledge and usage, include:
• Dual Age & Bilingual Option (Western & Chinese) • Na Yin narrations • 12 Life Stages evaluation • Death & Emptiness • Gods & Killings • Special Days • Heavenly Virtue Nobles

This software also comes with a Client Management feature that allows you to save and trace clients' records instantly, navigate effortlessly between BaZi charts, and file your clients' information in an organized manner.

The BaZi Ming Pan Version 2.0 Calculator sets a new standard by combining the best of BaZi and technology.

Joey Yap Feng Shui Template Set

Directions are the cornerstone of any successful Feng Shui audit or application. The **Joey Yap Feng Shui Template Set** is a set of three templates to simplify the process of taking directions and determining locations and positions, whether it's for a building, a house, or an open area such as a plot of land, all with just a floor plan or area map.

The Set comprises 3 basic templates: The Basic Feng Shui Template, 8 Mansions Feng Shui Template, and the Flying Stars Feng Shui Template.

With bi-lingual notations for these directions; both in English and the original Chinese, the **Joey Yap Feng Shui Template Set** comes with its own Booklet that gives simple yet detailed instructions on how to make use of the 3 templates within.

• Easy-to-use, simple, and straightforward
• Small and portable; each template measuring only 5" x 5"
• Additional 8 Mansions and Flying Stars Reference Rings
• Handy companion booklet with usage tips and examples

Accelerate Your Face Reading Skills With Joey Yap's Face Reading Revealed DVD Series

Mian Xiang, the Chinese art of Face Reading, is an ancient form of physiognomy and entails the use of the face and facial characteristics to evaluate key aspects of a person's life, luck and destiny. In his Face Reading DVDs series, Joey Yap shows you how the facial features reveal a wealth of information about a person's luck, destiny and personality.

Mian Xiang also tell us the talents, quirks and personality of an individual. Do you know that just by looking at a person's face, you can ascertain his or her health, wealth, relationships and career? Let Joey Yap show you how the 12 Palaces can be utilised to reveal a person's inner talents, characteristics and much more.

Each facial feature on the face represents one year in a person's life. Your face is a 100-year map of your life and each position reveals your fortune and destiny at a particular age as well as insights and information about your personality, skills, abilities and destiny.

Using Mian Xiang, you will also be able to plan your life ahead by identifying, for example, the right business partner and knowing the sort of person that you need to avoid. By knowing their characteristics through the facial features, you will be able to gauge their intentions and gain an upper hand in negotiations.

Do you know what moles signify? Do they bring good or bad luck? Do you want to build better relationships with your partner or family members or have your ever wondered why you seem to be always bogged down by trivial problems in your life?

In these highly entertaining DVDs, Joey will help you answer all these questions and more. You will be able to ascertain the underlying meaning of moles, birthmarks or even the type of your hair in Face Reading. Joey will also reveal the guidelines to help you foster better and stronger relationships with your loved ones through Mian Xiang.

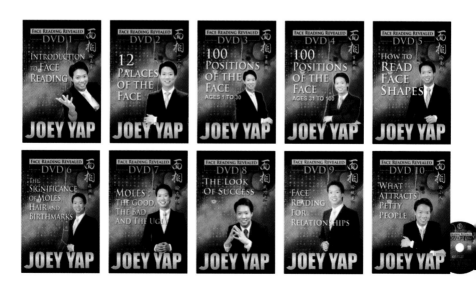

Feng Shui for Homebuyers DVD Series

Best-selling Author, and international Master Trainer and Consultant Joey Yap reveals in these DVDs the significant Feng Shui features that every homebuyer should know when evaluating a property.

Joey will guide you on how to customise your home to maximise the Feng Shui potential of your property and gain the full benefit of improving your health, wealth and love life using the 9 Palace Grid. He will show you how to go about applying the classical applications of the Life Gua and House Gua techniques to get attuned to your Sheng Qi (positive energies).

In these DVDs, you will also learn how to identify properties with good Feng Shui features that will help you promote a fulfilling life and achieve your full potential. Discover how to avoid properties with negative Feng Shui that can bring about detrimental effects to your health, wealth and relationships.

Joey will also elaborate on how to fix the various aspects of your home that may have an impact on the Feng Shui of your property and give pointers on how to tap into the positive energies to support your goals.

Discover Feng Shui with Joey Yap (TV Series)

Discover Feng Shui with Joey Yap: Set of 4 DVDs

Informative and entertaining, classical Feng Shui comes alive in *Discover Feng Shui with Joey Yap!*

Dying to know how you can use Feng Shui to improve your house or office, but simply too busy attend for formal classes?

You have the questions. Now let Joey personally answer them in this 4-set DVD compilation! Learn how to ensure the viability of your residence or workplace, Feng Shui-wise, without having to convert it into a Chinese antiques' shop. Classical Feng Shui is about harnessing the natural power of your environment to improve quality of life. It's a systematic and subtle metaphysical science.

And that's not all. Joey also debunks many a myth about classical Feng Shui, and shares with viewers Face Reading tips as well!

Own the series that national channel 8TV did a re-run of in 2005, today!

Continue Your Journey with Joey Yap's Books

Mian Xiang - Discover Face Reading (English & Chinese versions)

Need to identify a suitable business partner? How about understanding your staff or superiors better? Or even choosing a suitable spouse? These mind boggling questions can be answered in Joey Yap's introductory book to Face Reading titled *Mian Xiang – Discover Face Reading*. This book will help you discover the hidden secrets in a person's face.

Mian Xiang – Discover Face Reading is comprehensive book on all areas of Face Reading, covering some of the most important facial features, including the forehead, mouth, ears and even the philtrum above your lips. This book will help you analyse not just your Destiny but help you achieve your full potential and achieve life fulfillment.

Joey Yap's Art of Face Reading

The Art of Face Reading is Joey Yap's second effort with CICO Books, and takes a lighter, more practical approach to Face Reading. This book does not so much focus on the individual features as it does on reading the entire face. It is about identifying common personality types and characters.

Joey shows readers how to identify successful career faces, or faces that are most likely to be able to do well financially. He also explores Face Reading in the context of health. He uses examples of real people - famous and ordinary folk - to allow readers to better understand what these facial features look like on an actual face. Readers will learn how to identify faces in Career, Wealth, Relationships, and Health (eg. 'The Salesperson Face,' 'The Politician Face,' 'The Unfaithful One,' 'The Shopaholic One,' and plenty more.)

Easy Guide on Face Reading (English & Chinese versions)

The Face Reading Essentials series of books comprise 5 individual books on the key features of the Eyes, Eyebrows, Ears, Nose, and Mouth. Each book provides a detailed illustration and a simple yet descr explanation on the individual types of the features.

The books are equally useful and effective for beginners, enthusiasts, and the curious. The series is desig enable people who are new to Face Reading to make the most of first impressions and learn to apply Face R skills to understand the personality and character of friends, family, co-workers, and even business associa

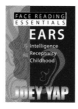
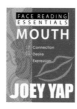

Continue Your Journey with Joey Yap's Books

hree Levels of BaZi Profiling (English & Chinese versions)

1 BaZi Profiling, there are three levels that reflect three different stages of a person's personal ature and character structure.

Level 1 – The Day Master

The Day Master in a nutshell is the BASIC YOU. The inborn personality. It is your essential character. It answers the basic question "WHO AM I". There are ten basic personality profiles – the TEN Day Masters – each with its unique set of personality traits, likes and dislikes.

Level 2 – The Structure

The Structure is your behavior and attitude – in other words, how you use your personality. It expands on the Day Master (Level 1). The structure reveals your natural tendencies in life – are you more controlling, more of a creator, supporter, thinker or connector? Each of the Ten Day Masters express themselves differently through the FIVE Structures. Why do we do the things we do? Why do we like the things we like? – The answers are in our BaZi STRUCTURE.

Level 3 – The Profile

The Profile reveals your unique abilities and skills, the masks that you consciously and unconsciously "put on" as you approach and navigate the world. Your Profile speaks of your ROLES in life. There are TEN roles – or Ten BaZi Profiles. Everyone plays a different role.

What makes you happy and what does success mean to you is different to somebody else. Your sense of achievement and sense of purpose in life is unique to your Profile. Your Profile will reveal your unique style.

The path of least resistance to your success and wealth can only be accessed once you get into your "flow." Your BaZi Profile reveals how you can get FLOW. It will show you your patterns in work, relationship and social settings. Being AWARE of these patterns is your first step to positive Life Transformation.

Continue Your Journey with Joey Yap's Books

Walking the Dragons

Walking the Dragons is a guided tour through the classical landform Feng Shui of ancient China, an enchanting collection of deeply-researched yet entertaining essays rich in historical detail.

Compiled in one book for the first time from Joey Yap's Feng Shui Mastery Excursion Series, the book highlights China's extensive, vibrant history with astute observations on the Feng Shui of important sites and places. Learn the landform formations of Yin Houses (tombs and burial places), as well as mountains, temples, castles, and villages.

It demonstrates complex Feng Shui theories and principles in easy-to-understand, entertaining language and is the perfect addition to the bookshelf of a Feng Shui or history lover. Anyone, whether experienced in Feng Shui or new to the practice, will be able to enjoy the insights shared in this book. Complete with gorgeous full-colour pictures of all the amazing sights and scenery, it's the next best thing to having been there yourself!

Your Aquarium Here

Your Aquarium Here is a simple, practical, hands-on Feng Shui book that teaches you how to incorporate a Water feature – an aquarium – for optimal Feng Shui benefit, whether for personal relationships, wealth, or career. Designed to be comprehensive yet simple enough for a novice or beginner, *Your Aquarium Here* provides historical and factual information about the role of Water in Feng Shui, and provides a step-by-step guide to installing and using an aquarium.

The book is the first in the **Fengshuilogy Series**, a series of matter-of-fact and useful Feng Shui books designed for the person who wants to do fuss-free Feng Shui. Not everyone who wants to use Feng Shui is an expert or a scholar! This series of books are just the kind you'd want on your bookshelf to gain basic, practical knowledge of the subject. Go ahead and Feng Shui-It-Yourself – *Your Aquarium Here* eliminates all the fuss and bother, but maintains all the fun and excitement, of authentic Feng Shui application!

The Art of Date Selection: Personal Date Selection

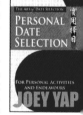

In today's modern world, it is not good enough to just do things effectively – we need to do them efficiently, as well. From the signing of business contracts and moving into a new home, to launching a product or even tying the knot; everything has to move, and move very quickly too. There is a premium on Time, where mistakes can indeed be costly.

The notion of doing the Right Thing, at the Right Time and in the Right Place is the very backbone of Date Selection. Because by selecting a suitable date specially tailored to a specific activity or endeavor, we infuse it with the most positive energies prevalent in our environment during that particular point in time; and that could well make the difference between `make-and-break'! With the *Art of Date Selection: Personal Date Selection*, learn simple, practical methods you can employ to select not just good dates, but personalized good dates. Whether it's a personal activity such as a marriage or professional endeavor such as launching a business, signing a contract or even acquiring assets, this book will show you how to pick the good dates and tailor them to suit the activity in question, as well as avoid the negative ones too!

Pure Feng Shui

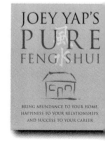

Pure Feng Shui is Joey Yap's debut with an international publisher, CICO Books, and is a refreshing and elegant look at the intricacies of Classical Feng Shui – now compiled in a useful manner for modern-day readers. This book is a comprehensive introduction to all the important precepts and techniques of Feng Shui practice.

He reveals how to use Feng Shui to bring prosperity, good relationships, and success into one's life the simple and genuine way – without having to resort to symbols or figurines! He shows readers how to work with what they have and make simple and sustainable changes that can have significant Feng Shui effect. The principles of Classical Feng Shui and Chinese Astrology inform his teachings and explanations, so all that the readers need are a compass, a pencil, some paper, and an open mind!

Continue Your Journey with Joey Yap's Books

eng Shui For Homebuyers - Exterior (English & Chinese versions)

:st selling Author and international Feng Shui Consultant, Joey Yap, will ide you on the various important features in your external environment that ve a bearing on the Feng Shui of your home. For homeowners, those looking build their own home or even investors who are looking to apply Feng Shui their homes, this book provides valuable information from the classical Feng ui theories and applications.

is book will assist you in screening and eliminating unsuitable options with gative FSQ (Feng Shui Quotient) should you acquire your own land or if u are purchasing a newly built home. It will also help you in determining iich plot of land to select and which to avoid when purchasing an empty rcel of land.

eng Shui for Homebuyers - Interior (English & hinese versions)

book every homeowner or potential house buyer should have. The Feng Shui r Homebuyers (Interior) is an informative reference book and invaluable ide written by best selling Author and international Feng Shui Consultant, ey Yap.

is book provides answers to the important questions of what really does atter when looking at the internal Feng Shui of a home or office. It teaches u how to analyze your home or office floor plans and how to improve their ng Shui. It will answer all your questions about the positive and negative flow Qi within your home and ways to utilize them to your maximum benefit.

oviding you with a guide to calculating your Life Gua and House Gua to fine-ne your Feng Shui within your property, Joey Yap focuses on practical, easily plicable ideas on what you can implement internally in a property.

eng Shui for Apartment Buyers - Home Owners

nding a good apartment or condominium is never an easy task but who do you ensure that also has good Feng Shui? And how exactly do you apply Feng Shui to an apartment or ndominium or high-rise residence?

ese questions and more are answered by renowned Feng Shui Consultant and Master ainer Joey Yap in **Feng Shui for Apartment Buyers - Home Owners**. Joey answers the y questions about Feng Shui and apartments, then guides you through the bare basics like king a direction and super-imposing a Flying Stars chart onto a floor plan. Joey also walks u through the process of finding an apartment with favorable Feng Shui, sharing with u some of the key methods and techniques that are employed by professional Feng Shui nsultants in assesing apartment Feng Shui.

his trademark straight-to-the-point manner, Joey shares with you the Feng Shui do's d dont's when it comes to finding an apartment with favorable Feng Shui and which is nducive for home living.

Continue Your Journey with Joey Yap's Books

Stories and Lessons on Feng Shui (English & Chinese versions)

Stories and Lessons on Feng Shui is a compilation of essays and stories written by leading Feng Shui and Chinese Astrology trainer and consultant Joey Yap about Feng Shui and Chinese Astrology.

In this heart-warming collection of easy to read stories, find out why it's a myth that you should never have Water on the right hand side of your house, the truth behind the infamous 'love' and 'wealth' corners and that the sudden death of a pet fish is really NOT due to bad luck!

More Stories and Lessons on Feng Shui

Finally, the long-awaited sequel to *Stories & Lessons on Feng Shui*!

If you've read the best-selling Stories & Lessons on Feng Shui, you won't want to miss this book. And even if you haven't read *Stories & Lessons on Feng Shui*, there's always a time to rev your Feng Shui engine up.

The time is NOW.

And the book? *More Stories & Lessons on Feng Shui* – the 2nd compilation of the most popular articles and columns penned by Joey Yap; **specially featured in national and international publications, magazines and newspapers.**

All in all, *More Stories & Lessons on Feng Shui* is a delightful chronicle of Joey's articles, thoughts and vast experience - as a professional Feng Shui consultant and instructor - that have been purposely refined, edited and expanded upon to make for a light-hearted, interesting yet educational read. And with Feng Shui, BaZi, Mian Xiang and Yi Jing all thrown into this one dish, there's something for everyone…so all you need to serve or accompany *More Stories & Lessons on Feng Shui* with is your favorite cup of tea or coffee!

Even More Stories and Lessons on Feng Shui

In this third release in the Stories and Lessons series, Joey Yap continues his exploration on the study and practice of Feng Shui in the modern age through a series of essays and personal anecdotes. Debunking superstition, offering simple and understandable "Feng Shui-It-Yourself" tips, and expounding on the history and origins of classical Feng Shui, Joey takes readers on a journey that is always refreshing and exciting.

Besides 'behind-the-scenes' revelations of actual Feng Shui audits, there are also chapters on how beginners can easily and accurately incorporate Feng Shui practice into their lives, as well as travel articles that offer proof that when it comes to Feng Shui, the Qi literally knows no boundaries.

In his trademark lucid and forthright style, Joey covers themes and topics that will strike a chord with all readers who have an interest in Feng Shui.

Xuan Kong: Flying Stars Feng Shui

Xuan Kong Flying Stars Feng Shui is an essential introductory book to the subject of Xuan Kong Fei Xing, a well-known and popular system of Feng Shui, written by International Feng Shui Master Trainer Joey Yap.

In his down-to-earth, entertaining and easy to read style, Joey Yap takes you through the essential basics of Classical Feng Shui, and the key concepts of Xuan Kong Fei Xing (Flying Stars). Learn how to fly the stars, plot a Flying Star chart for your home or office and interpret the stars and star combinations. Find out how to utilise the favourable areas of your home or office for maximum benefit and learn 'tricks of the trade' and 'trade secrets' used by Feng Shui practitioners to enhance and maximise Qi in your home or office.

An essential integral introduction to the subject of Classical Feng Shui and the Flying Stars System of Feng Shui!

Continue Your Journey with Joey Yap's Books

Zi - The Destiny Code (English & Chinese versions)

...ding Chinese Astrology Master Trainer Joey Yap makes it easy to learn how to ...ck your Destiny through your BaZi with this book. BaZi or Four Pillars of ...tiny is an ancient Chinese science which enables individuals to understand ...r personality, hidden talents and abilities as well as their luck cycle, simply ...xamining the information contained within their birth data. The Destiny ... is the first book that shows readers how to plot and interpret their own ...tiny Charts and lays the foundation for more in-depth BaZi studies. Written ... lively entertaining style, the Destiny Code makes BaZi accessible to the ...erson. Within 10 chapters, understand and appreciate more about this ...undingly accurate ancient Chinese Metaphysical science.

Zi - The Destiny Code Revealed (English & Chinese versions)

...this follow up to Joey Yap's best-selling The Destiny Code, delve deeper ... your own Destiny chart through an understanding of the key elemental ...tionships that affect the Heavenly Stems and Earthly Branches. Find out ... Combinations, Clash, Harm, Destructions and Punishments bring new ...ension to a BaZi chart. Complemented by extensive real-life examples, The ...tiny Code Revealed takes you to the next level of BaZi, showing you how to ...ck the Codes of Destiny and to take decisive action at the right time, and ...talise on the opportunities in life.

...e Ten Gods
Introduction to The Ten Gods in BaZi

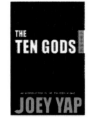

... Ten Gods, being an integral and core component of the study of BaZi (Chinese Astrology), ...the key to Decoding the Destiny Code. Anyone who wishes to make use of BaZi must have ...rong foundation in the Ten Gods.

... Ten Gods represent every conceivable aspect, object and item in life, both the tangible and ... intangible. As such, a person's life, in every sense of the word, is ultimately defined by the Ten ...ds present (and absent) in a BaZi chart.

...owing how to identify the Ten Gods of each of the Ten Day Masters, and understanding the basic fundamentals of ... of the Ten Gods is a breakthrough step in analyzing and accurately deriving information about a person, be it their ...racter, or their destiny, from their BaZi chart.

...s book presents a one-of-a-kind reference designed to provide a thorough introduction to the specific subject matter, ...Ten Gods in BaZi.

...rovides readers with a 360-degree perspective - a well-rounded standpoint - on the subject, covering the discussion ...ut each of the Ten Gods written to include both the traditional, orthodox and conventional perspective, and ... modern, less traditional perspective, along with the pros and cons of each of the Ten Gods attributes. It also ...nonstrates simple but useful methods of analyzing a BaZi chart using the Ten Gods.

Annual Releases

Chinese Astrology for 2011

This information-packed annual guide to the Chinese Astrology for 2011 goes way beyond the conventional 'animal horoscope' book. To begin with, author Joey Yap includes a personalized outlook for 2011 based on the individual's BaZi Day Pillar (Jia Zi) and a 12-month micro-analysis for each of the 60 Day Pillars – in addition to the annual outlook for all 12 animal signs and the 12-month outlook for each animal sign in 2011. Find out what awaits you in 2011 from the four key aspects of Health, Wealth, Career and Relationships…with Joey Yap's **Chinese Astrology for 2011**!

Feng Shui for 2011

Maximize the Qi of the Year of the Metal Tiger for your home and office, with Joey Yap's **Feng Shui for 2011** book. Learn how to tap into the positive sectors of the year, and avoid the negative ones and those with the Annual Afflictions, as well as ascertain how the annual Flying Stars affect your property by comparing them against the Eight Mansions (Ba Zhai) for 2011. Flying Stars enthusiasts will also find this book handy, as it includes the monthly Flying Stars charts for the year, accompanied by detailed commentaries on what sectors to use and avoid – to enable you to optimize your Academic, Relationships and Wealth Luck in 2011.

Pro Tong Shu Diary 2011

An ideal Tong Shu tool for professionals and experienced Feng Shui practitioners, the Professional Edition is designed to fulfill the requirements of those who need to perform Date Selection on a regular or specialised basis. This handy edition eliminates the need to search through many references when all the required information to select a good date is contained within this volume.

The Professional Edition comes in an elegant cover - a must-have whether you're a practitioner, student or simply a keen enthusiast.

Tong Shu Diary 2011

Enhance and organize your career and personal paths with Tong Shu Diary 2011. It will serve as your professional organizer, with a twist: You will hold the higher ground in determining the suitability of dates for your entire year's activities! This holistic Diary fuses the elements of the Chinese Solar and Lunar Calendars, with the lingua france of the Gregorian Calendar.

Weekly Tong Shu Diary 2011

Organize your professional and personal lives with the **Tong Shu Diary 2011**, with a twist… it also allows you to determine the most suitable dates on which you can undertake important activities and endeavors throughout the year! This compact Diary integrates the Chinese Solar and Lunar Calendars with the universal lingua franca of the Gregorian Calendar.

Tong Shu Monthly Planner 2011

Tailor-made for the Feng Shui or BaZi enthusiast in you, or even professional Chinese Metaphysics consultants who want a compact planner with useful information incorporated into it. In the **Tong Shu Monthly Planner 2011**, you will find the auspicious and inauspicious dates for the year marked out for you, alongside the most suitable activities to be undertaken on each day. As a bonus, there is also a reference section containing all the monthly Flying Stars charts and Annual Afflictions for 2011.

Tong Shu Desktop Calendar 2011

Get an instant snapshot of the suitable and unsuitable activities for each day of the Year of the Earth Rat, with the icons displayed on this lightweight Desktop Calendar. Elegantly presenting the details of the Chinese Solar Calendar in the form of the standard Gregorian one, the **Tong Shu Desktop Calendar 2011** is perfect for Chinese Metaphysics enthusiasts and practitioners alike. Whether it a business launching or meeting, ground breaking ceremony, travel or house-moving that you have in mind, this Calendar is designed to fulfill your information needs.

Elevate Your Feng Shui Skills With Joey Yap's Home Study Course And Educational DVDs

Xuan Kong Vol.1
An Advanced Feng Shui Home Study Course

Learn the Xuan Kong Flying Star Feng Shui system in just 20 lessons! Joey Yap's specialised notes and course work have been written to enable distance learning without compromising on the breadth or quality of the syllabus. Learn at your own pace with the same material students in a live class would use. The most comprehensive distance learning course on Xuan Kong Flying Star Feng Shui in the market. Xuan Kong Flying Star Vol.1 comes complete with a special binder for all your course notes.

Feng Shui for Period 8 - (DVD)

Don't miss the Feng Shui Event of the next 20 years! Catch Joey Yap LIVE and find out just what Period 8 is all about. This DVD boxed set zips you through the fundamentals of Feng Shui and the impact of this important change in the Feng Shui calendar. Joey's entertaining, conversational style walks you through the key changes that Period 8 will bring and how to tap into Wealth Qi and Good Feng Shui for the next 20 years.

Xuan Kong Flying Stars Beginners Workshop - (DVD)

Take a front row seat in Joey Yap's Xuan Kong Flying Stars workshop with this unique LIVE RECORDING of Joey Yap's Xuan Kong Flying Stars Feng Shui workshop, attended by over 500 people. This DVD program provides an effective and quick introduction of Xuan Kong Feng Shui essentials for those who are just starting out in their study of classical Feng Shui. Learn to plot your own Flying Star chart in just 3 hours. Learn 'trade secret' methods, remedies and cures for Flying Stars Feng Shui. This boxed set contains 3 DVDs and 1 workbook with notes and charts for reference.

BaZi Four Pillars of Destiny Beginners Workshop - (DVD)

Ever wondered what Destiny has in store for you? Or curious to know how you can learn more about your personality and inner talents? BaZi or Four Pillars of Destiny is an ancient Chinese science that enables us to understand a person's hidden talent, inner potential, personality, health and wealth luck from just their birth data. This specially compiled DVD set of Joey Yap's BaZi Beginners Workshop provides a thorough and comprehensive introduction to BaZi. Learn how to read your own chart and understand your own luck cycle. This boxed set contains 3 DVDs and 1 workbook with notes and reference charts.

Interested in learning MORE about Feng Shui? Advance Your Feng Shui Knowledge with the Mastery Academy Courses.

Feng Shui Mastery Series™
LIVE COURSES (MODULES ONE TO FOUR)

Feng Shui Mastery – Module One
Beginners Course

Designed for students seeking an entry-level intensive program into the study of Feng Shui , Module One is an intensive foundation course that aims not only to provide you with an introduction to Feng Shui theories and formulas and equip you with the skills and judgments to begin practicing and conduct simple Feng Shui audits upon successful completion of the course. Learn all about Forms, Eight Mansions Feng Shui and Flying Star Feng Shui in just one day with a unique, structured learning program that makes learning Feng Shui quick and easy!

Feng Shui Mastery – Module Two
Practitioners Course

Building on the knowledge and foundation in classical Feng Shui theory garnered in M1, M2 provides a more advanced and in-depth understanding of Eight Mansions, Xuan Kong Flying Star and San He and introduces students to theories that are found only in the classical Chinese Feng Shui texts. This 3-Day Intensive course hones analytical and judgment skills, refines Luo Pan (Chinese Feng Shui compass) skills and reveals 'trade secret' remedies. Module Two covers advanced Forms Analysis, San He's Five Ghost Carry Treasure formula, Advanced Eight Mansions and Xuan Kong Flying Stars and equips you with the skills needed to undertake audits and consultations for residences and offices.

Feng Shui Mastery – Module Three
Advanced Practitioners Course

Module Three is designed for Professional Feng Shui Practitioners. Learn advanced topics in Feng Shui and take your skills to a cutting edge level. Be equipped with the knowledge, techniques and confidence to conduct large scale audits (like estate and resort planning). Learn how to apply different systems appropriately to remedy situations or cases deemed inauspicious by one system and reconcile conflicts in different systems of Feng Shui. Gain advanced knowledge of San He (Three Harmony) systems and San Yuan (Three Cycles) systems, advanced Luan Tou (Forms Feng Shui) and specialist Water Formulas.

Feng Shui Mastery – Module Four
Master Course

The graduating course of the Feng Shui Mastery (FSM) Series, this course takes the advanced practitioner to the Master level. Power packed M4 trains students to 'walk the mountains' and identify superior landform, superior grade structures and make qualitative evaluations of landform, structures, Water and Qi and covers advanced and exclusive topics of San He, San Yuan, Xuan Kong, Ba Zhai, Luan Tou (Advanced Forms and Water Formula) Feng Shui. Master Internal, External and Luan Tou (Landform) Feng Shui methodologies to apply Feng Shui at every level and undertake consultations of every scale and magnitude, from houses and apartments to housing estates, townships, shopping malls and commercial districts.

BaZi Mastery Series™
LIVE COURSES (MODULES ONE TO FOUR)

BaZi Mastery – Module One
Intensive Foundation Course

This Intensive One Day Foundation Course provides an introduction to the principles and fundamentals of BaZi (Four Pillars of Destiny) and Destiny Analysis methods such as Ten Gods, Useful God and Strength of Qi. Learn how to plot a BaZi chart and interpret your Destiny and your potential. Master BaZi and learn to capitalize on your strengths, minimize risks and downturns and take charge of your Destiny.

BaZi Mastery – Module Two
Practitioners Course

BaZi Module Two teaches students advanced BaZi analysis techniques and specific analysis methods for relationship luck, health evaluation, wealth potential and career potential. Students will learn to identify BaZi chart structures, sophisticated methods for applying the Ten Gods, and how to read Auxiliary Stars. Students who have completed Module Two will be able to conduct professional BaZi readings.

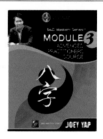

BaZi Mastery – Module Three
Advanced Practitioners Course

Designed for the BaZi practitioner, learn how to read complex cases and unique events in BaZi charts and perform Big and Small assessments. Discover how to analyze personalities and evaluate talents precisely, as well as special formulas and classical methodologies for BaZi from classics such as Di Tian Sui and Qiong Tong Bao Jian.

BaZi Mastery – Module Four
Master Course in BaZi

The graduating course of the BaZi Mastery Series, this course takes the advanced practitioner to the Masters' level. BaZi M4 focuses on specialized techniques of BaZi reading, unique special structures and advance methods from ancient classical texts. This program includes techniques on date selection and ancient methodologies from the Qiong Tong Bao Jian and Yuan Hai Zi Ping classics.

Xuan Kong Mastery – Module One
Advanced Foundation Course

This course is for the experienced Feng Shui professionals who wish to expand their knowledge and skills in the Xuan Kong system of Feng Shui, covering important foundation methods and techniques from the Wu Chang and Guang Dong lineages of Xuan Kong Feng Shui.

Xuan Kong Mastery – Module Two A
Advanced Xuan Kong Methodologies

Designed for Feng Shui practitioners seeking to specialise in the Xuan Kong system, this program focuses on methods of application and Joey Yap's unique Life Palace and Shifting Palace Methods, as well as methods and techniques from the Wu Chang lineage.

Xuan Kong Mastery – Module Two B
Purple White

Explore in detail and in great depth the star combinations in Xuan Kong. Learn how each different combination reacts or responds in different palaces, under different environmental circumstances and to whom in the property. Learn methods, theories and techniques extracted from ancient classics such as Xuan Kong Mi Zhi, Xuan Kong Fu, Fei Xing Fu and Zi Bai Jue.

Xuan Kong Mastery – Module Three
Advanced Xuan Kong Da Gua

This intensive course focuses solely on the Xuan Kong Da Gua system covering the theories, techniques and methods of application of this unique 64-Hexagram based system of Xuan Kong including Xuan Kong Da Gua for landform analysis.

Mian Xiang Mastery Series™
LIVE COURSES (MODULES ONE AND TWO)

Mian Xiang Mastery – Module One
Basic Face Reading

A person's face is their fortune – learn more about the ancient Chinese art of Face Reading. In just one day, be equipped with techniques and skills to read a person's face and ascertain their character, luck, wealth and relationship luck.

Mian Xiang Mastery – Module Two
Practical Face Reading

Mian Xiang Module Two covers face reading techniques extracted from the ancient classics Shen Xiang Quan Pian and Shen Xiang Tie Guan Dau. Gain a greater depth and understanding of Mian Xiang and learn to recognize key structures and characteristics in a person's face.

Yi Jing Mastery Series™
LIVE COURSES (MODULES ONE AND TWO)

Yi Jing Mastery – Module One
Traditional Yi Jing

'Yi', relates to change. Change is the only constant in life and the universe, without exception to this rule. The Yi Jing is hence popularly referred to as the Book or Classic of Change. Discoursed in the language of Yin and Yang, the Yi Jing is one of the oldest Chinese classical texts surviving today. With Traditional Yi Jing, learnn how this Classic is used to divine the outcomes of virtually every facet of life; from your relationships to seeking an answer to the issues you may face in your daily life.

Yi Jing Mastery – Module Two
Plum Blossom Numerology

Shao Yong, widely regarded as one of the greatest scholars of the Sung Dynasty, developed Mei Hua Yi Shu (Plum Blossom Numerology) as a more advanced means for divination purpose using the Yi Jing. In Plum Blossom Numerology, the results of a hexagram are interpreted by referring to the Gua meanings, where the interaction and relationship between the five elements, stems, branches and time are equally taken into consideration. This divination method, properly applied, allows us to make proper decisions whenever we find ourselves in a predicament.

Ze Ri Mastery Series™
LIVE COURSES (MODULES ONE AND TWO)

Ze Ri Mastery Series Module 1
Personal and Feng Shui Date Selection

The Mastery Academy's Date Selection Mastery Series Module 1 is specifically structured to provide novice students with an exciting introduction to the Art of Date Selection. Learn the rudiments and tenets of this intriguing metaphysical science. What makes a good date, and what makes a bad date? What dates are suitable for which activities, and what dates simply aren't? And of course, the mother of all questions: WHY aren't all dates created equal. All in only one Module – Module 1!

Ze Ri Mastery Series Module 2
Xuan Kong Da Gua Date Selection

In Module 2, discover advanced Date Selection techniques that will take your knowledge of this Art to a level equivalent to that of a professional's! This is the Module where Date Selection infuses knowledge of the ancient metaphysical science of Feng Shui and BaZi (Chinese Astrology, or Four Pillars of Destiny). Feng Shui, as a means of maximizing Human Luck (i.e. our luck on Earth), is often quoted as the cure to BaZi, which allows us to decipher our Heaven (i.e. inherent) Luck. And one of the most potent ways of making the most of what life has to offer us is to understand our Destiny, know how we can use the natural energies of our environment for our environments and MOST importantly, WHEN we should use these energies and for WHAT endeavors!

You will learn specific methods on how to select suitable dates, tailored to specific activities and events. More importantly, you will also be taught how to suit dates to a person's BaZi (Chinese Astrology, or Four Pillars of Destiny), in order to maximize his or her strengths, and allow this person to surmount any challenges that lie in wait. Add in the factor of `place', and you would have satisfied the notion of `doing the right thing, at the right time and in the right place'! A basic knowledge of BaZi and Feng Shui will come in handy in this Module, although these are not pre-requisites to successfully undergo Module 2.

Walk the Mountains! Learn Feng Shui in a Practical and Hands-on Program

 ## Feng Shui Mastery Excursion Series™: CHINA

Learn landform (Luan Tou) Feng Shui by walking the mountains and chasing the Dragon's vein in China. This Program takes the students in a study tour to examine notable Feng Shui landmarks, mountains, hills, valleys, ancient palaces, famous mansions, houses and tombs in China. The Excursion is a 'practical' hands-on course where students are shown to perform readings using the formulas they've learnt and to recognize and read Feng Shui Landform (Luan Tou) formations.

Read about China Excursion here:
http://www.masteryacademy.com/Education/schoolfengshui/fengshuimasteryexcursion.asp

Feng Shui for Life

Feng Shui for life is a 5-day course designed for the Feng Shui beginner to learn how to apply practical Feng Shui in day-to-day living. It is a culmination of powerful tools and techniques that allows you to gain quick proficiency in Classical Feng Shui. Discover quick tips on analysing your own BaZi, how to apply Feng Shui solutions for your own home, how to select auspicious dates for important activities, as well as simple and useful Face Reading techniques and practical Water Formulas. This is a complete beginner's course that is suitable for anyone with an interest in applying practical, real-world Feng Shui for life! Enhance every aspect of your life – your health, wealth, and relationships – using these easy-to-apply Classical Feng Shui methods.

Design Your Destiny

This is an introductory Program tailored for beginners on the study of BaZi. The Program teaches students the fundamentals of Personality Profiling and Destiny Analysis using BaZi, and guides them on plotting and reading the BaZi chart with confidence. This interactive workshop-style course encourages an enjoyable learning experience with proven fast results where students were able to apply what they've learnt instantly.